HIGHER
CONNECTIONS

Humor and Inspiration from a
Certified Public Pothead

ERIC & ALEXANDRA RIGHT

Editing, design, and distribution by Bublish, Inc.
Published by OJDM, LLC

ISBN: 978-1-64704-569-2 (eBook)
ISBN: 978-1-647045-96-8 (paperback)

CONTENTS

INTRODUCTION

HI, I'M ERIC. WELL, CRAP, I HAVE LIED TO YOU ALREADY AND I WASN'T even three words in. My name is not really Eric. For many reasons, primarily career related (but also to protect whatever shred of self-respect I have for myself), I am anonymizing my real name for now. However, I do promise everything else that I have written in this book is true, I think.

The name "Eric" was chosen by my significant other because of her love for Eric Bana, who I must admit is a pretty manly man, especially in *Troy*.

Maybe when I retire, I will feel comfortable exposing myself. (Yeah, I said it.) Or maybe once the media has spent a long enough time clamoring, I will reveal my true name. I envision it as the most anticipated reveal in history, even more than the revelation that Andy Kaufman has been alive for the past 38 years.

I admit, there are some weird and "out there" concepts in this book. There are also some very personal revelations. However, both myself and my significant other—whom I will henceforth call "Alexandra" (in honor of the love of my life, Alexandra Daddario, whom I have permission from my "Alexandra" to leave her for)—felt like we wouldn't be revealing the true impact of my experiences with cannabis if we didn't talk about the good, the bad, and the ugly. We wanted to be completely truthful, open, and honest with you so that you can hopefully apply what we have gone through to your life.

Whether this is with your parents, your siblings, your significant other, or even your guinea pigs, we hope you can take what we have been able to experience and find a way to make deeper connections with those in your lives. Your connections may not look exactly like ours, but that's okay. The point is to help you identify if and when these connections are taking place, and what to do when they present themselves in your life. To us, these connections have been life changing and eye-opening. Please know that I would not use that phrase if I didn't feel like using cannabis has significantly changed my life in a positive way.

For those of you who may think everything in this book is insincere or made up to try to make money selling books, that's okay, I may never be able to convince you otherwise. However, I swear that my only intent is to help others feel what I have felt and experience what I have experienced.

For full disclosure, most of what I have written has been thought of while I am high on cannabis.

ALEXANDRA'S NOTE:

It's true!

So, if I have intrigued you, please keep reading. I wish you luck.

Before we get into anything else, I have a quick request of you, the reader: Picture yourself sitting in your living room after what may have been the longest day of your life. The day could have been long for a multitude of reasons: an awful day at work; your significant other nagging you about a million things they needed you to do; dealing with a toilet that has exploded in your house; driving your kids to countless sporting events before realizing you had to take a trip to the grocery store, Home Depot, Target, and then the vet to figure out why your dog has been having diarrhea for the past week; receiving twenty-five phone calls from your mother asking about your COVID results; dealing with the home insurance company who canceled your policy last week for no reason; and trying to figure out how you're going to afford replacing both a refrigerator and a washing machine that broke on the same day. You get the picture. Now, imagine how you might feel after this type of day. Think about the options you have at your disposal to take the edge off and help you relax.

> **Option 1:** This option results in arguments about anything with anyone, depression, poor decision-making, eating something disgusting and greasy, passing out on the couch at 2:00 a.m. (hopefully without puking up what you have consumed), and waking up totally hungover the next day.

Option 2: This option will likely result in diarrhea or constipation (or both), feelings of guilt, depression, and the overwhelming desire to get to the gym the next day.

Option 3: This option results in reading until you hopefully pass out twenty minutes later.

Option 4: This option results in funny, crazy, and intense discussions with anyone around, forming insane connections with anyone around, trying to figure out the meaning of life, laughing at anything you see on TV, eating half a pizza or a gallon of ice cream, passing out without puking, getting a great night's sleep, and waking up totally refreshed and ready to tackle the day like the king or queen that you are.

Option 5: This option results in picking up the Bible, Torah or Quran to say some prayers and turning on CNN or Fox News to see what holy war is starting in what part of the world.

Now, without any other information about what the above options are, which one would you choose?

Personally, while it would be tempting to choose Option 5, as I do love me some Fox News and I am constantly praying for my fantasy football teams to do well, unfortunately, that is not my final answer. Now, if you did choose Option 5, I may suggest putting this book down right now and asking for a refund as this may not be for you. If you do choose to continue, I accept no responsibility for what you will read later on.

If you chose Option 1, then I assume you enjoy alcohol—be it liquor, beer, wine, or rubbing, and I think we can work with you here. While I used to enjoy alcohol and consumed it much more frequently than I do now, I have cut my alcohol use by 95 percent over the past twelve to eighteen months, mostly because the above description is pretty much what happens to me when I drink. Keep reading, and maybe after seeing the benefits I've experienced, you will put down the glass or bottle and pick up something else to consume after the next long day you have.

If you chose Option 2, then you enjoy a good meal after a day like the one I described—and I certainly cannot blame you for choosing this. I'm craving pizza, chicken parm with ziti, a hot turkey sandwich, and penne vodka while I write this. (I should have been born Italian!)

If you chose Option 3, then you're probably a smart cookie who opts for literary escapism to alleviate your stress—and I thank you for buying my book. Hopefully you have an open mind and a good sense of humor and can hang with me through the end.

If you chose Option 4, then you and I are best friends, and we should talk because this item is . . . drumroll please . . . cannabis! You can call it marijuana, weed, dope, grass, pot, reefer, ganja, hash, herb, chronic, Mary Jane, or whatever your favorite musician calls it. I will primarily call it "cannabis" and "marijuana" throughout the book, primarily because I was too lazy to use the "find and replace" option in Word. Hopefully you're not high as you're reading this because it may take you fifteen years to finish. Most likely, you can relate to some of what I write about in this book.

For those of you who have not consumed cannabis before, I understand you may be hesitant to try it because of historical misconceptions or stereotypes you may have heard. Some people believe it's a gateway drug, or that it's sinful.

Many have just never had the desire to try it, which I can certainly relate to. For these folks, I'm sure their idea of a pothead is somebody who does nothing more than sit in their bedroom watching their hair grow or watching a frisbee spin for an hour while debating the meaning of life. Most of this stigma comes from movies like *Cheech & Chong*, *PCU*, and *Half Baked,* which portray potheads as guys and girls with nothing to achieve in life and who are more worried about protecting the inchworm crawling up their arm than how they're going to fund their 401k and get that big promotion at work. These people certainly don't think of marijuana users as being able to give much insight into anything about life, other than what midnight snack is the best to quench their "munchies."

Now, don't get me wrong, if someone put a spinning frisbee in front of me while I'm high (especially a glow in the dark one), I'm not moving for at least forty-five minutes. I have easily stared at the cool glow-in-the-dark light in my bedroom for thirty minutes, and it has definitely taken me two hours to walk my dog around the block while high before (and it's not a long block).

However, for better or worse, I am not one of those guys who has the time to watch a frisbee spin for an hour, and I certainly don't consider myself a "junkie" or a "toker." I'm just a forty-something dude who leads a fairly normal life living in the suburbs with Alexandra, whom I have been with for a *loooooooonnggg time*—as she often reminds me. I have three kids (that I know of) who drive me nuts daily but whom I love deeply, a dog that was not my idea to get but is basically another child, three guinea pigs who poop more than anything on earth, two goldfish, seven koi fish, and a partridge in a pear tree (I literally have no idea what a partridge is). I have family that lives nearby, including two brothers and parents who are local and help with the kids as they are able.

I grew up in a fairly normal environment. However, years of therapy have taught me that I do have some unresolved issues from childhood that have affected my adult life—naturally, due to my parents and their interactions with each other, my siblings, and me. I suffered with normal teenage angst involving my looks, my friends, dating, and what I wanted to be when I grew up (which I'm still trying to figure out).

I went to college to study science, but after failing calculus multiple, multiple times, I came to the conclusion that maybe science wasn't for me. (I can only assume whomever came up with calculus was really high when they did so, because the normal human brain should not be able to figure that out.) I ended up switching majors and graduated with a bachelor of science in accounting. If you don't know much about accounting, just look up "double-sided entries" and tell me there isn't anything more exciting in life than recording a debit *and* a credit for the same amount.

I was raised in a Jewish household and, from a very young age, was exposed to everything Judaism had to offer (circumcisions being the primary and most wonderful of the traditions I was exposed to). Suffering through Hebrew School on Sunday mornings, I remember asking myself, "What the heck is this all about?" I would hear stories of fathers sacrificing their kids, God talking to Moses on a mountain to lay down the ten most important rules that we all need to follow, and the discussion of pigs and shellfish being dirty, and therefore, not to be eaten. I questioned pretty much everything I was told and was always wondering how anyone could believe this stuff. I don't want to seem like I don't believe in a higher power, because I do. However, the thought that Earth was formed in a week approximately 6,000 years ago and that we all came from Adam and Eve just never jived with me.

As I became older, I naturally questioned everything more, and I felt the societal pressure to succeed in a traditional way get worse. I had to go to college, become successful in my career, marry a nice Jewish girl and buy us a house with a white picket fence, and have children who would grow up to be nice, Jewish kids. However, I found my thoughts drifting to bigger things than social media likes or what type of car I should drive. I was more interested in how the universe works, how our minds work, and why we care about so many materialistic things in a lifespan that is not even the blink of an eye compared to the age of the universe. For most of us, it can be too overwhelming or even scary to consider some of the largest questions we can ask as humans, such as: Where did we come from and where do we go after we die? Why consume ourselves with those thoughts when we can focus on which celebrity broke up with which celebrity to date some other celebrity and how it will affect their Instagram followers?

If you step back and think about what we, as the human race, really know about our universe, it isn't much. Thousands of years ago, most people thought Earth was the center of the universe. Today, some of the smartest people on the planet are researching things like how big the universe is, whether there are multiple universes running in different directions, whether the Big Bang was the beginning of the universe or just the start of one universe, whether we are in a simulation, and whether our brains can actually "sync up" to other brains. So, if we are still learning about how our brains function and some of the fundamentals of our universe, how can we begin to understand deeper concepts like other dimensions, souls, and the meaning of life? Our brains are just not currently capable of grasping these concepts.

This is not to say I don't care about the important things down here on Earth—my family, my friends, my career, college football, my favorite hockey team, and my five fantasy football teams—but those are the things that get me through the day. I have tried to live a good life: be a good dad, a good significant other, a good friend, and a good steward of the planet by using solar panels on my house, driving an electric car, recycling, and donating to environmental organizations. But most of that feels somewhat trivial in the grand scheme of things and not central to the meaning of my life.

I am sure a good portion of you reading this find comfort in organized religion or faith in something else in your life, and that can certainly be a good thing for you, but that has just never been for me.

The reason I wanted to write the above is three-fold:

1. I have always questioned what people think is appropriate or what the status quo is, especially when it comes to societal norms and religion. Maybe that's a good thing, maybe it's just caused me more grief—who knows. But I have always felt that human beings are comforted by things they can understand: marriage, a career, a being who sits in the sky to watch out for them, and familiar and comforting stories shared from generation to generation (religious or otherwise). I get all of that; it's good to be comforted. And why spend your entire life questioning norms when it's easier not to? But that's just not me.

2. When I am sober, my life is generally draining and exhausting. Between work, kids, relationships, friends, family events, and other life demands, the ability to step back and just pause from the day-to-day grind is limited. I try relieving stress at the gym, but I just find myself more annoyed by the narcissism of half the people there who spend more time staring at themselves in the mirror or filming a TikTok video than working out. In the past, drinking alcohol would relax me a little bit, but it would also make me horny and depressed, and led to poor decision-making, lots of crying, and awful hangovers (none of which resulted in anything positive).

3. Since I started using marijuana in late 2019, I feel like I have found more peace and comfort with my life and with the universe. When I use marijuana, the world drifts away and I feel like everything I worry about on a daily basis is replaced with happiness, peacefulness, and the ability to connect with other people in a way that I cannot when I'm sober or when I'm drinking.

I know it may be easy to dismiss what I write in this book or assume that I'm making these experiences up, but please believe me when I say I am not. I'm not the type of person who would do so just to sell a few books. I genuinely believe that what I have experienced is something new and deeper than I have ever experienced before. Alexandra has seen what I've gone through while I have documented my experiences. She will tell you that she has seen me change for the better, become happier, and be more connected with her. This doesn't mean that she and I will stay together forever, because nothing in life is guaranteed, but I do feel we understand each other more and are more connected. I will get into other benefits I've experienced later in the book, but for now I will say this: **cannabis has been a positive influence in my life**.

This book primarily focuses on two things: First, the connections I have experienced while using cannabis, and second, a few of the predominant observations and general thoughts I have experienced while high. Some of these observations are deep, some are funny (hopefully), and some might be viewed as utter nonsense.

Generally, there are a few things that happen whenever I get high and am around people:

1. I have a connection to someone else's feelings and thoughts (usually Alexandra's, but they can also be with my kids, my friends, my dog);
2. I recognize the connection and tell Alexandra about it;
3. I document the experience if I can;
4. I have a "deep" visualization or revelation about how to explain some phenomenon or human experience like paranoia or multiple personality disorders;
5. I think of something funny (at least funny to me), which I've included in the back of this book. Sometimes I will have random thoughts and observations, which I've also included later in the book.

Please note that I am not professing to have any of life's answers or saying that what I have felt is the way things are actually working. If I was, I would be no different than religious prophets that claim to have all the answers about God and the afterlife. I am also not trying to be offensive or be perceived as derogatory to anyone who is religious. You are entitled to your own beliefs and nothing you read here is likely going to change the beliefs you've held for your entire life. But maybe, just maybe, everybody is right when they say, "Insanity is doing the same thing over and over again and expecting different results." By opening yourself up to trying something new, it's possible that your life will change for the better, the same way mine has.

While I am not advocating that people take marijuana in order to achieve these deeper connections or as some form of therapy, I do sincerely believe that the benefits of marijuana need to be explored and researched further, as there has been a lack of significant research due to the federal illegality of cannabis. For what it's worth, I do not believe that everyone needs to be high to form some of these deeper connections. Some people, like Alexandra, may not need marijuana, or other drugs, to form these connections. But for me, it appears that I need to be high.

However, as marijuana becomes legal in more states and its use becomes more widely accepted, we may discover more about the plant's impact on our brains, our bodies, and who knows what else. Hell, millions of people have been using another plant—sage—as a way to cleanse bad energy and spirits for thousands of years, so why would marijuana be much different? As it turns out, scientists have observed that sage can clear bacteria, disinfect air, put people in a positive mood, and has been associated with increasing wisdom, clarity, and spiritual awareness.[1]

If you can honestly say that you are deeply connected with the people in your lives, kudos to you. I am happy you have been able to achieve that level of connection. However, if you think about your daily life, can you really say that? Or are you so absorbed with your day-to-day tasks that the ability to look for deeper meaning in your life is generally lost (beyond the latest show on Netflix or when your kid's next baseball game is)?

The reality is, I do not see how most people can be happy when we're all so busy working ten-hour days, staring at screens for sixteen hours a day, and getting less than six hours of sleep. We have lost the ability and the desire to try to find something deeper in our lives. Some people turn to religion for that, but a lot of people, like me, don't, and identify themselves as atheist or agnostic.

There is a reason concerts, live sporting events, comedy clubs, movie theaters, houses of worship, and charitable events make us feel so good inside. We yearn for connections with other people. Think about your life and how good it made you feel to see your favorite band, sports team or comedian in a live environment. If there was one thing the COVID-19 pandemic taught us, it's how much we desire for and cherish connecting to other human beings—even if it is just going out to dinner with friends and family.

The experiences I've had while high that I've documented in this book have been life changing for me, and I hope you enjoy what I have written, or at the very least find it interesting and food for thought (damn it, now I'm hungry).

If the experiences in here resonate with you and you would like to share similar experiences or would just like to reach out, please do so at higherconnectionsnow@gmail.com. Alexandra and I also hope to continue talking about our experiences on our podcast, Higher Connections, which will be available through our websites higherconnectionsnow.com (Ok -shameless plugs are done).

ALEXANDRA'S NOTE:

Eric and I met when I was nineteen years old. We were friends for a couple of years before we started dating. We aren't the most obvious match, as we come from completely different backgrounds. I guess I am what you would consider religious; I pray on a daily basis, believe in angels, and grew up doing the rosary almost every Friday. However, as you'll read throughout this book, Eric isn't a very religious person. None of that mattered. I found him to be super cute, funny, charming, smart, and thoughtful. **(Eric's note: Obviously this is all true.)** I never imagined at the time that it would turn into something serious. But eighteen years later, here we are with a house, three kids, a dog, and a solid life together. Just like any other relationship, we've had our fair share of ups and downs, with some downs being more serious than others. However, we've always pulled through.

During the COVID-19 pandemic, Eric and I started arguing a lot more than ever before (I'm sure being cooped up together 24/7 didn't help). Besides being stressed from home schooling two kids and watching another young child, we were both working from home and working around each other all the time. However, we just weren't connecting at all. Personally, I felt resentful, overwhelmed, and generally unhappy with Eric. I didn't feel like he cared about anything but work, and the weight of everything at home somehow fell on me. At some point, I decided that it was time to give up and started trying to figure out the best path forward for us, apart from each other.

Just before the pandemic started, Eric started his journey with marijuana. Initially, I did not know what to make of it. I assumed it was just a coping mechanism for us falling apart and his stressful job, which I think it was for him, initially. The first few times he used marijuana at home, I found myself laughing hysterically because he would say and do funny things—things very outside of his normal comfort zone.

When Eric first started using marijuana, I thought he just wanted to try something new because he was bored with his life. I wouldn't blame him—you read how he described his life, right? I did not know what to make of it, though. But after a while, I noticed he was more relaxed, more talkative, more empathetic. I started to like him more when he was high. To be honest, I'd been making plans to leave him before he started using marijuana. I'd spoken to lawyers and was just waiting for the pandemic to stop. Later on in this book, I'll tell you how this experience saved our relationship (at least as of the writing of this sentence—he might have done something stupid after writing this that caused me to punch him in the balls).

As time went on, his experiences evolved into something more meaningful, which started to have a profoundly positive effect on me and on our relationship. I slowly began to recognize that these experiences were changing him and changing us as a couple in positive ways. This evolution started small, but it has really helped us in so many ways. He went from not being able to hold a serious, emotional conversation to asking me to "go deeper" in our discussions. He was not one to *ever* express himself, let alone tell me to go deeper on any given subject that was personal to me. Now, we talk more, and he is more patient with me, the children, and himself. He is more thoughtful, empathetic, caring, and generally happier. His "elevator music stopping," as he explains it later in this book, has helped him really focus and appreciate all the good things in his life.

We are friends again, which I really did not think would ever happen. Whatever meaning you take from the experiences and observations in this book, just know that I will always be grateful for what they have done for our relationship and family. I hope on some level you can experience this as well.

1

My (Very Brief) History with Marijuana

I, LIKE MANY PEOPLE, TRIED CANNABIS IN HIGH SCHOOL AND COLLEGE a few times, but it never really did anything for me. I found myself paranoid and hungry. So, like most college kids, I stuck with the Natty Lights, Gold's Best, and Jager Bombs to get me drunk on the weekends (and the weekends only, of course). Cannabis was always around, but it just wasn't something I was into—my throat hurt when I smoked it, I never really got to enjoy the impact of it because we would always drink alcohol with it, and it left me with a bad feeling afterward (of course, that could have just been the 2:00 a.m. breakfast buffets).

Furthermore, I was naturally shy around girls, and alcohol loosened me up and gave me the guts to go up to girls I never would have otherwise. Unfortunately for me, this very rarely resulted in a positive outcome. (However, there were definitely a few hookups that likely would not have happened while sober.)

In my twenties and thirties, I generally stuck with alcohol, but I'd graduated to the harder stuff—whiskey, tequila, wine, and good beer like Tröegs. However, as I got older, I found myself enjoying alcohol less and less. My tolerance decreased, I felt more hungover in the morning, and my decision-making abilities lessened with every passing year, leading to questionable life choices, to say the least.

I took breaks from alcohol from time to time to see how I did without it. These breaks would usually last a few months, maybe half a year, and then I would lapse right back into drinking. Doing so was generally just a way to escape the day-to-day grind of having a tough career, young kids, and the general annoyances of life. What's better than a whiskey on the rocks after a long day? Hint: It starts with an **M**, ends with an **A** and has *arijuan* in the middle.

This brings me to my late thirties, when I was dealing with some pretty large stressors: three young kids, a recent switch to a more stressful job, a stressful relationship with Alexandra that I wasn't sure would survive or not, the loss of some friends for a variety of reasons, and the overall state of the world—politically, socially, and environmentally. In general, I was sick of drinking alcohol and the hangovers that came with it.

So, one day when I was on a business trip to a state where cannabis is legal for recreational use, I thought why not do what every responsible businessman does? I went to a dispensary in a suit and bought some edibles. I could see the guys behind the counter rolling their eyes when I asked questions like, "How long does it take to set in?" "Can I drink alcohol as well?" and "Will I be okay if I take more than 10 mg?" Looking back, I should have just punched myself in the balls and saved myself the humiliation, but I was an edible virgin (that sounds delicious, by the way) and wanted to make sure I didn't end up walking around naked at 5:00 a.m. with a tiger, a baby, and Mike Tyson passed out next to me (*The Hangover,* anyone?).

So I didn't start off with much. I went with 10 mg, and it certainly led to an interesting night, which involved walking around the downtown area for two hours with nary a care in the world, ordering room service at 2:00 a.m. (best meal ever), and getting a pretty good night's sleep considering I only slept for four hours. I didn't really think much of that experience—it was cool, but it was more about people watching than anything. I felt relaxed and calm, and the best part was that I slept well and woke up without a hangover the next day.

Since that day, I have sourced my edibles from states where it is legal when I travel for work. I am confident enough to bring the edible back through airport security (sorry TSA). Only one time did I have a scare when I brought back bath salt mixed with THC (tetrahydrocannabinol, marijuana's main ingredient) in a bag that looked like normal Epsom bath salt. TSA was nice enough to take that bag out of my suitcase to "test it." Naturally, my heart was pounding for the fifteen minutes it took TSA to test the bag while I tried coming up with all sorts of excuses—it's for my significant other, my mom, my dog, my neighbor's uncle. Finally, TSA released me and sent me on my way without an issue, and I proceeded to the airport bathroom to change my soiled underwear. (For the record, I can only assume they were testing for explosives and not THC.)

ALEXANDRA'S NOTE:

Is it bad that I died laughing when he told me what happened? I just pictured him trying to lie his way out of it. Ha ha. Okay, you can call me evil now. But I do appreciate him risking his freedom to bring me back some bath salt.

When I first started doing edibles, it was primarily to help me relax after a long week. Generally, I would take between 10 mg and 20 mg and would just relax, watch TV, and zone out from the world before passing out and getting some great sleep. Eventually, I began thinking of certain funny things while high. I likened them to comedic "bits" that I thought were funny. Some of these are noted later in this book, in Chapter 16, so you can make your own judgement on whether they are truly funny or not. For the record, I am certainly *not* a comedian and respect comedians a great deal for what they do.

At some point in my early marijuana journey, I found myself recognizing that my thoughts were crisper, and I was more aware of them on a consistent basis. Some were bad thoughts, some were good thoughts, but they were mostly interesting thoughts that I really enjoyed working through. For example, if I was doing laundry, I would recognize that I was getting high because I couldn't focus on doing the laundry — I would think about what will happen when I die, followed by why my dog likes to sniff her own poop, and then I would try to figure out how a washing machine works.

I started having very deep thoughts about life, death, the universe, what was happening in my brain while I was high, and other things that most people do not think about while sober. At first, I chalked it up to just being high and chemicals splashing around in my brain, and I figured they were likely not meaningful in any way. However, the thoughts continued to be very profound and intense, to the point where I wondered whether I should write them down. But I kept convincing myself that the thoughts were stupid, and that they were nothing anyone would be interested in reading or hearing about (sometimes I still think that).

However, after several months, I worked up the nerve to talk to Alexandra about what I was thinking and feeling. The people who really know me would tell you that I usually do not open up or express myself in any meaningful way, other than to talk about things that annoy or frustrate me, which can be a significant number of things.

ALEXANDRA'S NOTE:

He's not exaggerating here. Trust me, it's a long list!

This lack of expression was always frustrating to Alexandra because she is the exact opposite. She could talk for sixteen days about some article she read on *Maxim* about how and why couples don't communicate well enough with each other.

I must admit that talking to Alexandra about these thoughts felt very freeing. I was expressing things that seemed so profound to me, but I kept asking her if she thought they were stupid or not. I didn't necessarily feel weird about expressing them; I felt like if they made sense to me, they would make sense to her.

So then I started getting high not just to relax but to see what crazy ideas and feelings would come out of my brain. Alexandra began documenting them—maybe to placate me or maybe because she thought they were interesting. Either way, we began discussing the thoughts and experiences I was having to see if they made any sense at all. Some of those are documented in this book and you can make up your own mind as to whether they make sense or not.

For the record, I am not addicted to marijuana. It has not led me to do other psychedelics like LSD, acid, or mushrooms, and my basic health has not changed in the two years I have been doing marijuana.

I am able to limit my consumption to once or twice a week (although some weeks I feel the need to consume more often than others—generally around the same time every month and I'll let you guess what is going on that drives *that* need) and am not nervous about losing the ability to control my intake. I rarely, if ever, do marijuana when I am working and never take it when I have to drive anywhere—in fact, 99.9% of the time, I consume marijuana when I have nothing to do or nowhere to go, which is generally during the weekend after the 5,214 things the kids have planned are finished.

As I'll get into later, the health impacts of marijuana are still being researched, but at this point, they do not appear to be any worse than most of the other things most people consume. However, before that, I will give you a brief history of the plant so you can get to know my new best friend.

2

A Brief History of Marijuana

SOME PEOPLE MAY HAVE GROWN UP HEARING THAT MARIJUANA IS A gateway drug while others grew up hearing that it is generally evil, but not many people understand the history of why marijuana was considered an evil drug to begin with.

Cannabis as a plant has been around for millions and millions of years. From what scientists can tell, humans started using it four to five thousand years ago to make oil, fiber, and ropes. Exactly when people began smoking the plant is still under debate, but most scientists believe it was between two to three thousand years ago in China and other parts of what is now known as Asia.

Cannabis and other psychedelics were likely used very heavily during the era in which the Bible was written, which makes sense. I can imagine a lot of the stories in the Bible being influenced by mushrooms or other psychedelic plants, as they were likely widely available in the Middle East and Africa when the stories in the Bible were initially created. Think about some of the biggest stories in the Bible.

- **Adam and Eve:** A garden, a snake, some ribs, and a forbidden fruit—sounds like something I would think of while high.
- **The Ten Commandments:** Moses stands on a mountain and speaks to God to receive the Ten Commandments, which God

has commanded all humans to follow. Yeah, great story—and only something that could be created when high.

- **Joseph in a Whale:** I mean, come on.
- **Jesus Walks on Water:** I've definitely seen things walking on water while I've been high, so why wouldn't others back in the day?
- **The Coat of Many Colors:** This refers to the name of the garment that Joseph wore, which was given to him by his father, Jacob. I can *definitely* see this being made up while someone was high on shrooms.
- **The Creation of the Heavens and the Earth:** I'm not saying this didn't happen the way the Bible describes it, but if it didn't, this is certainly something I could see being created while some guys were sitting around a campfire talking about how life started. It's very creative and very dramatic—something people could believe, with no way to prove it didn't happen. Brilliant and only something that people on drugs might think up.
- **The Resurrection of Jesus:** Is it possible the son of God died and then was resurrected? Sure, I guess it is. I think it would take a big leap of faith regarding the soul and what happens after we die. However, when it comes to Jesus and the people that claim they saw him, mainly his disciples, is it more likely that some of them were hanging out, high on cannabis, and one of them saw someone that looked like Jesus, and the others said they could see him too so they didn't feel left out? Who knows. All I know is that when I die, I certainly hope people see me and I freak them the hell out.

Regardless, in America, cannabis was not very widely known or used until the early 1900s, when the start of the Mexican Revolution in 1910 drove many Mexicans to the United States, bringing cannabis with them, as the plant was widely grown in Mexico. As is truly only something that could occur in America, hysterical claims about the drug began to circulate, such as allegations that it caused a "lust for blood." In addition, the term *cannabis* was largely replaced by the term *marijuana*, which some speculated was done by Americans to promote the foreignness of the drug and thus stoke xenophobia. Around this time, many states began passing laws to ban marijuana. In the 1930s, the Federal Bureau of Narcotics turned the battle against marijuana into an all-out war in order to promote their newly created department. Without any scientific basis, the department sought a federal ban on the drug, relying on marketing campaigns that relied heavily on racism. The head of the Federal Bureau of Narcotics, Harry Anslinger, claimed the majority of marijuana smokers were minorities, including African Americans, and that marijuana had a negative effect on these "degenerate races," such as inducing violence or causing insanity. Furthermore, he noted that "Reefer makes darkies think they're as good as white men," and that smoking the plant would result in white women having sex with black men.[2]

The passage of the Marihuana Tax Act in 1937 effectively made the drug illegal across the United States. Although this act was declared unconstitutional in 1969, it was replaced by the Controlled Substances Act the following year. That legislation classified marijuana as a Schedule I drug—putting it in the same category as heroin and LSD.[3]

As with most things, the rationale for illegalizing marijuana was not based on any scientific basis by the federal government. However, one of the worst side effects of this law being passed is that the ability of scientists to fully research the effects of THC—the active ingredient in marijuana—is still limited to this day. As such, trying to figure out the long-term effects of marijuana on humans is not very well understood. However, as I'll touch on next, you have to put these effects in context with everything else humans consume on a daily basis.

Furthermore, I don't know anyone who has used marijuana and then run to their local drug dealer to secure a line of cocaine or heroin. I think most people that use marijuana recreationally are not moving on to harder drugs. However, as with most things, I am sure there are exceptions to the rule.

As we stand (or sit) today, United Nations estimates put the number of people that use marijuana around 159 million, or about 4% of the total population of the planet.[4]

In 1996, California was the first state in the United States to legalize medical marijuana and since then, additional states have legalized marijuana for both medicinal and recreational purposes, with 15 states having fully legal status for the drug, and New Jersey and New York being the latest states to fully legalize it as of this writing. Additionally, only six states have total bans on marijuana use: Idaho, Wyoming, South Dakota, Tennessee, Alabama and South Carolina.[5]

The severity of punishment for possession of and consumption of marijuana has long been a thorn in the side of many communities, especially communities of color, where African Americans were almost four times as likely to be arrested for marijuana possession.[6]

I am not going to go into a socio-political rant about how unfair and unjust that is and, regardless of how you feel on the issue, the legalization of marijuana in more and more states has reduced the total arrests for possession of the drug since their peak in 2008, when over 800,000 marijuana-related arrests were made.[7]

In the years to come, my guess is federal legalization will become more possible as more research is done into both the potential consequences and health benefits of consumption, which I will get into in the next chapter.

3

Wait–There are Worse Things Than Marijuana?

A GOOD PORTION OF THE POPULATION IS SCARED OR HESITANT TO TRY marijuana, probably because they have heard marijuana is bad since they were young. I get it—I still don't eat lobster, crabs or other shellfish because when I was young, I heard they were bottom dwellers, and thus, inedible. Meanwhile, for most people that grew up in the 1970s and 1980s like I did, their parents were busy feeding them cheeseburgers, fried chicken, french fries, donuts, cupcakes, soda, ice cream, and countless cereals laced with more sugar than you can count. Some parents were likely driving their kids to and from school without seatbelts while smoking a pack of cigarettes around them daily.

However, if you think about what you eat and drink on a normal basis (seriously, write it down) from the time you get up to the time you go to bed, there is a good likelihood that whatever is on your list is as bad or worse for your health than marijuana (unless you are a vegan or are eating a Mediterranean diet).[8,9] Additionally, there are likely things that are entering your body that are out of your control, like air pollution, chemicals, microplastics, and spiders (hopefully only while you're asleep).

So, let's compare marijuana to other things in our everyday environment that most adult humans consume without a care in the world, and the known health impacts of these things.

Alcohol: Drinking alcohol is known to cause cancer, heart damage, stroke, high blood pressure, liver damage, pancreatitis, behavior changes, hallucinations, slurred speech (that can be hilarious, though), a shrinking brain, frequent diarrhea (also hilarious), infertility (clearly not an issue for me), and sexual dysfunction (definitely an issue for me). And this doesn't include the number of deaths caused by drunk drivers, drunken fights, and people falling off roofs in New York City (this happens more than you think). Yet, the average American drinks 2.3 gallons of alcohol per year,[10] and the average number of deaths associated with excessive drinking (almost 90,000) is higher than the total number of people who die from opioids each year.[11] A recent study led by King's College London (KCL) has found that drinking four small glasses of wine or four pints of beer per week damages short-term memory and spatial awareness and increases the risk of developing dementia in older age.[12] Cheers!

Tobacco: Smoking tobacco is known to cause cancer, diabetes, gum disease, lung disease, heart disease, stroke, emphysema, COPD, arthritis, and eye disease. Not only do you get the benefit of all of this for yourself, but you can also cause damage to others through secondhand smoke, which causes some of the above issues in non-smokers. More than 16 million Americans are living with a disease caused by smoking according to the US Department of Health and Human Services.[13] Furthermore, you get the added benefit of awful teeth, bad breath, and cracked, dry skin. It's a winner!

Red and processed meat: Eating red and processed meat can raise the risk of type 2 diabetes, coronary heart disease, stroke, and certain cancers, especially colorectal cancer.[14] Not to mention the delicious french fries that accompany your medium-well burger, which may cause an elevated risk of all-cause death, especially death from cardiovascular disease.[15]

Fried foods: Do I really need to get into how bad fried foods are for you? See above. Or just go to a state fair and look at the amount of fried food available and the people that are consuming said food. Case closed.

Fish: Although most fish is generally good for you, there is still some elevated risk of consuming too much mercury, which can damage your central nervous system.[16] Ironically, listening to the band Phish too much can also affect your central nervous system.

Desserts and junk food snacks: These delicious bastards can lead to higher cholesterol and diabetes. However, I will say if anything besides marijuana is worth dying for, a warm molten chocolate lava cake with vanilla ice cream is the next best thing. It could be one of the best things on earth.

Pollution: Studies have linked living in a city with high air pollution to smoking a pack of cigarettes a day for twenty-nine years.[17] Which would be just great if city life didn't also mess with people's mental health, leading to more people with mood disorders and anxiety.[18]

Smartphones and social media: Don't get me started on smartphones. Most adults (and kids) are so addicted to their phones—tweeting, liking, replying, commenting, texting, and scrolling—that they can barely have a face-to-face conversation. Have you ever gone to a mall (you may need to look up what that is) or a restaurant and seen four teenage girls at a table who are *all* staring at their phones, trying to take a selfie, and not saying a word to each other for fifteen minutes? It's insane. Our teenagers literally spend 50 percent of their non-sleeping lives (seven to eight hours a day) on screens and smartphones.[19] And adults aren't any better—how much time do *you* spend staring at your screen? We have turned into narcissistic, socially dysfunctional idiots who are more concerned about selfies than selflessness. We've forgotten about going outside for a walk because we're too busy inside liking and commenting on some video on YouTube about how wonderful it is to take a walk outside. We're also *literally* getting hornier because we're creating horns on our skulls from looking down at our phones so much.[20] I apologize for that rant, and while I am as guilty with my smartphone as the next person, you can't tell me smartphones are good for us, physically, socially, or mentally. *But please like me on all social media platforms.*

Gambling and fantasy sports: These lead to stress, anxiety, anger, depression, migraines, financial ruin, loss of friends, and potentially divorce.[21]

Cars: Driving a car is known to cause stress, agitation, anxiety, pain, fear, crying, baby creation, and death. (Unless you drive an electric car, in which case all of those go away—except the baby creation.)

Refusing to wear a mask or get a COVID-19 vaccine: This is known to increase the risk of getting COVID. However, wearing a mask and getting vaccinated increases the risk of being punched by someone who thinks you're a Libtard Democratic supporter—so, there's that. But one approach is proven to save lives and the other isn't, so you take your pick.

Your kids' music: Listening to any music your kids are listening to is known to increase stress, anxiety, and anger, and cause overall confusion. Not to mention that it results in financial distress when they say they want to go to a concert that costs $250 per ticket plus fees, taxes, parking, food, drinks, and three bottles of Tylenol.

And I haven't even mentioned phthalates (essentially the chemicals that make plastics more durable), which at the time of this writing may cause around 100,000 deaths a year from any cause.[22] So, basically, the summary of all of this is that we're all screwed and we're all going to die from something we do every day.

In terms of the benefits of marijuana, there appear to be several which are still being researched. A few of the larger ones include:

1. Treatment of chronic pain
2. Depression, anxiety, and post-traumatic stress disorder
3. Nausea and vomiting, especially when caused by chemotherapy

4. Epilepsy
5. Regulation and prevention of diabetes
6. Autism
7. Glaucoma
8. Slows the development of Alzheimer's disease
9. Inflammatory bowel diseases
10. Tremors associated with Parkinson's disease
11. Multiple sclerosis[23]

I've read some studies that state there is a potential link between marijuana use and heart attacks and strokes in young people aged eighteen to forty-four.[24] To which I say, *no shit.* Whenever I'm high, I eat two gallons of ice cream (not that fat-free crap), two pizzas, and half an egg and cheese sandwich from two days ago. My cholesterol probably jumps twenty-five points in four hours, which is more than enough to cause anyone's heart to say, "Hell nah." But, as of this writing, there has been no direct link that I could find between the chemicals in marijuana and an increase in heart attack or stroke risk. THC does, however, increase your heart rate and expand your blood vessels, which does put more pressure on your heart.[25] For anyone with a higher risk of heart disease, this could increase your risk of a heart attack. THC also affects your respiratory system (especially if you smoke) and could lead to symptoms of bronchitis as well as affecting the central nervous system.[26, 27]

Clearly, consuming anything you put in your body has risks, but you know what other chemical affects your respiratory, circulatory, and central nervous systems? A small, unknown chemical called caffeine.[28] How many millions of people drink coffee every day without a care in the world? You will read all sorts of research that coffee or caffeine is bad for you, good for you, somewhere in between, or that it increases the chance of one cancer and decreases the chance of another cancer. Years ago, there was the notion that coffee was a potential carcinogen and yet people continued to ingest it every day without too much worry.[29] Is marijuana on the same level as caffeine? I don't know, but my point is simply that people consumed coffee for years while not knowing whether it was truly safe for them, yet marijuana has this stigma of being bad.

You know the best part of using marijuana? *No hangover.* Instead, you get a layover. What's a layover? It's the morning after you do marijuana. (Think about it, the opposite of hanging is laying on the ground, right?) Generally, a layover just involves brushing your teeth to get rid of your unusually dry mouth, craving French toast, and then feeling refreshed in the morning. For me, that's a wonderful morning.

I don't smoke, I rarely drink, and I work out (with both weights and cardio). I don't eat cookies, snacks, or desserts, and I don't eat red meat, too much cheese, or too many fried foods (other than Arby's seasoned curly fries, which are absolutely delicious). I get seven to eight hours of sleep a night (assuming none of my children or the dog is sick, which is rare). All in all, I am doing well health-wise. If doing marijuana once a week is something I enjoy and if it comes with a little bit of risk, then I am okay with that. If you ask me, if I'm going to die from something, I'd prefer to die from something that makes me happy, relaxes me, and allows me to feel connected with the universe. But maybe that's just me.

There's also the view that marijuana is a performance enhancing drug. The World Anti-Doping Agency (WADA, which sounds like anyone in Boston saying "water") suspended an Olympic athlete in 2021 from the summer Olympics for using marijuana before her race because her biological mother had just died.[30] Seriously? If you told me an athlete was competing in the "Sit on the Couch for as Long as Possible While Saying as Little as Possible and Eating Cheetos" event, then I totally agree that using marijuana before would give them an unfair advantage. But if you can sit there and tell me with a straight face that using marijuana before a 200-meter sprint gives an athlete an unfair advantage, then you should be entering poker tournaments for a living.

If Usain Bolt and I were racing in a 200-meter race and I gave him a 40 mg edible before the race, then I would bet one of my children that the race would be closer than anyone expected. All it would take is a bee flying by his head to distract him for long enough for me to attempt to win.

I am hopeful that in short order, marijuana becomes federally legal, which would allow for more research to be done on the impact of THC and other chemicals in marijuana on the human body. At that point, if marijuana is found to be really bad for you, then we can reassess. People would be able to make more informed decisions about their bodies, their health, and the amount of THC they consume.

As I talk about in the next chapter, for me, the benefits of marijuana have outweighed the negative side effects so far. Maybe that will change in the future, but not yet. Not yet.

4

How Marijuana Impacts Me When I'm High

BEFORE I GET INTO THE DEEPER CONNECTIONS I'VE EXPERIENCED with Alexandra and others, I want to summarize how marijuana affects me each time I consume it. For those of you who have never tried it, consuming marijuana is slightly different than consuming alcohol in that alcohol initially makes you feel good (or "buzzed"), but then you generally get depressed, tired, nauseous, and sick if you drink too much. Alcohol seems to trigger the release of dopamine, which initially makes us feel good but, after too much alcohol, other brain chemicals are altered, which enhances the feeling of depression (and drunk crying).[31]

You could die from alcohol poisoning if you drink too much since alcohol is technically a toxin that kills cells.[32] Comparatively, marijuana, at the right dose, makes most people just feel relaxed, at ease, lighter—like a weight lifted off your shoulders. For me, it does all of this, but it also makes me feel more connected to things and to people. This connectivity can be summarized a few ways, but, in general, marijuana makes me more aware of my feelings and the feelings of others.

I have summarized a few ways that marijuana makes me feel as follows:

- **I am more aware of my thoughts**. I generally feel more aware of what I am thinking and feeling. For example, think of my thoughts like the wheel on *Wheel of Fortune*. As the wheel spins and that stupid little triangle thing goes from one number to the next, I can feel my thoughts change. As my brain moves from the $500 slot (e.g., a thought about me needing to do the laundry) to the $1,250 slot (e.g., a thought about how I can't wait to eat a slice of pizza later) to the $750 slot (e.g., I need to lose ten pounds), I can *feel* each thought leave my brain and the next thought come into my brain more clearly than when I am sober.

  As another example, think about when you're in a nice hot shower with awesome water pressure and you just get lost in your thoughts. You are hopefully able to tune out all of the troubles of your day—kids, significant other, work, financial issues, physical issues—and just focus on yourself and your thoughts. (Unless, of course, you bring a waterproof phone into the shower with you, but why would you do that? Don't you get enough screen time during non-showering hours?) Think about what happens when you're in this zone—your thoughts are likely all over the place and generally freeing. Some people sing in the shower, some people cry in the shower, some people are creative in the shower. Whatever the case, you are letting your mind wander free and it hopefully feels damn good. That's how I feel when I'm high.

- **I am more aware of my senses.** When I'm high, I can hear, feel, smell, taste, and see things better. I feel my heart beat more intensely, I can feel muscle twitches more intensely, and my senses are crisper and deeper than normal. This can get a little weird when you're using the toilet—not going to lie—but it feels like I am more connected to my body.

- **I am able to connect things more easily.** One of the first major thoughts and feelings I remember having was that marijuana increased my overall brain activity, which, in turn, increased the number of connections in my brain. It's like I was able to be quicker with my thoughts than I would be while sober. Think of it like the speedometer of my brain increases, resulting in more thoughts, deeper thoughts, and an increase in overall connectivity of my brain. I did some research on whether this has been scientifically proven and found a few interesting things:

  a) In a study published in 2014 in the journal *Proceedings of the National Academy of Sciences*, researchers compared forty-eight adults who used marijuana at least three times a day, for an average of eight or nine years, and sixty-two people who didn't use marijuana. It turned out that the brains of the chronic marijuana users showed greater connectivity, which is generally a measure of how well information travels between different parts of the brain. The researchers said they don't know for sure why chronic marijuana use is linked to these brain changes, but they think it may have something to do with THC (tetrahydrocannabinol), marijuana's main psychoactive ingredient, which affects cannabinoid receptors.[33]

  b) THC may increase the level of "neural noise," or random neural activity in the brain. In a 2015 study published in the journal *Biological Psychiatry*, researchers measured the levels of this random neural activity in twenty-four people under two conditions: after they had been given pure THC, and after they had been given a placebo. They found that the people showed greater levels of neural noise after they received the THC compared with their levels after they took the placebo.[34] The neural noise seems to be an increase in certain neurotransmitters, which are often referred to as the body's chemical messengers. They are the molecules used by the nervous system to transmit messages between neurons or from neurons to muscles. Sometimes neurotransmitters can bind to receptors and cause an electrical signal to be transmitted down the cell (excitatory). Marijuana seems to increase the activity of certain neurotransmitters, including GABA, dopamine, and noradrenaline.[35]

So, according to this research, the greater connectivity I feel while high *is* happening, and theoretically, it increases my ability to form and sense thoughts, more so than when I am sober. When I take edibles, I feel like my mind is going at warp speed for two to three hours afterward, and then my mind needs to cool down after generating so many thoughts and connections. Most of the concepts I've written about in this book have been while my mind has been in this warp-speed phase. After my warp-speed phase, I go into my staring-at-the-TV phase for two to three hours before "knocking out" (picture Jim Breuer's character in *Half Baked*, or go watch the movie if you haven't seen it). I will go into more detail about what I think is happening during this warp-speed phase later in this book.

- **I am more aware of others.** I feel how others around me are feeling and can sense their energy better. It's a bit hard to explain, but I am more sensitive to other people's feelings. I can be talking to Alexandra, my mother, my kid's karate teacher, or my local post office worker, and I'll be able to sense their emotions. Some people call this type of person an "empath" or a "clairsentient." In general, I feel closer to people and sense their feelings more when I'm high than when I'm sober.

- **I think about "the steps" more.** For most of us, what we do daily comes naturally—we don't think about getting dressed, driving to work, working, eating, taking a shower, etc. For others, the daily grind of a typical day can be exhausting and cause anxiety or stress. Normally, when I am sober, I don't get too stressed out by the things I have to do; I can multi-task and manage just fine. However, when I am high, I can literally count the number of steps I need to do in order to relax, lie down, and watch TV. I can see the steps almost like in a timeline. I'll give you an example.

a) On a typical night, this is what I have to do before I can relax in bed: 1) poop; 2) take my contact lenses out; 3) give my daughter a bath; 4) dress my daughter; 5) put cream on my daughter; 6) brush her teeth; 7) brush my teeth; 8) brush the dog's teeth; 9) put my daughter to bed; 10) get the laundry; 11) plug the electric car in; 12) let the dog out; 13) clean up after the dog; 14) set the alarm; 15) get my water with ice; 16) vacuum any remaining fruit flies in my kitchen; 17) shut off the lights; 18) pee; 19) clean my glasses; 20) close the windows; 21) lock the windows; and 22) put cream on my hands. Then *finally*, I get blissful TV and relaxing time.

One night when I was high, I told Alexandra I felt I had about thirty-two things left to do before I could relax, and she told me that was *exactly* how she thinks normally. She constantly thinks about the number of things she has to do before she can relax. This is likely a function of her having some form of attention deficit disorder—we've talked about it before—but this in particular helped me understand how she normally thinks and processes information. When I'm high, it is almost like I become her and see how her brain works (for the record, from what I have seen, it is *always* racing a million miles per hour), then I slow down and go back to me. As a side note, what is interesting is that when she is high, her brain slows down and the steps seem to disappear, which is the exact opposite of how she normally thinks. I will talk later on about what might be causing this phenomenon.

- **I am a better debater**: Don't have an argument with me because it will not end well for you. When I get into debates or arguments with Alexandra or friends while high, I make more reasonable, succinct and intellectual arguments. Alexandra has told me as much. She can see my point of view much clearer when we get into arguments and my debating skills go "through the roof". I would make the argument I am a master-debater (yes, I said it). Now, don't get me wrong, I am not looking to get into arguments when I am high, but when I do, you best come prepared for battle. If I really was smart, I would save all my arguing for when I am high but, alas, I am still a dope.

- **I am better at callbacks**: When I am high, I can do "callbacks" with the best of them. What is a callback you may ask? It's essentially bringing something that was discussed earlier in a conversation into the current conversation, generally with a decent window between each conversation (i.e. at least 30 minutes after the original conversation). Comedians may use callbacks for jokes to essentially bring their "set" full circle. When we are out with friends or I'm just having a conversation with Alexandra, I am able to recall specific things that were discussed 30, 60, 90 minutes earlier and quickly bring them into the current conversation. I attribute this to my brain moving quicker leading to more and faster connections, which allows me to essentially think "quick on my feet".

- **The elevator music stops**. It's happened to all of us. We get in an elevator, hear "Hit Me Baby One More Time" by Britney Spears, and we want to hate it . . . but we don't. For the rest of the day, we find ourselves humming the lyrics to the song without thinking about it. Similar to this experience, we all have elevator music in our brains—the thoughts that are always circulating around, lurking in the background. Whenever you have a slow moment in the day, all your thoughts go back to that elevator music running in the back of your mind. Usually that back-track makes you stressed, anxious, angry, worried, or just plain miserable. For me, my elevator music is work—there is always something work-related in the back of my mind that I am thinking about doing or finishing. For Alexandra, it's the kids, our relationship, or her list of 6,000 things she must get done. For others, it could be a health issue, a work issue, a personal issue, or any number of things.

When I'm high, the elevator music that is my job is replaced with good and happy thoughts and feelings. I don't think about work, don't worry about work, and don't feel anxious about what I have to do next week. It's wonderful. Short, but wonderful.

Stop for a second and think about what your elevator music is. Is it related to work, family, relationships, politics, finances? How can you try to turn the "music" off? Maybe you don't need marijuana to do this, but is there another way to turn this elevator music off through meditation, therapy, or just putting your goddamn phone down and going for a walk?

ALEXANDRA'S NOTE:

This is very true for me. I have tried so many things to stop the elevator music, but nothing has worked as well as marijuana. I've tried various types of anti-anxiety medicine, yoga, meditation, and therapy. You name it, I've tried it. When I am high, the crazy cycle of thoughts stops, and I am able to be more present and enjoy the small moments (similar to how Eric thinks normally). I can cuddle with my kids on the couch and truly feel happiness and fulfilment. Under non-high circumstances, I struggle with this because, as any working mom with young children knows, there is always something to do or something else that is occupying my brain. So, for me, marijuana has a calming effect. Whereas Eric's brain moves faster, mine slows down, which is a very good thing for me.

- **I act and react differently.** At some point, many months after I started doing edibles, I realized that I was acting differently—not in the sense that I would punch a wall or get on stage to do a comedy routine—but I would act and react differently to everyday situations. Most people would say, "Duh, you have a crap ton of chemicals working through your body, so you're going to act differently." They may be right, but I will give you some examples.

a) I am chattier. When I am sober, I generally want people to leave me the hell alone, and I don't feel like carrying on a conversation. But when I'm high, I talk more and *want* to talk more.

b) My tone changes when I'm high. I'm calmer, more relaxed, and I enunciate more, which is *exactly* how Alexandra talks when she's not high.

c) I am more empathetic.

d) I am more worried about the kids (paranoid) and want to help out with the kids more.

e) I am more emotional and talk about my feelings more.

f) As I noted above, my mind thinks in steps, and I am constantly thinking about how many things I need to do before I can lie down in bed and just chill.

g) I generally act happy and free. I am certainly not like that when sober—I am stressed, annoyed, a little forlorn (I had to look that word up). But it's the opposite when I'm high. Whatever this lovely little plant does to us, I am *all* for it.

A lot of the changes in how I act are similar to how Alexandra normally acts. She is chatty, calmer, and more relaxed (except when she has her "special days" each month). She is definitely empathetic, she is definitely paranoid about the kids, and she is always willing and wanting to talk about her thoughts (it's awful).

Later on, I will get into what I think is happening, but for the next chapter, I will talk about some of the more memorable experiences I have observed and documented while high.

5

Gather Round . . . It's Story Time!

SO, WHAT EXACTLY WERE MY EXPERIENCES WHILE I HAVE BEEN HIGH that led me to believe something was going on that I could not explain?

I must admit that at first, I assumed what was happening was either due to pure coincidence or me simply being more in touch with my inner feelings and subconscious than I would be otherwise. However, when Alexandra and I started documenting these experiences, we soon realized it was impossible that all of them were either of the above.

Whatever happens to me when I'm high, I have enough of a sample size to truly say that I am connecting with others on a different level. Maybe when you read my stories below, you'll believe it too—or maybe not. That's up to you.

The experiences noted below are not all of our experiences where we believe we have been connected, but they are the ones that stood out to both of us as being the most interesting, the ones that made us laugh the most, or have an "Oh my God!" moment.

I hope you enjoy!

Is It Ever Too Hot for Butternut Squash Soup?

I hate soup. That's not just something I say to be dramatic. If you were to put a bowl of soup and a bowl of cow testicles in front of me, hold a gun to my head, and say "choose," I would have to think about it for a full minute. I think it's a pointless food; you can't eat it, but you can't drink it. It's hot, it drips all over you, and it generally just stinks. I have it two times a year: Jewish holidays and leftovers after the Jewish holidays, when I'm force-fed matzah ball soup by my mother.

Which is why this story is so interesting to me. Alexandra and I were spending a summer day in New York City without the kids for the first time in what felt like forever. I'd had an edible gummy in the early afternoon. We eventually wandered down to the Greenwich Village area of the city and stopped in a small restaurant to have a snack since we had been walking for nearly three hours. I looked at the menu and the first thing that caught my eye was butternut squash soup—it was practically calling me to order it.

Just to set the scene, this was a freaking *hot* summer day, which makes it even harder to believe that I would have wanted to order soup. We were both sweating by the time we sat down, and there were literally fifteen other things on that menu that I would have typically ordered. Prior to that day, I'd had butternut squash soup maybe once, so there's no statistical evidence that I usually enjoy it.

After I told her that I was going to order the soup, Alexandra looked at me and said, "You know, that's one of my favorites, and I was going to get that too."

We just looked at each other, smiled, and said, "Whoa!"

Now, is it possible that, after sweating for three hours and sitting down outside on a beautiful day in New York, somehow, some way, my body craved butternut or squash or soup? I suppose . . . but I don't think that's all there is to it. Don't get me wrong, the soup was *delicious*, and it's now my favorite soup—but I've had many a chance to order butternut squash soup since then when I'm sober and I've given a strong pass on it.

ALEXANDRA'S NOTE:

For the record, I completely disagree with Eric on this— soup is the best food ever. You can have tons of flavors and textures in one delicious bowl. He's clearly never had pho or ramen. But, on this particular day, he wanted it. This story is so interesting to me because butternut squash soup is one of my top five favorite soups.

Experience Summary:

Connection: Alexandra

Amount consumed: 20–25mg

Time until connection: 100–120 minutes

Cool connection rating: 9 (Mostly because this was one of the first times we realized something weird was happening to me while high. There were some prior times when I started to tell her what I was experiencing, but this was definitely one of the first where we both agreed something weird was happening.)

Meaningful connection rating: 8.5 (Similar reasons as those noted above made this meaningful to me.)

Total score: 17.5

The Air Conditioner Repair Man

I was in Chicago, or Detroit, or Indianapolis—I can't remember, some Midwest city—for work. I had popped a gummy an hour or so before arriving at my hotel room. It was summer, so when I got there, I quickly realized the air conditioning unit was broken. I called down to the front desk, and they apologized and sent someone up to fix it.

Typically, I would be annoyed that the AC was broken, complain to the front desk, and demand an upgrade to the presidential suite to compensate for the inconvenience. Alexandra has seen me behave this way multiple times while traveling. However, I realized that I wasn't annoyed at all; this time, I was relaxed and calm. I thought to myself, "It is what it is."

The repair guy got there about ten minutes later, and we started chatting. He started telling me about his life story—how he'd been

ALEXANDRA'S NOTE:

Seriously, he really is the master of getting free shit when annoyed while staying in a hotel or while flying.

out of work for a while, just got this job back, and was happy because he had five kids at home (or it may have been two or three) and was now able to provide for them. He told me how he immigrated from some European country and how he tried to also send his money back to his family.

We conversed for twenty to thirty minutes while he worked to get the AC running. I genuinely felt empathy for this individual. He was working hard to get the air conditioning back for my stupid ass, while telling me about his difficult situation. Eventually, when he did fix it, I realized I didn't have any money to tip him, which made me feel bad.

Now, bringing it back to how I typically would feel and react, believe you me, normally I would not feel empathy, at least not to the level I did. Maybe I'd feel sorry for the dude and go back to watching whatever stupid thing I was watching on TV. However, this time was completely different; I was interested in his story, felt bad for his situation, and felt even worse that I didn't have money to tip him.

After he left, I remember saying to myself, "WTF, this isn't normally how I would be feeling." I had to call Alexandra to tell her. She said, "Eric, that is exactly what I would have felt," and again, we both went, "Whoa!"

Now, could this be a coincidence, where his story was so sad that it made me feel more empathy than I normally would when sober? Absolutely. Could it just be that the drips of dopamine from consuming the edible triggered certain emotions that allowed me to recognize them in a different way than when I am sober? I do have to acknowledge that possibility. However, it was still an unusual moment for me that caused both Alexandra and me to wonder if I was connecting to her even if I wasn't physically around her.

ALEXANDRA'S NOTE:

I've known Eric for twenty years now, and I've always told him he lacks empathy. He is the smartest person I know, but the whole concept of walking in someone's shoes has always been a struggle for him. So, when he started to have more empathetic experiences while high, I was extremely happy for him and for myself. It was around this time that I realized we were connecting in a way we haven't for so many years. Shit, I'm not sure we *ever* connected like this. So while I wasn't there for this connection, he did call me right after and we talked about it, and we both said it was interesting how empathetic he was being.

Experience Summary:

Connection: Alexandra (remotely)

Amount consumed: 10–12 mg

Time until connection: 90–100 minutes

Cool connection rating: 8 (Mostly because this was the first time I felt like I connected with Alexandra when she wasn't physically there with me. So this helped support the fact that you may not need to be physically close to someone to connect with them in some way.)

Meaningful connection rating: 6 (It was one of the first times that I realized how empathetic Alexandra is. As I've already said, I am not empathetic, so this helped me realize how good it can feel to feel empathy for someone. It was also meaningful, as the AC repair guy fixed the air conditioning, which made for a very comfortable night's sleep.)

Total score: 14

My Smart-Ass Son

One of the more surreal experiences I've had while high was in September 2021. I had taken 15 mg a couple hours earlier. This was the first experience where I believe I physically reacted like Alexandra would due to a triggering emotion. We were in the kitchen, chatting about some nonsense while she was washing the dishes (I probably had to rewash a few dishes afterward). Her face was turned away from me because she was looking down at the sink. I was eating a piece of cake (of course; I was high) about ten feet away from her and was not looking at her.

My eleven year old son came into the kitchen, yelling and generally being a smart-ass about everything. I instantly cringed and felt my body tighten, and I remember clenching both of my fists because felt like I just wanted to slap him across his face due to his *smart-assness* (yes, that's a word).

He finally took his smart-ass upstairs, and I turned to Alexandra and asked her, "Do you normally feel like you want to slap him when he is being smart-ass?" She replied, in all seriousness, "Yes. I cringe, and my body tenses up." I responded, "That is *exactly* how I just felt. I literally clenched my fists into a tight ball and got tense." She said, "That's exactly what I was doing too!"

At that point, we both were like, "WTF!" We both agreed that, normally, I don't care that he's being a smart-ass. In fact, I encourage it and laugh it off. This time was the exact opposite. The anger and tension in my body was not something that would have ever happened if I was sober.

I expressed to Alexandra that this was the first time I felt like I reacted the same way as she did at the same time (or at least it was the first time I recognized it). The *really* freaky part is that afterward, as we were talking about what happened, all I wanted to do was bite the nail on my right middle finger. As Alexandra pointed out while I did so, that is the *exact* finger she bites whenever she's stressed (in this case, because of my oldest son being a smart-ass, which she absolutely hates). I never bite my nails—ever. I have beautiful nails and would do nothing to harm them.

Now, could all of this be a coincidence? Of course. Maybe what my oldest son said would have made me cringe even if I wasn't high. Maybe me biting my nail the exact same way as Alexandra was because I'd finally picked up her habit. I have no idea.

What is tough to express in words is how unbelievably happy I was when I realized that I was able to connect with her in a deep way and I was able to literally feel how she was feeling in that moment. What was that connection? I'll get into it more later, but it was a wonderful feeling to realize that this may be possible to do and it filled me with absolute warmth

ALEXANDRA'S NOTE:

Generally speaking, I *hate* smart-asses, especially when someone thinks they are smarter than you and trying to get away with something that way—which is what our son was doing that night. In my family growing up, sarcasm was not appreciated and was mostly considered disrespectful. Unfortunately, my eldest son has his father's *smart-assness* embedded in him, which is why I cringed that night (mostly so I didn't smack him). From what I remember, we were not looking at each other when this happened, so there was no way Eric could have seen me cringe.

and happiness. I hope other people will be able to experience this as well.

Experience Summary:

Connection: Alexandra with a physical reaction

Amount consumed:
15–20 mg

Time until connection:
90–100 minutes

Cool connection rating: 9 (Mostly because this was one of the first times I had a physically-similar reaction to her.)

Meaningful rating: 6.5 (While this was a very interesting connection to further my theories about me being able to connect to Alexandra without having to look at her, there wasn't anything terribly meaningful about the connection itself.)

Total score 13.5

Normally, Eric is the exact opposite; he typically encourages *smart-assness*. That's why it was so interesting to me when he said he felt the same way I did—he would *never* feel like that normally. Is he an empath while high? Maybe, as I do think empaths are able to feel and sense emotions more than the average person. The question is can empaths feel and sense things where either: 1) the two people are not talking to one another; or 2) the two people are not looking at each other (both of which were the case here)? I don't know but it is an interesting question.

Shut Up, Mattie

Dogs are great—every dog owner will say the same thing. But every dog owner will also admit there are times when you want to take your dog and lock them in the basement for a couple of days just to get a break from their constant whining, barking, eating food they shouldn't be eating, diarrhea-ing on the floor, pissing on the floor, vomiting on the floor, and just being a dog. In general, while I am patient with our dog, there are times that I do lose my patience with her—but Alexandra has far less patience with her than I do.

One night, our friend was over with her two kids. I had taken 10 mg about two hours earlier. Alexandra, our friend, and I were sitting in the kitchen talking (or trying to talk). Our dog, Mattie, in all her glory, decided she needed to be part of the conversation and started barking with a frequency and at a frequency (see what I did there?) that would cause the average person to think that they should move all the citizens of Kansas out of the state, erect a ten-foot-high electric fence around the entire state, move every dog into the state, and then let them fight it out until there is only one dog left in the entire country.

(By the way, if you want to see one of the more perfect comedic bits of all time that proves how some human beings are just creatively above others, please watch "George Carlin—Save Money on Prisons." Regardless of your beliefs, background, or views on politics, race, or religion, we should all marvel at how absolutely funny, creative, and brilliant George Carlin was.)

Anyway, back to the incident. After dealing with Mattie's incessant noise for five minutes, without looking at each other or giving each other any sort of cue, Alexandra and I said, at the same time, in long, drawn out voices, "Mattie, shuuuut uuuup."

What was most interesting was the way we said the phrase. We didn't shout or scream, we didn't say any other words. We said the same thing in *exactly* the same tone, length, and verbiage.

As soon as we said it, we both looked at it each other and started laughing. I don't think she knew I was high, but she said, "You're high, aren't you?" I looked at her and said, "We'll talk about this incident later," because I wasn't sure how our friend felt about marijuana.

I will reiterate that I *felt* myself needing to say "Mattie, shuuuut uuuup" in that drawn-out way. After we laughed it out, I had a few moments to think about what happened, and I realized it was honestly so amazing to be able to see how Alexandra was thinking in that moment.

ALEXANDRA'S NOTE:

I have to admit, this experience was pretty funny—both of us telling the dog to shut up at the same time, in the same way. It was a feel-good moment, for sure. This type of connection (saying the same thing, at the same time, in the same way) is somewhat common when he is high, but not when he is sober.

Experience Summary:

Connection: Alexandra, thanks
to our dog.

Amount consumed: 10–15 mg

Time until connection: 120–130 minutes

Cool connection rating: 8 (Mostly because this was one of the first times we said the same thing at the same time.)

Meaningful connection rating: 4 (My dog will hate me for this, but while it was cool, it wasn't terribly meaningful for me—sorry, Mattie.)

Total score: 12

The Damn Balloons!

One night, after we got back from dinner with friends, Alexandra and I were in the kitchen. I'd taken a gummy a couple hours before while at dinner, so we took an Uber home. Our three-year-old daughter had gotten her hands on some old balloons, still half-full of helium, that were floating around in our house from some event a month back. She proceeded to beat the ever-living shit out of the balloons with my son's drumsticks (which she'd also gotten her hands on somehow). After about twenty seconds of this lovely noise, I said, "I cannot tell you how fucking annoying that is." This wasn't directed to my daughter or to Alexandra, necessarily—it was just something I felt I needed to say. However, Alexandra was within earshot, and she turned to me and said with a smile, "I was just going to say, 'I cannot tell you how fucking annoying that is!'"

We both instantly cracked up. I said, "Write that one down before I forget!"

I had time to reflect on this experience afterward, and I kept asking myself if what happened could have been a coincidence. Could the fact that I said exactly what she was thinking at the same time be a stroke of chance? Sure. But I don't think it was, and I'll walk you through my reasoning:

1. What I said wasn't in response to a question asked by anyone.
2. This was a nine-word phrase (with a curse caught in the middle of it) that was in response to something random occurring in our world that generated a thought by both of us at the same time. In reality, either one of us could have had any number of responses to what was happening. Something along the lines of "Daughter, please stop doing that" or "Daughter, why are you doing that?" or "My God, I'm going to go insane if she keeps this up."
3. I think a coincidental response would generally apply to phrases that are five words or less (maybe six, if you push it) and don't have curse words in them. Here are some examples of phrases that would be pure coincidence:
   a) "No sir." — How my friend and I respond when an officer asks, "Were you two out tonight doing cocaine and hookers?"
   b) "We're not sure." — How Alexandra and I respond when my mother asks, "Will we see you in temple for Rosh Hashanah two years from now?"
   c) "That's what she said." — The response of two older brothers watching their youngest brother change the diaper of his firstborn son while making the following statements: "I don't know how it sticks together." "Does he have a package?" And finally, "It's supposed to be tighter than that." (This absolutely did not happen to me and my youngest brother).
   d) "No, Dad, we didn't." — The response by two sons to whether they ate the last piece of Dear Old Dad's crumb cake from some Lithuanian bakery (which makes the best damn crumb cake you've ever had in your life) that Dad was really looking forward to having but the damn kids didn't bother asking Dad if he wanted the last piece, knowing how much he loved it, so they just

decided to go ahead and chow down, leaving Dad with nothing for dessert but some of the dog's stuffed bacon chicken and peanut butter bones. Ah . . . I feel better now. We can move on.

e) "We are definitely not married." — The response by two straight, single guys to two straight, single girls asking if they are married.

f) "His name is Alan and he is eighteen years old." — A response by two coworkers to a police officer questioning a group of coworkers about whether they knew the name and age of a coworker that disappeared after attending a Justin Bieber concert two nights earlier. (This is a nine-word phrase, but with no curse word in it—in case you weren't paying attention.)

4. Also, by my calculations, there are a few things I could have said differently in the sentence:

a) I could have shortened "cannot" to "can't."

b) I could have used the word "express" instead of "tell you."

c) I definitely didn't need to throw the curse in there.

d) I could have substituted the words "balloon hitting" for "that."

e) I could have added the name of my daughter to the front of the sentence.

But I didn't. I said it exactly the way I said it, which was exactly the way Alexandra was thinking it. So, in my mind, there is no way this was just a coincidence. I'm sure there are language scholars and scientists that will say there is a perfectly rational explanation for why this happened, and I am all ears. They will probably say Alexandra just said she was thinking the same exact thing to appease me and maybe she did. I will let her respond.

ALEXANDRA'S NOTE:

Similar to some other experiences, there are times when Eric says out loud what I am thinking at that moment. This was one of those times. I hate that he seems to be "in my head," but it is pretty cool that we do this sometimes. And for the record, what he said was exactly what I was thinking in my head.

Experience Summary:

Connection: Alexandra

Amount consumed: 15–20 mg

Time until connection: 120–130 minutes

Cool connection rating: 8 (Mostly because this was one of the first times we realized I said the same thing she was thinking.)

Meaningful connection rating: 8 (For the same reason as previously noted.)

Total score: 16

Two "One Secs"

One Sunday evening, we were hanging out at home after I had taken 15 mg about an hour and a half earlier. I was helping my son do his homework (which I *never* do—yes, I'm an awful father, but you try doing third-grade homework and tell me how you feel about it). But that evening, I was happy to help my son out with his homework that he was struggling with. Again, this never happens—ever—so Alexandra and I started a conversation about how different I was behaving, and she smiled and said, "That's how I generally feel because I know he struggles with this stuff." We were attempting to continue this conversation when our three-year-old daughter, Ophelia, interrupted with some story about her doll's arm that had fallen off for the seventy-second time that night.

After about ten seconds of her talking over us while we were trying to have a conversation, we both said, at the same time, "One sec." Similar to prior experiences, I admit this could have been pure coincidence. However, I just want to lay out twenty different things we each could have said differently in that moment:

1. "One second."
2. "One second, please."
3. "Ophelia, one second."

4. "Ophelia, please, one second."
5. "One second, Ophelia."
6. "One sec, Ophelia."
7. "Ophelia, one sec."
8. "Ophelia, one second, please."
9. "Ophelia, one sec, please."
10. "Ophelia, stop."
11. "Ophelia, please stop."
12. "Stop, Ophelia, please."
13. "Stop please, Ophelia."
14. "Ophelia, can you stop please?"
15. "Ophelia, can you please stop?"
16. "Please, Ophelia."
17. "Please, Opheliaaaaaaa."
18. "Please, Ophelia, stop."
19. "Please, Ophelia, can you give us one second."
20. "Ophelia, holy hell, for the love of God, can you please give us one second." (This is the one usually used, for the record.)

These are the different phrases I came up with in a few minutes, but I'm sure there are more. Similar to prior experiences, I am sure there are people that will just say that when you're in the middle of a conversation, you naturally say the shortest thing that comes to mind. I can buy that, but again, we said it at the *exact same time*. Not two seconds earlier, or two seconds later, but at the exact same time. I will let you decide what you think.

ALEXANDRA'S NOTE:

I was happy Eric was helping the kids out with homework, which isn't something he normally does, as that is my territory. He usually does not have the level of patience needed to teach a nine-year-old how to multiply 5x5 using blocks. (If your kids follow Common Core, you know what I'm talking about.) While I was more focused on how he was being empathetic and bonding with his son than the connection we had over saying the same thing at the same time again, when I think back on this, it is pretty cool to realize we were potentially connecting. If this was a one-time occurrence, I would think of it as being a coincidence more than anything, but it has happened too many times while he's high to be able to chalk it up to just a coincidence at this point.

Experience Summary:

Connection: Alexandra

Amount consumed: 15–20 mg

Time until connection:
80 minutes

Cool connection rating: 7 (This was one of the first times Alexandra started recognizing the connections we were having as well, but there have certainly been cooler connections. This one was pretty funny, though.)

Meaningful connection rating: 5 (Not terribly meaningful, but it just continued to add to the evidence that we were connecting.)

Total score: 12

My Electric Car Is Too Powerful

If there is one thing that I own that would devastate me if it was destroyed or stolen, it's my electric car. It's a beautiful piece of machinery that I have received many compliments on. So one night, Alexandra and I were out with friends for dinner and, as I had taken about 20 mg of edibles about ninety minutes earlier, I was in no position to drive. She got in the driver's seat, and within ten seconds of me getting into the passenger's seat, I felt nervous and jittery and my legs started shaking uncontrollably. I realized I was nervous about having to drive the car—except I wasn't the one driving. So I told Alexandra what I was feeling, and she said that was exactly how she was feeling in that moment.

Anyone who's driven an electric car knows it is very different from a gas car. The acceleration is different, the one-pedal driving is different, the braking is different, and the steering is different. At that point, Alexandra had not driven my car enough to be comfortable with it.

Thus, it does make sense that she would be nervous to drive my car and risk messing it up. Plus, she had half a glass of wine, and anyone who knows her knows she gets sleepy after she has wine.

After a few minutes of her driving, I realized I was biting my nails, which, as I wrote about earlier, is something *she* does when she is nervous and something I never, ever do when I'm sober.

About five minutes later, as we were talking about what I had been feeling, she asked me, "How are you feeling now?" I responded that I felt better because I was distracted by our conversation, which was true. She said, "That's exactly how I feel right now; I am distracted and don't feel nervous anymore about driving."

I am happy to report that we and the car made it home just fine.

This was one more experience where the feeling of a connection was very apparent. The skeptic in me would say that I was just nervous that she was driving my car. She'd had half a glass of wine, and maybe I was nervous that she wouldn't be okay to drive, and my nerves were just enhanced by the marijuana. That is certainly a possibility. But I believe what I felt wasn't simply my own nerves—it seems more like it was me tapping into *her* nerves about driving.

Experience Summary:

Connection: Alexandra

Amount consumed: 20 mg

Time until connection: 90 minutes

Cool connection rating: 8.5 (This was really cool because it was another connection that manifested itself through changes in my physical behavior.)

ALEXANDRA'S NOTE:

I agree that I was very nervous about driving his car. It is fast, and I hate driving it because he considers it his "baby." That night, I was more nervous than usual because I had consumed half a glass of wine, which for most people wouldn't be much, but it makes me tired. Initially, I didn't pick up on his leg shaking, but once he pointed it out, it was pretty interesting to see. Also, from the way he was talking, it did sound like he was nervous. We had a good conversation on the way back, which did distract me, and we got home fine. We definitely should have planned that night better, but it made for a very interesting connection experience.

Meaningful rating: 5 (More meaningful because it reminded me how *awesome* and *fast* my car is.)

Total score: 13.5

I Just Want Her to Talk to Me

As I have noted already, I don't normally like to talk—about anything, but especially my feelings. And like every woman on Earth who is in a relationship, Alexandra only wants to talk—about absolutely anything at all. So, you can see where the conundrum usually lies.

One night, I had consumed around 50 mg of THC (by accident) a couple of hours earlier, while Alexandra was out at a friend's house. Once I realized I had probably taken more than normal, I started to freak out a bit. I tried calming myself down through deep breathing and drinking water, which is known to help relax you. Then my buzz hit, and I started getting a little paranoid, but nothing terrible. Eventually, I just really felt like I wanted Alexandra with me, and I wanted her to talk to me.

It didn't matter what we were going to talk about, I just felt the overwhelming need for her to talk to me and for me to talk to her. I distinctly remember sighing and saying, "I just need her to talk to me" in my head and then out loud (this was while I was alone in my bedroom—not creepy at all). I texted her right away and said, "I need you to talk to me. About anything. Just talk to me." A moment later, it hit me. I texted, "Omg, I'm *you*—all I want is for you to talk to me."

When she got home and we talked about it, she confirmed this is how she generally feels, especially when I travel for work, which I had done that week. She told me all she wants is to talk—about her day, work, family, friends, her feelings (*yech*), how she wants us to go away on vacation, life, anything.

In that moment, I realized I was likely connecting to her in a deep way; I felt what she always feels in the back of her mind—her elevator music. She just wants to talk to me.

As usual, I do have to leave open the possibility that I just wanted someone to calm me down after taking too much THC. It could be that this wasn't a true connection and just my way to calm myself down. It could also be that marijuana lowers my inhibitions, which results in me wanting to talk more in general.

For full disclosure, of all the experiences I have documented here, this one was the least convincing one to me, but because of the nature of the result, I still felt like it was interesting to document in order to show the benefits of consuming marijuana (i.e., being more open to communicating and connecting on a basic human level).

Experience Summary:

Connection: Alexandra

Amount consumed: 50 mg (whoops)

Time until connection: 100–110 minutes

Cool connection rating: 8.5 (I struggled with this ranking at first, but I realized I have to separate the feelings of being nervous about how much marijuana I had accidentally taken from the rest of this experience, which led me to realize that she just misses me and wants me to talk to her and be her friend. The coolness of that revelation really bumps this experience up for me. Although I did just throw up in my mouth a little bit after writing that.)

Meaningful connection rating: 8.5 (This was meaningful to me because it made me realize that no matter how much of a PITA (Pain In The Ass) she is or how annoyed I get with her, I need her in my life for her love and companionship. I realized that I maybe I do actually enjoy connecting with her through conversation. For this reason, I bumped up this score. Take that, Hallmark!)

Total Score: 17

ALEXANDRA'S NOTE:

I totally agree that this may have just been more about his freaking out than him connecting to me. But I'll take it! Even though I don't remember everything we talked about, I do remember that we were both really engaged and laughing. Eric is totally right—I genuinely enjoy talking and having adult conversations and while I am sure it is annoying for him when I talk his ear off (I don't know what that phrase means), this night wasn't like that. It was a great night.

Dad, Can We Skate?

While the above experiences have been with Alexandra, there are other times I've felt connected to my kids, my friends, and my damn dog. I have connected with my daughter when she's been tired and I could sense she wanted to lie down with me; I have connected with my older son when he's had a rough day and I could sense he needed some reassurance from me; I have connected with my dog while we were on a walk and I could sense she wanted to find the rabbit she saw twenty-five minutes earlier.

One really intense experience I had with my nine-year-old son occurred on a Saturday night when we were hanging out with friends at our house. I had taken 20 mg of edibles about two hours earlier and the adults were all sitting in our sunroom, talking about who knows what. At some point, I walked out of the sunroom and into the living room, where my middle son was sitting on the couch watching TV. As I walked back to the kitchen, with my back to him, he asked me, "Dad, what time can we do open skate tomorrow?"

To give some background, he was referring to the fact that we had gone to his buddy's birthday party at a roller-skating rink three weeks earlier, when he tried out rollerblading for the first time in a long time and had done well at it. Afterward, he asked me if we could go back. I told him we could go on a Sunday, because that was when they had open skating sessions for the public.

He asked me about it the week after, and I'd forgotten to look into it. A week later, he asked me again, and again I'd forgotten about it.

Finally, on this night, when he asked me about it for the third time, I *felt* a rush of disappointment and sadness in me, and I instantly knew it was coming from him. It took me a few seconds to remember why he was sad, until I realized I had forgotten about the roller skating multiple times and that it was something he really wanted to do.

This feeling was so intense that I started to tear up and had to get Alexandra (who was in the middle of talking to our friends) and take her outside to tell her what I felt. I was extremely upset; I was shaking and felt like I wanted to cry. I truly, with all of my heart, know that I had felt how my son felt in that moment, when I had completely forgotten about something he really wanted to do.

Anyone with a kid will tell you they would be sad if they realized their kid was disappointed in them. As such, it makes it hard to distinguish whether this feeling of sadness was my son's or mine. I would respond to that by saying the initial feeling that hit me was likely my son's (keep in mind that I could not see him when he said this but I likely heard it in his voice) and this feeling was then compounded by me being more sensitive and empathetic than normal, which resulted in disappointment in myself for forgetting.

I obviously have no way of proving that this sense of sadness was from him, but I do believe it was. It is not a great feeling to know that you have disappointed your kid, but I am happy to report that I was able to get him to the rink the next day and, I assume, he loves me again.

Experience Summary:

Connection: Younger son

Amount consumed: 20 mg

Time until connection: 120–130 minutes.

Cool connection rating: 4 (This was an interesting and deep connection, but any connection that makes you want to cry is not cool.)

ALEXANDRA'S NOTE:

This seems like it was one of the more meaningful connections for Eric because, regardless of the fact that it made him sad, I felt like it was a truly loving moment for him. Also, the level of connection was intense! I was very happy to learn that he felt the way he did, as I have tried to explain how I feel when I know the kids are upset, and I don't think Eric really understood until that night. I remember standing outside with him and asking him if he felt like crying. I was shocked when he said he did, and I saw tears welled up in his eyes. To me, that was a really beautiful moment, and certainly not something he ever would have felt sober. I really do believe he felt how my son was feeling and, while I certainly don't want my son to be sad, I am happy Eric was able to work through the emotions and get him to the roller rink the next day!

Meaningful connection rating: 9 (This was one of the deepest connections I have had to my younger son, so that jumps this experience up to a 9.)

Total score: 13

Panic Attacks

One night, after getting home from dinner out with friends, I had one of the weirdest experiences while high. When we came back home around 10 p.m., our three-year-old was up and running around all over the place (of course), but when I went upstairs, I found the two boys asleep in our bed. I shook them awake to get them the hell out of our room so I could watch some TV.

The eleven-year-old woke up just fine and said, "Goodnight, Dad," but the nine-year-old half shrieked as if he'd been startled awake and jumped up. It took him a few seconds to realize what was going on, but he eventually crawled out of my bed and stumbled to his room. I didn't think anything of it and I wasn't worried about him being freaked out so I went to go pee.

As I went into my bathroom, I immediately felt my heart starting to race—slowly, at first, but then faster and faster. It got to the point that I became scared about what was happening, so much so that I went downstairs to tell Alexandra that I didn't feel right and was nervous about my heart rate. Then I started getting chilly, and my body was trembling uncontrollably, as if I had a fever.

For the next twenty minutes, I was essentially experiencing a full-blown panic attack. I walked around my kitchen, trying to breathe deeply, drinking water, and talking to Alexandra about random topics to distract myself. She kept talking to me, and I kept breathing, and eventually I went upstairs to lie down and try to warm up while she made me some tea.

After another twenty minutes, the panic attack began to die down. I felt better, and my heart stopped racing. As I calmed down, I took some time to speak with Alexandra about what happened and why the hell I had a panic attack. After some discussion, we realized a few things that are important to note:

1. It is possible I had an increased heart rate because of the THC, and I freaked out and had a panic attack because of that. However, my heart had never raced that fast while high before, and I hadn't taken any more edibles than usual (around 20 mg). However, it could have been a different strain of THC that caused my heart rate to increase, which gave me a panic attack.

2. I have had a few panic attacks in my life, but the last one was close to twenty years earlier, when I was buying my first house. However, I haven't had any since then. There was nothing else going on that would have led to a panic attack in this moment.

3. My heart started racing almost immediately after I woke my son up from a deep sleep, and he appeared to be scared and didn't know what was going on.

4. I wondered whether, in that moment, I was connected to my son, which manifested itself through me physically reacting to how he was feeling—which was scared.

Interestingly enough, the next morning, we casually asked him how he'd felt when I woke him up, and he told us that he was scared, that his heart was racing, and that he was shaking in his bed from being woken up. We did not prod or lead him on in any way; we just asked him how he'd felt and that was what he told us, which leads me to believe he may have had a small panic attack.

So, the question is: What caused my panic attack? Was I connecting to my son because I was high, or was I just feeling the impacts of marijuana on my circulatory system and my heart? I can't answer it for sure—all I can say is that I believe I was connected to my son and that the connection physically affected me, similarly to some of the other experiences I have already summarized.

I also had a heart-warming moment after the panic attack, when I realized that Alexandra's voice and her reassurance that nothing was wrong were the main reasons I started feeling better. It was exactly what I needed at that moment. She explained to me later that my son has told her that the sound of her voice helps him whenever he is scared or panicking, which apparently does happen a lot.

Experience Summary:

Connection: Younger son

Amount consumed: 20 mg

Time until connection: 120 minutes

Cool connection rating: 9.5 (In the moment, it was not very cool, as I really thought something was wrong with me and I was scared. But after I talked to Alexandra about the experience, there was a lot of "Wow, did that just happen?" and "Holy shit" on my end. It got even crazier when we asked my son the next morning how he had felt the night before and he said his heart had been racing and he had been shaking.)

ALEXANDRA'S NOTE:

So this experience did freak me out a little, as Eric hasn't had a panic attack for twenty years. However, my son does get scared when woken up quickly like that, and the timing of Eric's panic attack and our son being scared is too much of a coincidence in my opinion. After Eric started to calm down, we had a really heartfelt conversation where I again finally felt like he understood me—particularly how I can feel what our kids are feeling and my need to make them feel better. As scary as it was to see him have this panic attack, I am happy that he did have that experience. In the past, he would have argued with me that I was "babying" the kids, whereas now he tries to soothe them more. Lastly, to know that my voice helped calm him down really warmed me, and to know I have that effect on him made me see him in a different light. I know we all get so busy with our daily lives—coordinating pick-ups, drop-offs, breakfast, lunch, dinner, homework, playdates—that I forgot that before we had kids, we did have a profound impact on one another. This experience reminded me of how much I missed that.

Meaningful rating: 9 (It was very meaningful to me, as I realized how my son feels when he is scared. This was one of the connections where I learned something about my kids that I didn't understand before. Understanding how scared he gets at times made me realize that he's still a little boy on the inside. That is what made this meaningful for me.)

Total connection score: 18.5

Water, Please!

I love drinking water, specifically water with ice (as long as it's not crushed ice, which I explain later). On any given day, I'll likely drink ten cups of ice water, which results in me peeing 500 times a day. Since the next experience involves water, I want to paint the picture that I always have a cup of water near me, day and night. So, one night, after I had taken 15 mg of edibles about ninety minutes earlier, I was standing by my bed when my son asked me what I was doing. I was busy with setting the lineup for one of my fantasy teams for the next day (I lost that week, I believe) on my phone and didn't really pay attention to him. However, in that moment, I sensed his need to hang out with me and for me to be "his bud." I think he had lost at his baseball game earlier in the day and was upset about that, or maybe he was just in a mood, but either way, I could strongly sense that he just needed to hang out with me. So, I said, "Let's watch a scary movie together," and he lightened up and lay down in my bed.

As I was looking down at my phone trying to sync a scary movie to our smart TV from my phone, out of the corner of my eye, I noticed him sit up. I didn't see his face, and he didn't say anything, but at that moment I knew he needed water. I handed him my glass, which he thanked me for by saying, "Thanks, I was thirsty."

I didn't recognize the connection at first because I was still busy trying to put the movie on the TV, so it took me a minute or so to realize that I had sensed that he was thirsty without any indication by him.

Again, he did not say he was thirsty, and I did not see his face because I was staring at my phone trying to figure something technical out on it (doing anything technical while high is pretty much like an accountant trying to repair the engine of a 757 jet), so there was nothing I saw or heard to tell me he was thirsty. Yet, somehow, I just knew he was and offered him water.

Of course, then he drank all of my water, which pissed me off, which made me lose the connection pretty easily. But as long as *he* wasn't thirsty anymore . . .

Experience Summary:

Connection: Older son

Amount consumed: 15 mg

Time until connection: 90–100 minutes

Cool connection rating: 7 (Definitely pretty cool because it was another time I made a connection without seeing or hearing anything that would have led to me reacting to someone, which has happened many times during my experiences.)

Meaningful rating: 9.5 (Very meaningful for me because it was one of the few times I have connected with my older son—or at least recognized that I was connecting to him.)

> **ALEXANDRA'S NOTE:**
>
> It is hard for me to comment on this experience because I wasn't there and didn't see what happened. Eric told me about it a little later on that night and I thought it was interesting that he felt he was able to recognize my son being thirsty without even looking at him. If this just happened in isolation, I would certainly say it was a coincidence. However, with everything else I have witnessed and experienced with Eric, I do believe him when he said he made this connection. And by the way, Eric is totally right about him always having water nearby. He drinks water until 10 p.m., which is probably why he gets up eighteen times a night to pee and proceeds to wake me up every single time he gets up. I'm just going to end up getting him a bedpan in the very near future.

Total score: 16.5

Mom! Get out of my head!

I have two experiences with my mom where I felt I was able to connect with her, both of them on different days. Here is the first.

Family events are always fun, especially holidays, where relatives are free to question everything you are doing with your life and make recommendations to correct whatever you are doing wrong—whether it's with you, your kids, your career, or the type of DustBuster you are using. So, prior to Thanksgiving of 2021, I decided I wanted to get high for a few reasons, primarily to stay calm throughout the day and also to try to connect with my mom. As such, at some point during the afternoon, I had taken 20 mg of edibles before the family arrived.

While I was in the kitchen making fried ravioli and chatting with family, one of my kids put some music on the refrigerator (yes, that's a thing now). As this music was playing, the kids were playing with the dog, the dog was barking, the kids were yelling and screaming, and Alexandra was trying to talk to me about some nonsense about getting a new oven. Pretty quickly, I became overwhelmed by all the noise, and I just felt the need for it to stop as I couldn't concentrate on whatever it was I was trying to do. So I asked (more like yelled at) one of my kids to turn down the music and stop screaming, which they eventually did after several attempts, and I started to feel a little better.

To be clear, I normally don't give a crap about loud music or loud noises—in fact, I encourage it. Usually, Alexandra is telling me to turn down the TV or music and I have been high while around loud music (I've been to a couple of concerts while high and it never bothered me), therefore, I don't think I would have had the same overwhelmed feeling if I had been sober. I also distinctly remember the *feeling* of being overwhelmed by the loud noise, which is what happens with auditory sensory overload when your brain becomes overwhelmed by the amount of sound it needs to process and cannot focus on other things.

After the music was turned down, I had a revelation that I was potentially connecting to my mother, as I know she hates lots of noise and definitely hates lots of *loud* noise. I always thought she was doing it just because she was worried that other people would complain, especially in their apartment building where they have ornery and cranky neighbors. However, after sensing this feeling, I now understand that she likely suffers from some form of auditory sensory overload. She is constantly telling the kids to quiet down whenever they get loud, and she is constantly turning down loud music or televisions. I talked to my mom about this afterwards, and she confirmed that this is how she feels in those scenarios.

I tried finding some research on whether marijuana impacts your sensitivity to hearing in a way that might explain why I reacted the way I did, but I couldn't find much. There have been studies that show THC does impact the parts of the brain responsible for auditory stimulation (noise)[36] but nothing that would truly suggest that THC causes you to react to loud noises on a consistent basis. Yes, I probably experience heightened sensory perception when I'm high, which makes sounds louder, but again, this was the first time I can recall that I had an overwhelming sensation of being bothered by these loud noises, which happened to be when my mother was present. Coincidence? Maybe—I will let you form your own conclusion.

Either way, after I realized I potentially connected to my mother, I felt pretty awesome, and it made me realize that she really is negatively affected by loud noises. So, for the rest of the evening, I ensured that my kids, the music, and TV weren't too loud. It turned out to be a great Thanksgiving!

I do realize this is similar to the "Shut Up, Mattie" experience, where I believe I connected to Alexandra's feeling of wanting Mattie to shut up because of the incessant barking. This time, I believe I connected to my mother's aversion to the loud noises. Two separate connections, but similar reactions.

Experience Summary:

Connection: Mother

Amount consumed: 20 mg

Time until connection: 90 minutes

Cool connection rating: 8 (The connection itself was pretty cool because it again helped me realize that I can

ALEXANDRA'S NOTE:

This is a tough one for me to comment on, as I don't recall the details of where Eric and his mother were when this was going on. While I am confident that he felt that connection with his mother, all I can remember is how I noticed that his mother was uncomfortable, which tends to happen a lot, especially when our kids are running around and screaming! While I don't think he could see or hear his mother when this was going on, what I do know is how happy he felt about understanding how she was feeling, which is a wonderful thing for him.

connect to someone without seeing their face or without them even being in the same room as me.)

Meaningful connection rating: 9 (This was very meaningful for me because this was the first time I felt like I had connected with my mom. I now understand how loud noise makes her feel, which really helped me going forward to try to control the noise around her: my kids, the dog, the volume on our TV or music player, etc. So, because I was able to understand my mom better, to me, this experience shows the power and benefit of being able to connect like this.)

Total score: 17

Yawwwwnnnnnnnn

One afternoon, my parents came to our house after my older son's black belt test (which he passed on the first try, by the way). I had taken 20 mg of edibles an hour and a half earlier—just because. Around 6 p.m., we were just hanging out and I was talking with my sons about something kid related when I felt an overwhelming desire to lie down and shut my eyes for a bit. It wasn't late by any means, so I didn't think it was because I was tired. There wasn't anything going on that would have led to me being mentally or physically exhausted (other than dealing with three kids). It took me a moment, but eventually I wondered if I was connecting with my mother and that she was ready to leave because she was exhausted and wanted to lie down.

For some background—when my parents come over, there's generally a time limit to my mother's energy level. As such, at some point, she will begin the process of stating her desire to leave. Usually it begins with a statement that she has something to do at home (laundry, Zoom meetings, cleaning, etc.) I always attributed this to her just losing her patience or wanting to go home to do chores. I'd suspected she gets tired earlier than most people, but even when she wanted to leave as early as 4:00 p.m., I never really thought much about it.

On this day, she'd had a rough day for a couple of reasons, and my guess is that it must have led to a higher level of exhaustion than normal. So, after I felt this rush of exhaustion come over me and realized that I could be connecting to my mother, I told my dad to start saying his goodbyes and helped them get on their way. If I'd been sober, I likely wouldn't have cared how quickly they left and would not have been so inclined to help my mother get out of the house. But that day, because I felt this level of exhaustion, I wanted to make sure she could leave in time to get home and rest.

You may think this was just me being empathetic because I was able to read my mother's face, and it is fair to think that. However, although she was in the same room, I certainly wasn't looking at her or talking with her at the time I felt this. I distinctly remember how strong the wave was that came over me, and I strongly believe that it wasn't my exhaustion I was feeling but my mother's.

> **ALEXANDRA'S NOTE:**
>
> Similarly to above, I'm not sure I can be totally impartial here. However, it was pretty funny, because before I even knew what was happening, I thought, "What the fuck—why is he acting like his mom right now?" He was telling his dad to get up and saying, "It's time to go," which made me laugh so hard because he *never* does that.

Experience Summary:

Connection: Mother

Amount consumed: 20 mg

Time until connection: 75–80 minutes

Cool connection rating: 8 (Mostly because I was not looking at my mom when this happened, and the tired feeling was overwhelming.)

Meaningful connection rating: 9 (It was very meaningful for me because I feel like this was another connection with my mom where I was able to understand her better. Now when she gets like this, I try to help her by telling her to sit down, or by getting her a glass of wine or something else to relieve her level of stress and exhaustion.)

Total score: 17

Out-Of-Body Experience

One of the most intense experiences I've ever had on marijuana was in early 2021, after I had accidentally consumed between 50 mg and 60 mg of THC due to a misread of the dosage on a box of edible chocolates. (Yeah, that can happen. *Whoops.*)

This experience was one of the most emotional nights I've ever had in my life. It got to the point that I was crying outside, on the ground, in front of Alexandra, saying, "I love you so much!"

During this experience, I had an intense vision of how my soul interacts with other souls around me, like planets rotating around the sun. This vision led me to a lot of the thoughts and processes regarding the soul that I describe later in the book. At first, I was pretty freaked out by what I felt. However, after calming down a bit, I realized that I felt comforted by and at ease with what I had seen. I wasn't scared or fearful of anything I experienced. In many ways, this was the catalyst to a lot of what I have written about in this book.

I can't explain what exactly happened but I distinctly remember myself starting to leave my body, which freaked me the fuck out and I felt like if I kept going, I would have started flying above my body. I can only say that I know what I felt. It was real, and it was intense.

That night was particularly emotional for me and for a solid fifteen to twenty minutes, I was completely uninhibited with expressing my emotions and felt like all of my negative emotions were pouring out of my body and there was nothing I could do to stop it. I do feel like something left me that night and went into the universe at large—call it negative energy, my inner demons, everything I had held inside for so long but was afraid to express, etc. Either way, I do think that was the night I began to change for the better.

Yes, of course, there is the possibility that it was just chemicals in my brain reacting in such a way that caused me to think I was leaving my body and seeing things around me. However, after the experiences I've had over the past year and a half, I have to believe it was more than that.

There has been some research done on out-of-body experiences and astral projections, which is when you feel like your spirit (or astral body) leaves your physical body. Some theories link them to epilepsy, brain injuries, stress, sleep deprivation, and anxiety.[37] (With the amount of stress and sleep deprivation I have, I would be experiencing this daily if that were the case.) Of course, drugs like marijuana, LSD, and shrooms have also been linked to these experiences. However, there's nothing that I have seen that truly explains why using cannabis would cause an out-of-body experience to occur other than cannabis being a "psychedelic."

If anyone reading this has had similar out-of-body experiences, please email me and let me know what you think is happening to you; I would love to hear about them.

Experience Summary:

Connection: Not a bloody clue. Anyone and everyone who was around and potentially some people that were not around. Can't really say who/what I connected to that night.

Amount consumed:
50–60 mg (Again, *whoops.*)

Time until connection:
75–80 minutes

ALEXANDRA'S NOTE:

This was by far the craziest experience I've had with Eric. We both went through a whole range of emotions that night. At first, I thought it was hysterical that he'd taken too many gummies and was high as a kite. That quickly turned into me thinking, "Oh shit, do I have to take him to the hospital? If so, who is going to watch my kids?" I imagined all of us getting kicked out of the hospital because my kids were being too loud or crying because it was late at night. I remember Eric telling me he felt like he was leaving his body. He was visibly freaking out, but he kept talking through it and telling me everything he was feeling. To me, it seemed like it was a cathartic experience for him; he apologized for past mistakes while telling me how much he loves me and our kids. Again, if you know Eric, you know he does not express anything, let alone something like this. I almost felt like this was a cleansing for him—all of the stress and anxiety he had been feeling left his body. Since that night, I have noticed a change in him. There are some days when he seems to revert to the old Eric, but for the most part, he has been a much different person. I don't know if he actually left his body, but I feel like his demons, so to speak, left him in some way that night.

Cool connection rating: 9 (Similarly to the time I had a panic attack, I have to separate some of my fear during the experience from the rest of what I felt. I was scared shitless when I felt like I was coming out of my body, but after I calmed down, I thought it was pretty amazing. There was a lot about that night that moved me, but something about the raw emotions coming out of me that night sticks with me to this day, which makes this one of the coolest and most interesting experiences I have gone through.)

Meaningful connection rating: 8.5 (Alexandra and I agreed that something in me changed after that night. It was like I got out all the bad and raw emotions I'd been holding inside for so long, which allowed me to be freer with myself. It was after that night that I started documenting these experiences, so that was also the night that started this journey for me. For these reasons, I have given this experience a very high score.)

Total score: 17.5

Spirit of Christmas Eve

It was Christmas Eve, and I had taken some edibles about an hour earlier (because, as a Jewish person, I strongly believe that this is what Jesus would do). I was watching TV, minding my own business, when Alexandra came in and asked if I was okay. I said I was fine, and right as I said that, our dog Mattie—who was lying on the floor next to me—made a growling noise. This caused Alexandra to think of an interesting experience she'd had earlier in the week, while I was traveling for work, that she hadn't told me about yet. As she explained it, she'd woken up in the middle of the night with a very high fever (she had been sick for a few days, and I know, I'm an asshole for leaving her alone while sick), and when she got up, she saw the light in the extra bedroom was on. She started walking to turn it off, and as she was walking down the hall, she heard someone say, "Mama, Mama." She checked on the children, but they were all fast asleep.

I asked her if she thought it was the boys or our young daughter and she said she didn't think it was them. She said it sounded like a six- to eight-year-old boy. I asked her how hearing that voice made her feel, and she said that she hadn't freaked out like she normally would have—it just made her feel like they needed her help.

A bit of very personal backstory here. In 2014, Alexandra and I found out she was pregnant with what would have been our third child at the time. There was an issue with the pregnancy, and we had to make the decision to terminate the pregnancy or risk complications at birth. This was a very difficult decision, and we have had to live with that decision and our feelings about it since then—albeit in different ways for each of us. I think she would agree it affected her much more profoundly than it affected me, which I am sure is true for any woman that has had to make a difficult decision about a pregnancy.

So, with this in mind, I asked if she thought the voice she was hearing was "Quarter," which is what we had named it when we made the decision to end the pregnancy. She said she hadn't thought about whether that was a possibility. Then we got into a deep discussion about what happened and the fact that she needed to forgive herself for the decision. We also spoke about the fact that we had never really talked in detail about the pregnancy afterward, but that it was something we both decided together was the best decision for her and our family. I kept telling her, "You need to forgive yourself if you want to move on; you need to get the negative energy out of you."

As we continued to talk, I had a moment where I felt an absolutely overwhelming sensation. I remember grabbing her arm and saying, "Wow, I feel an overwhelming sensation of love right now." I distinctly remember it taking over me like a wave, first starting in my head, then my chest and arms, and finally down through my legs. There was also a buzzing in my head that just felt like pure love and warm energy. The sensation lasted for a minute or two, and the entire time I was holding onto Alexandra's arm and saying, "Wow, wow. We have a strong connection right now."

As the sensation began to end, I told her that it felt like, because of the discussion we were having, a little bit of negative energy that she associated with this topic was released from her, and I picked up on it, though it turned into positive energy for me. What could this have been? I don't know. But the sensation was so overwhelming that I had to pause for a few minutes to just collect my thoughts. I lay there for fifteen minutes and just kept telling Alexandra that it was the most intense and longest connection I felt like I had ever had.

Of course, the topic at hand was a difficult one. However, the feeling I had that she'd let go of some of the negative energy around this topic was strong, and she agreed that discussing it helped her feel a little better, but that she still had a long way to go before she could fully forgive herself. Please keep in mind, this is very personal for us to be writing about, but the connection I had was so strong and so emotional for me that we felt this story should be included in the book.

What we took away from this is that we think that it is possible that when one person releases negative energy, it can turn into positive energy for whoever is able to connect to that person. I felt so good afterward and it turned the rest of the night into a great Christmas Eve. I will let her summarize her reaction to this experience in her note below (as of this writing, I have no idea what it will be, but I hope it is as positive as mine!).

ALEXANDRA'S NOTE:

Eric is right; this is a deeply personal issue for me and not one I ever speak about. I was sick with the flu and had a 103.5 fever when I woke up at 3:00 a.m. to pee and heard a little boy's voice saying, "Mama, Mama." I normally would have freaked out, but this night I didn't at all; I just felt like this voice needed my help.

Since I was so focused on trying to get better, I didn't think about it again until a few nights later. I told Eric about it on Christmas Eve, which somehow led him to ask me if I thought that voice was perhaps our third child from years ago. I had a very hard time discussing this topic because, while it was a difficult decision we both made together, it's not something I have ever forgiven myself for—or him, if I'm being honest. In that moment, I felt myself getting angry and resentful toward him because of all the months I'd cried myself to sleep, the depression that followed, and the downward spiral of stupid shit he did afterward. The negative emotions in those few minutes were all-consuming. However, it did make me realize there were so many unsaid things about that topic, things I've always wanted to say to him but never did because I felt like it would have only led to an unproductive argument.

I told him I never felt like it'd been a "we" decision because I hadn't been strong enough in the moment to fight for "Quarter." That is probably why I haven't been able to fully forgive myself; I was already a mom of two beautiful boys, and I should have fought harder for our third. But I didn't, and I will have to live with that decision for the rest of my life.

I did notice that as I started revealing more and talking about it more, Eric started to feel a deeper connection, and he said he felt an overwhelming sense of love surrounding him. He touched my arm and told me to let him feel the moment because something was happening. Personally, I didn't feel anything of what he felt, but I did feel myself calming down and gaining a greater sense of peace. It was cathartic, and maybe this was the first step toward forgiving myself.

As hard of a conversation as it was, it did not ruin the night at all. It was quite the opposite, actually. We had a great dinner and a fun time opening presents. That night, for the first time in a long time, I wanted to go to church. I felt I had forgiven myself enough that I could go back to church and face God. I then went to mass with my mother and had a nice, long conversation with the "big man in the sky," as Eric calls him.

This connection was meaningful for me, but in a different way than it was for Eric. I truly do believe that he was feeling something come off of me. I don't know what it was—maybe he could sense the negative energy leaving my body somehow—but I do believe that he felt something powerful that night, and I will take that as a very positive takeaway from this experience.

Experience Summary:

Connection: Alexandra

Amount consumed: 15 mg

Time until connection: 80–90 minutes

Cool connection rating: 9.5 (The overwhelming sensation of the connection flowing through my body was very vivid; I felt it so strongly in my forehead that I started rubbing it, then felt it in my chest, my arms, and eventually my legs, which started shaking. I never felt scared that something bad was happening to me. I just let the feelings take over my body, and it was very positive. I somehow knew that she had let go of a little something in her that I was picking up on. I can't give this a 10 because I don't know how much cooler a connection can get (yet), but this is right up there with the highest score I can give.)

Meaningful connection rating: 9.5 (This was very meaningful for me because the conversation started with Mattie making a noise and turned into a deep discussion about the decision we had made years earlier. We never had a discussion like this about it, but I told her that she needed to let it go and start forgiving herself, and then moments later, I had these feelings. I don't know how much this helped her at the end of the day, but for me, it was the most meaningful and warm connection I have had since documenting these experiences.)

ERIC'S NOTE:

As a short follow-up, this feeling happened once more (as of the time of this writing) when we were discussing another serious topic, and I felt another sense of warmth and love take over my body. We will talk more about this experience on our *Higher Connections* podcast.

Total score: 19

My Summary Thoughts on These Experiences

There's a song I love by The Head and the Heart called "Missed Connection." The song is apparently about how the band met each other, but it's also about how one member of the band met his girlfriend; one of the lines of the song is *"But I see it and I feel it in my soul"* and is essentially how I feel. There is no proof about what I'm feeling when I make these connections other than what I tell Alexandra when it happens. So, it's hard to summarize what I am feeling, other than to say it feels surreal.

As I've noted, I'm also aware that everything I've experienced could be chalked up to chemical reactions in my body impacting my sensitivity to those around me, or that I've just become more empathetic to those around me in general. However, the number of experiences I've had—especially the ones where the person I felt I was connecting to was either not in the same room or out of sight—has led me to believe that there is something else going on, something that cannot be explained away as easily as this.

Is it possible that everything I have experienced is just my subconscious surfacing while I'm high, and it turns out I am more like Alexandra than I thought? Absolutely. Most of my experiences could be chalked up to my normally suppressed feelings coming out. However, what makes me confident that something unusual is happening is the timing of everything I have experienced—the congruity and synchronization of my thoughts and feelings in relation to somebody else's. If I'd said, "Shut up, Mattie" a few minutes after I heard Alexandra say the same thing or if I hadn't tensed up at the exact same time in the exact same way as Alexandra when my son was being a smartass, I obviously wouldn't think anything of it. How these experiences could be just a coincidence each and every time is actually the part I can't get my head around.

The experiences I have shared above are some of the more notable ones. There have been many more where Alexandra and I have said, done, or felt the same thing at the same time. As I noted above, I have also had experiences with my kids where I can tell how they are feeling and why while I am high. For example, my daughter wanting to start her bedtime routine, my older son's need for reassurance after a tough baseball game, or my dog needing to go pee without her sitting by the door begging to go outside. Being able to feel these connections allows me to have the proper conversations with Alexandra or my kids in reaction to their feelings. What's more is that I *want* to do this, and it doesn't feel forced or pressured or shameful to *want* to do this.

I will admit that my family was not very open growing up and we never spoke about our feelings and thoughts for a variety of reasons. I am sure a lot of you reading this can relate to that. I always admired my friends who had open and honest relationships with their families but, for whatever reason, I never had that growing up. So now, the realization that it *is* okay to share my thoughts and feelings with my family is wonderful and something I certainly wish others could do as well.

Is it possible that human brains are able to connect with each other naturally, like a cranial Wi-fi network? Sure. Some scientists are already starting to research whether human brains are able to connect to share thoughts amongst the different human subjects that are being studied, which would allow subjects to collaborate and solve a task during direct brain-to-brain communication.[38] Additionally, some scientists have also done research into whether our brains sync purely due to interactions with each other, especially when cooperation is the primary purpose of the interaction.[39]

It is entirely possible that at some point before I die, scientists will be able to prove the existence of a brain-to-brain connection that is possible between people, whether that connection is just due to the energy that our brains generate or something else that I will get into later in the book.

There is something called the *filter theory of consciousness* whereby scientists believe the brain acts as a filter for consciousness and is essentially a receiver, and this filtering can be altered to tap into information that is normally not accessible by our brains, whether this is through meditation or psychedelic drugs. It's basically saying that most of us should be able to tap into our natural abilities to be intuitive or clairvoyant, but because we are so consumed by the day-to-day focus of surviving, our brains are not able to tap into this greater power.[40] Some people believe there are ways to harness this greater power, such as meditation, yoga, and connecting to nature.

Regardless of what is happening, I feel like I have become more connected with Alexandra because of this, in a very positive way, since I believe I can understand how her brain works and how she thinks. I'm not saying this is better than traditional therapy, but I know I feel much closer to her and understand her better than I did before I started all of this. What if marijuana is the ultimate way to become closer with your "Alexandra" by understanding who they are as a person and how they operate? I say it's worth a shot if you and whomever you want to connect with are both open to it, but it's obviously up to you to decide. I do lay out the steps for doing so later in this book.

While the title of this book is *Higher Connections*, the focus of this book is really trying to find deeper and more meaningful connections. Think of some of the greatest inventions in human history:

- cavemen learning how to communicate through grunts, mumbling, pointing, and, eventually, language

- the Vikings (not the football team; I mean the dudes with axes and perfect six-packs) crossing the ocean on boats to see the world
- the invention of the automobile (by whomever actually did it)
- the invention of the airplane
- the invention of the telephone
- the creation of the internet by Al Gore
- the evolution of social media and dating apps (Facebook, LinkedIn, Instagram, NextDoor, TikTok, Grinder, and most importantly J-Date)
- the current evolution of virtual reality and AI

All these inventions have one thing in common: humans were looking to create new ways in which to facilitate human connection, whether physically or otherwise. While each of these inventions has allowed us to have *more* connections to other humans, did they really improve the quality or deepness of the connections?

Ask yourself this question: If you could choose between 1) connecting to 1,000 people with whom you have very little things in common and never develop deep, meaningful relationships, or 2) connecting with 10 people that you can fully understand and connect to on a deep and meaningful level, which one would you choose? Maybe some of you would choose quantity over quality. That is your choice. I can certainly tell you after going through what I have, nothing can replace connecting deeply to a person in your life.

It's been proven that connecting and interacting with other people results in the release of dopamine, which is linked to positive emotions.[41] This is why social media platforms are so successful; they are designed to get you hooked on that little drip of dopamine you get every time someone likes your picture or comments nicely on your post about your kid winning a participation trophy in basketball. If you imagine how good you feel when you see those likes or those comments on your post, and then multiply that by 100,000, maybe you will understand how I feel when I am deeply connected to Alexandra and others.

The truth is we spend too much time staring down at our phones, posting, commenting, scrolling, liking, disliking, texting, emailing, and recording that we have all lost the ability to look inward at ourselves and outward at those around us in order to try to understand each other and the deeper meaning to our lives here on Earth. You don't have to be a priest, rabbi, shaman, or theologian to find this deeper meaning; I'm a friggin' accountant whose biggest worry prior to starting this journey was which wide receiver to start in fantasy football. I truly believe that if you keep an open mind, you can experience your own meaningful connections.

The last thing I'll include here before moving on is from the movie *Contact*, starring Jodie Foster and Matthew McConaughey, which summarizes how I feel pretty well. At the end of the movie, Jodie Foster is at a Senate hearing trying to describe an experience she went through where she believes she traveled through a space wormhole in a pod made on Earth based on designs that she believes were sent by aliens through signals that she and her team identified. While she has a space traveling experience that lasts about eighteen hours—where she travels through space, meets an alien disguised as her dead dad, and then comes back to Earth with her pod crashing into the Pacific Ocean—the people on Earth just see the pod falling right into the ocean, only five seconds after it was dropped. So at the Senate hearing afterwards she is grilled by a senator, and she basically gives the Senator a middle finger and tells him that while she can't prove or explain her experience, everything about it makes her believe it was real, it was something that changed her forever and it was something she wishes everyone could feel.

Preach on Jodie.

6

Happy Happy, Peace Peace, Joy Joy!

BEFORE THIS BOOK GETS REALLY WEIRD AND DEEP, I WANTED TO SUM-marize the benefits of these experiences and how they have changed me (hopefully for the better) in the brief time I've been having them. I kind of look at these experiences as my personal therapy. I have tried regular therapy, and it's hard because it can take a long time to have a "breakthrough" moment, when you realize what is happening and how to change it.

In fact, there are some therapists who have suggested that their clients get stoned before a session as a way to relax and help them process thoughts they might not have while sober. While I'm not suggesting you and your significant other dose up before going to visit your therapist, maybe you should consider trying it on your own to see if it helps open the lines of communication between you. What's the downside? You have a craving for pizza, have sex, pass out, and get eight hours of great sleep. Sounds wonderful to me.

Yes, marijuana is still federally illegal, but more and more states are opening up to recreational marijuana, so I hope it's only a matter of time before it is federally legal. Yes, there are risks with too much consumption, as there is with anything you're putting into your body (ooh, baby). I could walk outside my door tomorrow and get run over by a bear (you thought I was going to say a bus, but we have a lot of bears by where I live). If you can moderate what you consume and are self-aware enough to realize if you have an addictive personality, I think it's worth a shot.

So, take everything I say with a grain of kosher salt. You need to find your own path to whatever will make you happy, and this may not work for you. But I hope it does.

All I can say is that since expressing my thoughts and feelings while high, my overall stress levels have come down, I feel happier with my relationship and my life, and I have (for the most part) stopped worrying about the day-to-day bullshit. I focus more on my thoughts and feelings, and I also communicate them more (for the most part) to Alexandra than I ever have.

I've gone from someone who was, years ago, getting drunk fairly often, making poor personal decisions, and sometimes feeling unhappy with my life, to someone who is more at peace with the world and not afraid of death. So, I would say I have come a long way in a short amount of time.

Here are some of the positive impacts that my getting high has had on my relationship and other areas of my life:

1. **I feel closer to the people and things I connect with (yes, I have connected with my dog).** Because I am able to understand how Alexandra and others think, I can be more patient with them when they drive me fucking insane (which is often). I understand what they feel, why they feel the way they do, and what really gets under their skin. I understand how my nine-year-old is naturally fearful of a lot of things and therefore scares easily, so I try to reassure him as much as possible. I understand how my friend needs to tell stories to get a laugh out of people as a way to get the love from them that he probably never got from his parents. The best example is the connection I had with my mom, when I felt how overwhelmed she gets with noises. I will now try to limit the loud noises around her so she doesn't get flustered. In the past, I would just dismiss it as her

being a Jewish mother and being worried about her neighbors complaining, but now I know *exactly* how she feels when this is happening. I would have been unlikely to realize this if I hadn't gone through this high experience.

2. **I am at peace.** Some people will say they find peace once they have found God. In this case, I have found my God and it is me (just kidding... kind of... well, not really). But seriously, these experiences have allowed me to find a peace I never would have experienced before, and it's awesome. For example, I still don't want to die anytime soon, but I don't think death is anything to be scared of. I think it is a beautiful thing that everyone will go through and is not something to fear.

3. **I focus on the important things.** A lot of people take marijuana for medicinal purposes, but it can also help people forget about what may be painful in their lives (physically or otherwise). I spoke earlier about the elevator music of my mind going away when I'm high, which helps me focus on the good things about life and remember to be grateful for what I have: Alexandra, my kids, my dog, my health, my house, my friends. When I'm high, I rarely, if ever, think about work. Which is why I usually only get high on the weekends, so that getting high doesn't interfere with work. Not that my career isn't important, because it is and I am proud of what I have accomplished in my career so far, but I always go back to the old saying that no one ever says on their deathbed that they should have spent **more** time working. We all need to remember that.

4. **I talk more.** This could be a good thing or a bad thing depending on what I am talking about. Regardless, I am more communicative and actually enjoy talking about my feelings and experiences. You may not want that in your life, which I certainly understand, but it is nice to really talk to somebody and be able to express yourself from time to time. (Unless it's about how many Instagram followers you have—in which case, fuck off, no one wants to hear it.)

5. **I am more accepting and more humble.** I am more accepting of others and their beliefs, and I understand where people are

coming from. I may not agree with those beliefs, but at least I can understand why people have them. I have had conversations with people about politics while I am high, and I find myself saying, "Yeah, I get it, you're right." Imagine that.

6. **I am happy.** There's really no other emotion that covers how I feel when I'm high. I am truly, genuinely happy. Beat that, whiskey.

However, the above benefits don't mean that Alexandra and I don't have day-to-day problems, especially about things like how messy the house is, why there's no milk in the fridge, why there are so many fruit flies in the kitchen, why the dog wasn't put in her crate at night, why my DVR recordings were deleted, why she didn't take the boys to get haircuts when she said she would three weeks ago, why she didn't tell me her sister was coming to visit tonight for twelve days, why I can't have my next birthday party in Nashville with my boys, why she hates Tool (the band), and why we don't have any toilet paper. However, it does mean I understand her better and will hopefully continue to be more understanding of her.

ALEXANDRA'S NOTE:

I know I've touched on some of the benefits Eric's experiences with marijuana have had on me previously, but to summarize them more fully:

a) He is more empathetic with people. I feel like his connections have helped him understand the people he is connecting with better, which allows him to have more patience.

b) We communicate more. We talk more about real and meaningful topics, not just what activities the kids have or what's for dinner. They are topics that allow us to understand each other more deeply.

c) We became friends again. Before the kids, before the other events and circumstances that have defined our relationship, and before the craziness of the COVID-19 pandemic, we were friends first. Good friends. I believe him taking marijuana has allowed us to become friends again.

I don't know if we would still be together if he hadn't gone down this road. When he drank instead, it was never great; he would be funny and charming around others, but when we got home, he was a different person when we were alone—angry, mean, and depressed. Now that he has given up alcohol and does marijuana instead, I feel like we have connected in a very deep way, and I hope that it continues. As Eric mentioned earlier, nothing in life is guaranteed and I don't know what the future holds for us, but I hope it continues this way, because I feel like this is the person that I know he can be.

With all of these benefits, think about if our world leaders partook in marijuana before a major world conference. Our world is not exactly in the best place politically, socially, economically, or environmentally. Imagine if every world leader was required to take 15 mg before negotiating major economic, environmental, and social agreements. My guess is we would have world peace, fair trade, and environmental policies that actually put the planet first. Imagine that.

When you think about all the bad things that have happened historically—world wars and other major conflicts—would anyone be surprised to learn alcohol was involved somehow? Alcohol makes people aggressive, belligerent, and narcissistic. (Of course, there are certain world leaders—who will remain nameless—who are all of these things without drinking.) Think of how many fights you have seen because alcohol was involved? It's like paying for beer and getting front row seats for *Royal Rumble*. But can you imagine anyone ever getting into a fight while high? I can imagine it, but the participants would be as likely to fall down laughing from someone farting than from a punch to the face.

I really think we should create a cannabis summit, invite world leaders to participate, and require that they all agree to something while they're there. We'd likely walk about with life-altering accords on climate change, trade, social issues, and stem cell research, as well as agreements to finally acknowledge that social media is the worst thing to ever happen to humanity and must be destroyed. And that would be after just one day. Imagine if the summit lasted a week—we'd be able to spend the trillions of dollars we put into the military on other causes that don't result in our mutual destruction. (You know, things like solving poverty, free healthcare, and free education for everyone.)

So, if any of you know a world leader, please bring this up with them and let me know what they say. Thank you. Also, please invite me to the summit.

You may not put a lot of stock in my arguments, and that's okay. I am not writing this to make money or become famous as someone who has all the answers to the meaning of life. I'm just sharing how marijuana has changed my life for the better. I hope you can experience the same benefits and feel more connected to other people on a much deeper level. In the next chapter, I'll describe how you can embark on a journey similar to mine.

7

Buckle Up—It's Your Turn

SO, I HAVE SHARED MY EXPERIENCES AND THE BENEFITS I'VE ENJOYED from having these experiences. Now, the question is: What can you do to connect to someone in a profound way? Remember, the goal is to come to the realization that you are thinking or feeling something different than you normally do.

I want to be clear that some people may not need to be high for this to happen. One thing I have learned along the way is that certain people, like Alexandra, seem to be able to connect to other people all the time and don't need to be high, which I'll discuss later in the book. So even if you don't like marijuana (How dare you!) or don't want to get high (What are you thinking?), you still may be able to connect in this way if you train your mind to recognize others' feelings. See Step 6 below.

Now, there are a few caveats I have to note:

- I do not understand how these connections happen. I am not a psychologist or a medium. I am not sure of the science behind how I am able to connect to other people, or if there even is a science behind it. Maybe it's like in the movie *Avatar* when the Na'vi connect those weird braids to each other or to their animals and can bond with them. Or maybe it's like in the movie

Pacific Rim when the two main characters, Raleigh Becket and Mako Mori, form a neural connection and become one in order to sync their movements. I honestly do not know.

- I am not sure if the person you are trying to connect to has to have an open mind at the same time. I do not think so, based on my experiences, but it's a possibility.

- I am not sure if you need to be physically close to someone to make the connection, although I would recommend you are so that you can talk about the experience in real time. I would think you could be on the phone or on Teams, Zoom, Skype, Google Duo, WhatsApp, or whatever else is out there by the time this comes out. While I've had some experiences connecting to Alexandra when I was not physically near her, most of the experiences were when we were in close proximity.

- I do not know if blood relation vs. non-blood relation matters. I have connected to Alexandra, my kids, my mother, my brother, and my friends. I think the connection may be stronger with a blood relation, so keep in mind that your experience may differ between a blood or non-blood relation.

- I don't know if everyone can do this. There's the possibility that only certain people can connect like this—call them empaths, mediums, or whatever you want—so it is possible you may not be able to. Please don't send me hate mail if this is the case. Keep in mind, though, that it took me a solid six months to master the ability to realize when I was connected. I had to train myself to recognize when I was feeling something different than I normally would. It's not hard, but it does require self-awareness and the desire to recognize it.

So, with that said, here are the steps I suggest following in order to try to achieve this connection:

Step 1: Choose Your Person

Figure out who you want to connect with. They could be a parent, child, significant other, or friend. Make sure they are fully aware of what you are trying to do. After they laugh it off as ridiculous, ask them to be open-minded and honest with their feelings as well while you are trying to do this.

Step 2: Have an Open Mind

If you go into this without the desire to truly connect, you'll be doomed from the start. Both people should have an open mind that this may work for them and may be pretty cool.

Step 3: Be Prepared to Recognize and Express Your Thoughts and Feelings

You should be prepared to recognize and talk about your feelings and thoughts, especially during the first couple of hours after you've taken an edible. Avoid situations where you get high and then go to a concert or watch a movie for two hours. You must be open and available to do this exercise.

Step 4: Get High

This only applies to those of you who may not be able to connect to other people normally (like Alexandra). If you are able to connect to others' feelings normally, I salute you and I envy that you don't need the added expense of buying marijuana. If that's the case, feel free to skip this step.

If you think you do need to get high to connect, it's definitely the best part! I strongly suggest eating something before you are ready. Make sure you have your phone near you and maybe download a nice voice recording app in case you want to speak about what may happen rather than write it down. Now, take an amount of marijuana that gets you high but not so high that you can't talk or

ERIC'S NOTE:

For those of you that wear contacts, I strongly suggest taking your contact lenses out before getting high. There may not be anything worse than trying to get a contact lens out that has been lost in your eye when you're high. **Absolutely. Nothing. Worse.**

function. For me, it's generally between 10 mg and 20 mg, but you have to figure out what is best for you. I don't suggest smoking, as it doesn't last long enough, and the effect is immediate rather than gradual.

Step 5: Be Natural

Both of you should go about your normal day or night and do whatever activities you usually would. In other words, you shouldn't just sit around a Ouija board waiting for something to happen, or get a babysitter for your kids while you just stare at each other for five hours. Let the other person continue with their day so that they can experience their normal emotions and feelings. However, try to ensure you are both able to talk, if needed. If you are high, do not drive. I would also try to avoid something that both of you are experiencing for the first time, like skydiving or a threesome, because you both likely have no idea how each other would normally react.

Step 6: Be Aware of Your Feelings

If you are the person that is high or trying to connect, be aware of your thoughts and feelings so that you can compare those feelings to how you would normally think or react. These feelings should come naturally to you; do not try to react like the person you're trying to connect with. You can write these thoughts down or record them for later so that you can compare them with whomever you're trying to connect with. The discussion about the experience doesn't necessarily have to be a real-time conversation. **The most important thing is being able to recognize when your feelings and thoughts may be different than normal.**

For example, if you are a middle-aged married dude and feel the desire to watch *Pretty Woman* and then cry at the end of the movie, then you may be connecting to your wife or girlfriend whose favorite movie is *Pretty Woman*. (By the way, no, that has absolutely never happened to me.)

It's important to understand that the thought or feeling may not be something crazy or special; it will likely be a response to a regular, everyday occurrence, like watching a movie, having a conversation with your kids, dealing with a pet, etc.

As I noted above, you may have to train yourself to recognize when you're feeling something you normally wouldn't. It took me six months to be able to do this, but it does become easier to identify the feelings that aren't normally yours.

Step 7: Talk About It!

If you think a connection has happened, talk about it with whomever you feel you have connected to. Remember, the other person needs to be open and willing to express themselves to you so they can give you an honest description of how they were feeling and what they were thinking when the connection may have occurred. Only then will you be able to determine if what you were feeling was also what they were feeling at that moment.

Again, I want to express that it's very important that you are able to: 1) recognize the emotion; 2) correlate it to how the other person might be feeling in that moment; and 3) remember to tell someone or write it down so you can talk about it later in order to confirm what happened.

If you can be patient with this exercise, I truly hope you will be able to connect to the person you are trying to connect with. If you do, it can be an intense, yet awesome, emotion or feeling. It can truly make you feel like everyone in this crazy world is connected to each other and that there is some greater force at work here.

If you don't connect for a while, don't get too down, as it may take some time. You might actually be connecting with someone else, even if they're not directly in front of you, so be open to this possibility as well.

If you have any questions or if this actually worked for you, please contact me via email to let me know how the experience was and whether you think you had a connection. I would love to read about your experience.

8

So You're Telling Me What Now?

NOTE THAT ALL OF THE CONCEPTS AND THEORIES I DISCUSS BELOW came to me while I was high. However, most of the research was done while I was sober because it takes me thirty minutes to type out a URL when I'm high (there's no easy way to do research under the influence).

So, after everything I have experienced, seen, and felt, what do I think is happening to me when I make these connections? What allows me to do this?

The answer to that may be as simple as I am an "empath," which is defined as someone who feels empathy more than the average person. Perhaps I am just more cognizant of others' feelings when I'm high and am also able to express that to others. However, I believe what is happening is more than that and is tied to a concept that has been around for a long time. Essentially, I believe my third eye opens when I am high.

I believe that when I'm high, there is an increased level of connections in my brain that essentially allows my brain to speed up and become more active with more synapses firing. As I noted earlier, there are certain studies that support the fact that your brain is firing more under the influence of THC, which results in more "neural noise." So, as my brain speeds up and the connections increase, I believe this allows my third eye to open (like a portable generator you have to crank up hard in order to generate electricity). The more active my brain is, the more energy is created which I believe opens my third eye.

For those of you who aren't familiar with the third eye concept, it is centered around open-mindedness, perception, intuition, and knowledge. You can call it whatever you want—a third eye, a portal, a window, a door—but the central concept is that it is something that allows you to be more connected to the universe and provides you with perception beyond ordinary sight. Think of the third eye as something that allows you to tap into your "sixth sense"—an additional sense beyond sight, sounds, smell, taste, and touch.

I hate (love) going back to the movie *Contact,* but what I believe happens in my brain when high can be likened to the machine that was used to send Jodie Foster's character across the universe. As the speed of the machine increases, the energy field gets stronger and more intense until it is at full energy, at which point a portal opens that sends her sailing across the universe. If you don't know what I am talking about, go watch the movie to get a visual of it.

I also correlate it to a compass with a big needle in the middle that shows the direction you are going. When I am sober, my "brain compass needle" (BCN) spins to the different directions (east, west, north, south) slowly, and I take more time with my thoughts to focus and get things done. When I am high, my BCN is generally moving all over the place very quickly, resulting in lots of thoughts and lots of connections to be made.

Alexandra talks about the fact that sometimes she thinks she says something and she doesn't. I actually witnessed it one night when we were having a conversation and she thought she said "that's so cool" but she didn't. Those words never made it to her mouth because she had a pain in her neck that made her BCN go in another direction to focus on the pain instead of speaking the words. I feel like her BCN is always all over the place since her brain is constantly going a million miles an hour and she can't focus on any one individual task. How this would physically happen is something that is beyond me. My guess is it has something to do with the right parts of our brains being energized in a way that allows us to connect to the energy of others. I am not a scientist and certainly would not profess to have a scientific explanation for how this could happen. Similar to the lyrics and meaning of the song "Third

Eye" by Tool (one of the best fourteen-minute songs ever), I believe that marijuana allows me to connect to the energy of the universe and the energy of the souls of people around me. As I described earlier, you can think of these souls as always near you, like planets near the sun (you get to be the sun). Some souls are closest to you (like Mercury), and some souls are farther (like Pluto...wait, is Pluto still considered a planet?).

Historically, there has been a link between the third eye and our brains, the most complex organ in our body. The primary view is that the third eye was an actual eye at some point in human history (similar to other animals that have a third eye associated with them like lizards, sharks, and frogs) but eventually this eye retreated into the brain and is now located there.

A few parts of the brain are typically associated with the third eye: 1) the pineal gland; 2) the pituitary gland; and 3) the pre-frontal cortex. What is interesting is that the consumption of cannabis impacts several areas of the brain, including the pineal and pituitary glands, through increased blood flow and the altering of chemicals, such as melatonin and N-dimethyltryptamine (DMT), that are regulated by these glands.[42, 43]

For those of you who aren't familiar with these glands, they serve very different purposes but have historically been connected to the third eye concept for a multitude of reasons I've outlined below.

THIRD EYE AND BRAIN CONNECTION FOR DUMMIES

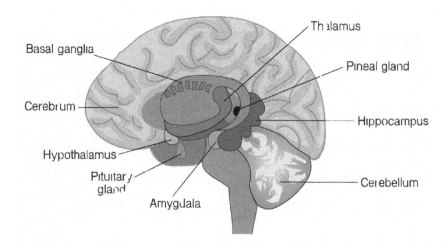

PINEAL GLAND
Referred to as the seat of the soul.
Is believed to have been an actual eye in early humans that sank back into its current location in the brain.
Produces melatonin, which affects circadian rhythms and reproductive hormones.
Produces DMT, which has been called the "spirit molecule."
Impacted by THC because of changes in melatonin, DMT, and other chemicals.

PREFRONTAL CORTEX
Involved in higher cognition, planning, personality, and proper social behavior.
Plays an important function in calming certain other parts of the brain.
Mediates stress hormones.
Impacted by THC.

> PITUITARY GLAND
>
> Known as the "master gland" as it produces many hormones throughout the body.
>
> Controls reproduction, blood pressure, growth, metabolism, etc.
>
> Frequently known as the third eye chakra, which is connected with intuition and insight.
>
> Impacted by THC because of changes in multiple chemicals, including thyroid stimulating hormone and other hormones.

Pineal Gland

This very tiny gland is a light-sensing organ that's located in the front part of your forehead and is structurally similar to your eye. The pineal gland's main function is to produce melatonin, a hormone derived from serotonin, which helps moderate and regulate sleep and our circadian rhythm.

Research into the pineal gland has led some people to refer to it as a "visual" gland. As noted in the graphic, some call it the "seat of the soul" or the "third eye," believing it holds mystical powers. Others believe it produces and secretes DMT, a psychedelic so powerful that it has been dubbed the "spirit molecule" for its spiritual-awakening type trips. Graham Hancock, a British author, has suggested that DMT could be the "lens" of the pineal gland, allowing us to expand our concept of reality and thereby find profound wisdom from its effects.[44] Many cultures, such as the ancient Egyptians and Hindus, have symbolized the third eye concept with dots in the middle of the forehead where the pineal gland is located.

Psychoactive chemicals hit the pineal gland much quicker, which means it is significantly impacted by THC due to the ability of cannabinoids to attach to cannabinoid receptors in your brain.

The pineal gland was one of the last parts of the brain discovered, and has since become the subject of much mythology and speculation. The seventeenth-century French philosopher Rene Descartes thought the soul was located in the pineal gland. This is what he wrote:

My view is that this gland is the principal seat of the soul, and the place in which all our thoughts are formed. The reason I believe this is that I cannot find any part of the brain, except this, which is not double. Since we see only one thing with two eyes, and hear only one voice with two ears, and in short have never more than one thought at a time, it must necessarily be the case that the impressions which enter by the two eyes or by the two ears, and so on, unite with each other in some part of the body before being considered by the soul. Now it is impossible to find any such place in the whole head except this gland; moreover it is situated in the most suitable possible place for this purpose, in the middle of all the concavities; and it is supported and surrounded by the little branches of the carotid arteries which bring the spirits into the brain.[45]

Pituitary Gland

Due to the pituitary gland's constant interaction with messages from glands throughout the brain, which are relayed from all three of its lobes, it is known as the "master gland." It regulates body temperature, blood pressure, and water and salt concentrations throughout the body, as well as the kidneys, thyroid, and some functions of the sex organs.[46] Even our sleep patterns are the result of the pituitary gland, as it works with the pineal gland to produce the sleep-promoting hormone melatonin, setting our bodies into ritual circadian rhythms every night. Therefore, its regular functioning as a glandular "switchboard" is thought of as the key to our well-being. The pituitary gland is frequently connected with the body's third eye chakra, which is considered the place of intuition and insight and involves connection to subtle energies that allows us to achieve a greater sense of connection with spirituality, nature, and universal wisdom.[47]

Prefrontal Cortex and Amygdala

The prefrontal cortex is thought by neuroscientists to be part of the mental processing system of humans, and it appears to help control emotions. Brain scans done with PET imaging equipment show that when a person meditates there is a lot of activity triggered in the medial prefrontal cortex, which includes the amygdala and lies in the same general area as the "third eye" from Eastern spiritual literature. Brain research informs us that people who regularly meditate physically evolve their brain structures with neural changes that promote higher consciousness, and neuroimaging has confirmed that meditators actually shrink their amygdala, which helps control the "fight or flight" reaction in most people.[48] As such, when the amygdala shrinks, people become more emotionally stable, and this equates to the Buddhist concept of mindfulness.

Does this mean that these glands are actually related to the third eye? I am sure any brain researcher reading this can explain how these glands work and whether there is any possibility that they could act as some sort of pathway to another sense humans don't normally tap into. To be clear, there is no scientific evidence that any third eye exists, and the brain is a complex organ that is still being researched and its functionalities are still being discovered.

It is also possible that marijuana allows the brain to revert to a more intuitive state by activating certain regions that are more "animalistic" or intuitive in nature while deactivating the parts of our brain that are worried about meaningless shit. So, without all the worries of a typical day, we are more able to look inward at ourselves and outward at others, and therefore able to connect with people on an innate and deeper level.

VISUAL OF THE THIRD EYE OPENING
BASED ON MY EXPERIENCES

If you are anything like me, visuals are always helpful to understand new concepts. I am an accountant, so charts, graphs, shapes, pictures, and sparklines are my friends. As such, I've tried to compare in the visual below when I feel my third eye is open based on how long after I have taken an edible. (Note that smoking cannabis would likely shorten the window for which your third eye is open.)

The pattern below is based on the typical amount of THC that I consume (between 15 mg and 20 mg).

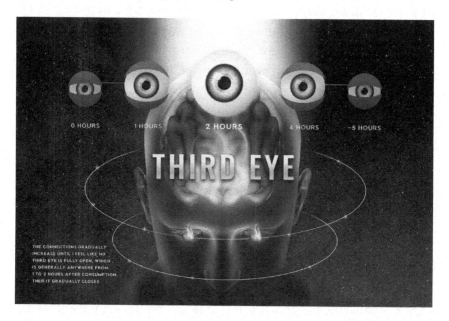

The following stages demonstrate the general pattern of my connections. However, this can vary depending on whether I am out to dinner with friends, watching a game, or doing something where I may not be focusing on the energy being generated. But if I am home and ready to focus on my feelings, this is the general pattern:

Consumption: Take the edible at zero hour.
And We're Off: I start to feel my brain moving and connecting about 45–60 minutes after consumption, which is the typical time it takes for an edible to work through my body.
It's Officially Open: This is when I feel like my third eye is open and when I feel the most energy, typically around the 90- to 120-minute mark. This time frame is generally when I have felt most of the connections I documented above. The trip generally lasts for a couple of hours, and hopefully I am able to

generate a connection with someone around me. Ironically, it doesn't seem like the amount of THC I take impacts the length or deepness of a connection. While my out-of-body experience did occur on more THC than I normally take, some of the more intense and warm feelings came after only 10–15 mg, which isn't that much (at least for me).

Time to Shut Down: Around 2.5 hours after consumption, the connection starts to fade, and I feel like my brain starts slowing down. I may still have a connection here, but it's usually pretty quick and not as deep. I also feel drained mentally, but not physically (which I will touch on in a bit), and I begin my "cooldown" phase where I just want to relax. I enjoy this phase, especially after making a connection, because I usually feel awesome for doing so and can then just relax.

Chill Mode: This is usually my creative phase, where I'll think of something funny or interesting to write down. A lot of the observations later on in this book were thought of during this phase. Clearly my brain is still moving during this phase in a way that allows me to be creative, but it's a different feeling than in the "It's Officially Open" phase.

This pattern may differ if you smoke, meditate, or do something else to open your third eye. As I have noted, some people may have their third eye open all the time and are constantly able to make connections (e.g., mediums). How do they do this? I don't know—maybe some people are just born with that ability. For me, I get a solid ninety minutes to two hours to experience these connections. For you, it may be shorter or longer. Eventually, you should be able to recognize your own pattern for when you feel the connections taking place.

Can the third eye open in two directions?

One night, Alexandra and I were talking about whether the connections I have had were good connections. I said to her, "I'm not sure how you measure good or bad, but to me they were all good—or interesting, at the least."

She then told me that she also feels these connections, but they are sometimes bad or negative connections, where she feels paranoid or scared. She doesn't like the feelings that result from these connections, as they generally lead to anxiety, paranoia, and fear. She is also someone whose brain is constantly in motion and who is always thinking, regardless of what she puts in her body (ooh, baby).

So we started wondering whether your third eye can open in two different directions—one direction opens it up to a good place (equivalent to the concept of heaven), and the other direction opens it up to a bad place (equivalent to the concept of hell). Maybe it's not necessarily two directions but more of a connection to either positive or negative energy—but I don't feel like you can connect to both at one time. I think it has to be one or the other.

Think of it like the picture below:

The questions for me are: What do the good directions and bad directions represent? Are they different planes of existence, different dimensions, different types of energy? I don't have an answer to that, but I do believe different states of mind can lead to different types of connections occurring—one being warm and positive, and the other being cold and negative. The question then becomes: Can our third eyes open to different dimensions that contain different types of energy?

I am sure most of you reading this know people in your lives that seem to exude good energy and some that seem to exude bad energy. You can never pinpoint it—it is just something you intuitively feel—but you know some people are good and some people are bad. Maybe this concept applies to all types of energy, emanating from a human origin or otherwise.

I correlate this to the movie *The Mist* (which has one of the best and worst endings ever—go watch it), where a town is invaded by a mist and taken over by a swarm of alien-looking creatures that seem to be from another world. Eventually, it is revealed that there was a government project to discover other dimensions being conducted at a local military base and that the scientists had opened a doorway into a dimension containing these evil creatures. At the end of the movie, the doorway is somehow shut, and the evil creatures are eradicated. While I am not suggesting that evil monsters are lurking on the other side of our third eyes, there are different types of energy throughout the universe, so it's not a huge leap to think that different types of energy may exist in dimensions or planes that we currently cannot see with our eyes or any other senses.

It is certainly an intriguing theory, and one I may never have an answer to. It also begs the questions of how and why this would happen? Is there something in our genes or how we grow up that influences which way our third eye opens?

What comes to mind is the Nature vs. Nurture concept, which argues that certain things are inherent in us genetically (*nature*) that we can't change, and other things are learned through life experience and exposure (*nurture*).

Could the mix of nature and nurture influence the type of connection we have when our third eye is open? Or are the connections we have a representation of the type of energy we surround ourselves with in life? It's possible that some people, such as Alexandra, are naturally inclined to connect to negative energy when their third eye is open, which may come from their past experiences or from their natural inclination to be a positive or negative person (i.e., glass half full vs. glass half empty). The question for me (and you) would be: Can you stop those negative connections and switch them to positive ones?

When Alexandra is high, her negative feelings cease to exist, and they are replaced with a general lack of caring about anything. It's as if her third eye shuts down and her brain is able to stop worrying and being paranoid about everything. It's beneficial for her, but in a different way than it's beneficial for me.

There is some science that indicates marijuana affects men and women differently, with the biggest effect seeming to be that women's sexual urges increase under the influence of cannabis (sweeeet) and men get hungrier under the influence (I can certainly attest to that).[49] However, I don't know if the different responses to cannabis between her and me is just due to gender. I think her brain just functions differently than mine when sober and so the impacts on the brain because of cannabis result in a completely different experience for her when she is under the influence.

I correlate it to a miner (someone that goes into mines to search for gold, not an underage person, just to be clear) who has a flashlight on their helmet that helps them see where they are going in a mine. That beam of light is only focused on a small area of the mine at a time. This may be how your third eye works—it is searching for a connection when it is open, and hopefully, if you have good energy around you, this results in a warm and positive connection. However, if you have bad energy around you when your third eye is open, you may experience a bad connection filled with paranoia, fear, and anxiety.

When Alexandra is high, the flashlight on her mining helmet shuts off, her third eye seemingly closes, and she is generally calm and not worried about anything. When I am

ALEXANDRA'S NOTE:

So, for me, I do think my third eye is open all the time. I have always been someone who is very "in tune" with the emotions and feelings of those around me, which is typically known as an empath. Based on my life experiences, I am a very paranoid person and always think the worst, which I believe does create some negative connections for me. Marijuana helps to ease those tensions, those fears, and helps me to be more in the moment.

high, my mining helmet seems to be on and searching for connections, hopefully positive and warm.

Does Hypnosis Close Your Negative Third Eye?

Hypnosis has historically been used for a variety of conditions, including pain management, hot flashes, behavior changes, anxiety, and PTSD. Essentially, bad or negative things in your life can potentially be treated with hypnosis or hypnotherapy.

There is research that suggests certain parts of the brain are slowed down during hypnosis, including the prefrontal cortex and dorsal anterior cortex, which play a role in focus and attention.[50] I wrote earlier about the potential connection between the prefrontal cortex and the third eye. Are certain connections in the brain slowed down, allowing the person's negative third eye to close, and thus also allowing the person to replace negative feelings with warm and positive ones?

If this is truly what is happening, maybe you don't need to be hypnotized to get these results—maybe you just need to get high. It is ironic that several of the symptoms people get hypnotized for have also been shown to be helped by marijuana, especially pain management, anxiety, and PTSD. Maybe it's just a coincidence, but maybe it's not.

Can You See What Your Third Eye Is Seeing?

One night, I was ninety minutes into a session of being high and was feeling a lot of connections. At this point, I believe my third eye was fully open. I closed my eyes and concentrated on the blackness that enveloped me. As I focused on the blackness, I began to see shapes forming—some round, some triangles. Eventually, the shape of a sideways oval came to life and began flashing yellow very fast. I immediately opened my eyes, as it was a little creepy. I closed my eyes again, and I saw the same yellow, sideways oval flashing once again (think of the inner black part of the Eye of Sauron from *Lord of the Rings*, but yellow and horizontal instead of vertical).

I remember thinking, "What if I keep focusing on that yellow light? Will I eventually be able to head toward the light and see what it sees?"

This idea freaked me out a little bit, as you always hear of people seeing a light as they're dying (scientists are trying to find a reason for this), and I didn't really feel like testing that theory out at the moment.

Furthermore, when people have near-death experiences, they speak of a light they see that feels like warmth, love, and acceptance. Many people who have near-death experiences come back less afraid of death, saying death leads you to a place that is not to be feared. Could this light they see actually be their third eye, which is fully open right before death? Below, I speak more to what I think could happen, which I call the "Final Connection,"

However, it did make me wonder if I (or anyone else, for that matter) could focus enough, through meditation or otherwise, for that light to be recognized as the third eye. Please note that as I was trying to do this, I had two kids playing some sort of hockey game downstairs, the TV was on, and my daughter was watching *Frozen 2* for the 10,214th time, so my ability to focus was somewhat limited. But if someone was able to do this when they were able to completely focus, hopefully in solitude, could they actually see what their third eye can see? Maybe one day I will try that again and see what happens.

So, if you were able to open your third eye and see through it while you were alive, what would you see? Would you see another universe or dimension? Would you see souls of people you know hanging out? I know the theory sounds as loopy as the idea of heaven, but it is something to consider.

Are Dreams Our View of Our Third Eye?

I also wonder whether dreams and nightmares are a natural way to see what your third eye sees on a nightly basis. In the next chapter, I talk more about how our third eye could potentially be open during REM sleep, which leads to the ability to connect with people, and the concept of the "witching hour."

Most dreams and nightmares occur during the REM stage of our sleep cycle.[51] So, if our third eye is open during that cycle, could our dreams be a view of what our third eye is seeing? Maybe our good dreams represent when our positive third eye is open, and our nightmares represent when our negative third eye is open.

There are a lot of theories on why we dream, from processing the subconscious mind, to processing memories, to expressing our deepest desires.[52] There are also many types of dreams—dreams where we think we foresee future events, dreams where we are communicating with our subconscious, and even symbolic dreams that seem to guide the dreamer in either the present or the future.

I generally have a hard time remembering my dreams, so I suggest keeping a dream journal to record your dreams as best you can. Then think about whether the dream represents something you would be able to see with your third eye open, such as a connection to someone you know or a view into some other dimension. If you dream of someone, ask that person if they have been thinking about you recently (assuming they tell the truth, of course) to see if such a connection was made. Unless it's a celebrity—that could be weird and end up with you in jail.

My View of Our "Final Connection"

No, the "final connection" isn't a reality TV show where you try to meet the person you end up with for the rest of your life after knowing them for six weeks (although a TV show about meeting people when everyone is high sounds hilarious to me). When I talk about the final connection, I'm referring to my belief that as we pass from this life, there is one final connection we make as our third eye is fully opened right before death.

If you recall, I noted above that I get drained after making a connection, mostly mentally. However, I do feel a bit physically drained as well. It's not like I ran a marathon and can't move, but I do feel "wiped."

When Alexandra has a strong connection to someone in her family, she feels the same way. She says it feels like the "life is drained out of her." If you haven't heard this phrase before, it basically means that you feel lethargic, tired, and drained of energy after going through something intense, whether it's physical, emotional, or mental.

So, I began to wonder—if Alexandra and I feel drained after having a small connection when our third eye is open, what might happen if we had a much *larger* connection?

If you extrapolate the amount of energy that is drained from us after one connection, is it plausible to suggest that a much larger and deeper connection would drain all the life out of us—and result in death? Is this larger connection a connection to everyone we've ever known, everyone that exists, a connection to the universe itself? Obviously, I don't know, as I have not experienced death yet, but if I do, I promise to find someone to haunt and let you know what I think.

As you know from earlier, I love charts and graphs, so I decided to create the chart below to help visualize what I think might happen as we approach that final connection. I would say that usually I am toward the lower end of the range, but I have *definitely* felt pretty drained after a connection.

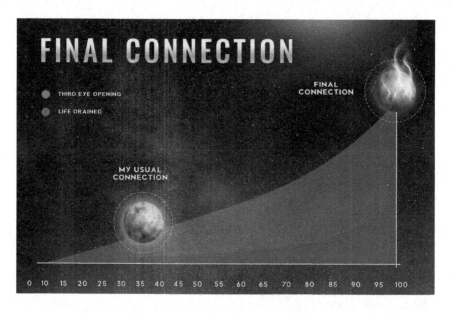

It could be a chicken or the egg dilemma where either: 1) when we are dying, our third eye opens to the point that we are connected to everything and that final connection drains the life out of us, or 2) we open our third eye naturally to the point where we have a final connection, and then die.

As far as I'm aware, no one has ever died from their third eye being open so much that all their life drained out of them, so I have to believe that the first scenario is more likely. As I noted above, when people have experienced a near-death experience (NDE), they generally have a few characteristics, including: 1) a perception of leaving the physical body; 2) passing into or drawn into a tunnel; 3) seeing a mystical or brilliant light; 4) intense and positive emotions; 5) a sense of unlimited knowledge; and 6) encountering deceased loved ones.[53] All of these characteristics could theoretically be explained by having some sort of final connection that is caused by your third eye opening as you approach death, which allows you to connect to everything and experience the universe in a different way than the vast majority of us have before.

I also believe that when people die and don't get to have a final connection for whatever reason (maybe they die tragically, maybe they aren't at peace when they die, maybe they just need to say goodbye to someone), they become a ghost or presence, and they stick around until they are acknowledged by the person they are trying to connect with.

As an example, Alexandra and I believe that her ex-boyfriend haunted our old house many years ago. There was a period of time where we had unusual things happening; our sons were hearing things, I was hearing things, and Alexandra was feeling things. Eventually Alexandra literally had a talk with him to tell him that he was scaring the kids and that while she missed him, he had to move on. I truly believe that her ex-boyfriend never got a positive final connection because of the way he died (in a car crash) and that he chose Alexandra to make this final connection with (they remained very close even up until his death). When he received that connection from her, he was able to move on.

Interestingly enough, in February 2022, it was revealed that scientists recorded the brain waves of a dying person for the first time ever. As part of this recording, scientists noted that different parts of the brain were active that are associated with memory recall, which could support a "Recall of Life" that may take place near death.[54] Perhaps these last activities of the brain are this final connection that our brains go through before death.

In general, I believe this final connection is a positive one; I see it as being filled with beautiful colors and warmth. I am certainly not suggesting that anyone try to get there on their own, but I do think this only happens upon your death, and I don't believe you can get there without it. I really have felt comforted by the thought that this final connection is something larger than anyone on Earth can possibly imagine, and I believe our souls, spirits, energies all go to the same place after death, wherever that may be. (I am not going to get into what that place is—you can theorize that for yourself.)

A visual of how I picture what I am able to connect to

In general, when my third eye is open, there are two things I feel like I am able to do: 1) sense someone's general feelings or aura, and 2) have real-time connections to thoughts and feelings with some-one which pop up based on certain experiences that lead to that feeling or emotion.

ALEXANDRA'S NOTE:

Honestly, I am still not sure what to make of this except that I am happy Eric feels that dying, or the "final connection," is a positive experience. I myself am still working toward feeling that way, and most of the time, dying does scare me. Not because I am scared for myself, but because it is hard for me to imagine a reality where I am not with my children. With regard to my ex who passed away several years ago, I have always felt bad that we did not get to say goodbye. He was my first everything, and I adored him. He was a good guy with a good heart. He called me two days before he passed away, but I did not pick up the phone because I was on the boardwalk with Eric. I thought to myself, "Oh, I'll call him back later." Unfortunately, later never came. Many years later, in our first home, I do feel we experienced hauntings of some sort, which we later thought was his way of wanting to say goodbye.

1. Connection to someone's aura: When I connect to someone's aura, I can get a sense of how someone is feeling that day—lonely, depressed, sad, needing to hang out, missing me, etc. It's like I am connecting to an invisible shield of emotions that hovers around the person's physical body (like the force field

around the Death Star in *Star Wars)*, and I can tap into that. I have trained myself to be able to recognize this connection if I am high because I now know that I am likely to get a sense of how they feel in general (though not a specific thought or emotion). The best examples of this are when I can feel like Alexandra misses me and just wants to talk to me, or when I can feel my kids are having a bad day or need some sort of comfort 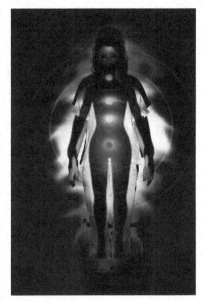 from me. I think the closer to someone you are, the more intertwined your auras become and the easier it is to feel what they are feeling on a more regular basis.

2. <u>Instant connections with people:</u> Instant connections are when I connect with someone's thoughts or feelings in real time, or as they are having them. Think of it like the solar flares on the surface of the sun that bubble up and explode into space. To me, these thoughts and emotions are little solar flares that come off the person's aura and connect with me. I've been training myself to recognize this connection to their "solar flare" as quickly as possible. The best examples of this are when I felt Alexandra's fear about driving my car or when I felt my son's panic when I woke him up out of a deep sleep. These are instant  connections that may not represent their overall feelings but do represent their feelings in the moment.

All of the experiences I shared earlier in the book were either a connection to someone's aura or connections to their real-time thoughts and feelings. Each one of the connections seems to be possible when I'm high, and I can still connect to someone's overall aura, even if they aren't having any significant thoughts or feelings, which is similar to what an empath can do.

Again, I feel like the closer you are to someone, the easier it is to connect to them because your auras are more connected than others. Think about those who are close to you, and especially someone that you have been with for many years—do you feel like you may be able to "connect" to them better or more frequently than someone else that you just met? Maybe you just need time to build this inter-connectivity with someone else, but once you have that connection, it is tough to break.

Either way, I believe this is what I am able to connect to with those I have experienced this level of connection with.

To me, instant connections are cooler, more intense, and seem to tire me out more. Maybe these are deeper connections that drain my energy more than a general connection to someone's thoughts and feelings.

9

Life's Mysteries in a Nutshell

STILL WITH ME? I KNOW SOME OF THE CONCEPTS AROUND THE THIRD eye may have been tough to follow, but there are other concepts that may be explainable by the third eye/connection concept that humans have been trying to explain for centuries.

The concepts below are things neither science nor religion can explain or prove (as hard as they try to) that have boggled humankind for a long time. While reading about these concepts, try to keep in mind that for your third eye to be open, you may not need to be high, so the people that go through these situations would not necessarily need to be high to experience them.

The Witching Hour

I'm sure you've heard stories of people swearing they saw their recently deceased loved one standing over them in the middle of the night or dreamed of having a conversation with a family member who had just passed away. Most supernatural experiences seem to occur in the middle of the night, around 3:00 a.m., but generally between 1:00 a.m. and 4:00 a.m. As such, this period is termed the "devil's hour" or the "witching hour." There are theories that this is related to when Christ died (because it's the inverse of 3:00 p.m.) or is based on mocking the Holy Trinity.[55] I think you can guess my reaction to that. However, there is some basis that a lot of paranormal phenomena seem to occur early in the morning (and yes, for the record, I do believe in paranormal phenomena). Most people will scoff at the idea of ghosts and think people are just seeing things—and that's okay—but I have certainly experienced enough to be open to the idea that there are spirits or energies that do not pass on after they die and stick around for some reason. If ghosts do exist, then we have to ask ourselves whether we are able to connect with them on a deeper level, similar to how we can connect with people who are still with us.

When you sleep, your brain is most active during the REM cycle, which for most people occurs throughout the night but gets longer the deeper into the night.[56] If most people go to bed between 10:00 p.m. and midnight, their brains would be most active at some point between 1:00 a.m. and 4:00 a.m.

If our brains are most active during this window, could this be a situation where our third eyes are open, allowing us to connect with someone who is either alive or has passed on? This could occur either through dreams (which are most vivid in the REM sleep cycle) or through some sort of physical manifestation of paranormal activity.

Earlier, I brought up the story of Alexandra's ex-boyfriend who died in a car accident many years ago. She was thinking a lot about him after he died, and I asked Alexandra to think about the times when she felt he was around. She said it was generally either in the middle of the night or when she was thinking about him. We both believe she was connecting with him while her brain was active and her third eye was open, and it manifested through her/our experiences. We cannot prove any of this, but we are okay with that. The point is that if our brains are most active in the middle of the night, does this allow connections to occur while we are sleeping and/or dreaming?

I have also thought about whether we can only connect to people we know or whether we can connect to anyone. Without any proof to back this up, I do believe that we are more likely to connect to people we know than people we don't. However, theoretically, there is the possibility we can connect with people we don't know, as well those who may still be hanging around (maybe an old owner of the house or someone else attached to the place we live in); I feel like that type of connection would be more likely to be filled with negative energy.

Think about any paranormal experience you may have had and whether your brain would have been more active than normal when that experience occurred. If it was in the middle of the night, were you dreaming about someone you knew who recently passed? Did you sense someone or feel like you knew someone was there without seeing them? Maybe you were connecting to someone who'd passed, and being asleep allowed you to do so.

So next time you hear a noise at 3:00 a.m., and it's not just you farting yourself awake, be comforted that you may have just connected to someone while you were sleeping and try to relax. As far as I'm aware, nobody has proven to have been hurt from a ghost attack. If you do feel there is a negative presence around, see if you can figure out why and what they need to move on. Bring in a medium, use a Ouija board, or whatever other way you feel like you can figure out who might be around and why they may need a "final connection" to move on.

If you feel you have connected to a spirit in the middle of the night (or otherwise), please reach out with your stories.

Possessions

We've all seen movies about possessions. For anyone born before 2000, you've likely seen *The Exorcist*. For anyone born after 2000, you've likely seen *The Exorcism of Emily Rose*. They're great movies—and likely exaggerated for Hollywood purposes—but the concept of possessions has been around for a long, long time. The question then becomes: Are possessions real? Lots of cultures believe in the ability of the human body to be possessed by spirits, which are typically evil in nature.

Usually, possessions have been explained as the devil or a demon entering a person's body and causing them to want to kill people. As I'm sure you can guess by now, I have never believed this was the case. I'm not saying I never believed that possessions could occur, just that I never believed they were the devil coming for a visit.

So, if it's not the devil, is there another explanation for what happens to someone who is possessed? If the third eye does allow for a connection to another person, whether dead or alive, are the people that are possessed making a strong negative connection while their third eye is open?

I did some research on whether there was a typical diagnosis for people who said they were possessed. Three main conditions were mentioned the most: Tourette's Syndrome, epilepsy, and schizophrenia (try spelling that when you're high).[57, 58] When I did some research into what causes each of these conditions, here is what I found:

1. Tourette's Syndrome: The exact cause of Tourette's syndrome is unknown. It's a complex disorder likely caused by a combination of genetic and environmental factors. Chemicals in the brain that transmit nerve impulses (neurotransmitters), including dopamine and serotonin, might play a role.[59]

2. Epilepsy: Epilepsy is a central nervous system (neurological) disorder in which brain activity becomes abnormal, causing seizures or periods of unusual behavior, sensations, and sometimes loss of awareness.[60]

3. Schizophrenia: Problems with certain naturally occurring brain chemicals, including neurotransmitters called dopamine and glutamate, may contribute to schizophrenia. Neuroimaging studies show differences in the brain structure and central nervous system of people with schizophrenia. While researchers aren't certain about the significance of these changes, they indicate that schizophrenia is a brain disease.[61]

There is also research that shows a correlation between traumatic injuries and spiritual possessions. These traumatic injuries could be PTSD, depression, or some sort of long-term substance abuse.[62] There is research showing that certain parts of the brain, like the amygdala and the mid-anterior cingulate cortex, become overstimulated when a person has PTSD, while other areas become under-stimulated.[63]

So, right off the bat, I admit that there is not a ton of information on what causes these conditions. However, from the research available, there is definitely a clear link: There seems to be a change in brain chemistry or brain activity that occurs with each of these conditions. When I first had this theory that possessions could be related to the third eye, I had no idea what research I would find that might support the idea. However, when I saw those three conditions were linked to possessions, I was very intrigued that each of them seemed to involve changes in the brain.

If these conditions do lead to affected individuals experiencing changes in brain activity, could they then also lead to their third eyes being open—which in turn leads to a negative connection with someone else that manifests through what we call a "possession"? Whether you believe in possessions or not, this is something to consider.

I personally think it is possible for people to be physically affected by a connection to someone else—hell, I think it's happened to me in spurts (see the "Panic Attack!" story above). I think if someone makes a deep, long-lasting connection with someone else, this could result in the traits and characteristics of what we normally think of as being possessed. However, I do think it is also possible that a lot of these cases are simply people needing some sort of medication to control whatever changes in their brain cause these reactions.

I will let you decide what you think. If you feel you know anyone that has been possessed before, please reach out and explain what you feel was happening.

The Feeling That Someone Died

I'm sure most of us have heard stories of, or even personally experienced, someone dying and another person feeling that the person has died before being told. Some people call it a sixth sense or a premonition. There have been numerous stories of this happening, even when the deceased person has died thousands of miles away from the person who senses it. All these stories cannot be pure coincidence, or hallucinations, or fabricated for attention. I believe these people truly felt something. So, the question is: How is this sensing of death possible? Is it possible that the people who experience this somehow have their third eye open at the time of death of the other person, which allows them to connect to the person who has passed on and sense that they have died? Is there a way for us to connect with those that are near death or have just died without being physically near each other (i.e., shared death experiences)? As I discuss later, I do believe that, at the time of death, the soul of a dying person disperses to those close to them.

There are stories of shared death experiences in which people have vivid and sometimes terrifying dreams of their loved ones appearing to them in order to tell them they have passed away, only for the person to wake up and find out that it is true. In a lot of these cases, their experiences are dismissed or they felt misunderstood.[64]

As I noted earlier, if your third eye is open when you're in REM sleep, could this be a way for your loved ones to connect with you if they pass away while you are sleeping? It's an interesting theory and is something that could be comforting for those who believe this is possible. But again, this may only be possible for those who have their third eye open when a loved one passes away. This could also be why most people don't experience this phenomenon and why those that do may be scared to admit it.

If you have experienced this, ask yourself what you were doing when you sensed it and whether you think your third eye may have been open at the time. Please reach out to me via email with your stories.

Power of Prayer

We have often heard the term "the power of prayer," which, for the purposes of this book, has two meanings: 1) the ability of prayer to help you in your personal life, and 2) the ability of prayer to heal the sick.

I am not one that prays by nature. However, there have been studies indicating that faith and prayer may help us experience greater health physically, mentally, and psychologically. Studies have indicated that people who engage in prayer and meditation on a regular basis have a change in their frontal lobes, which control concentration and focus.[65]

There have also been studies that show the power of prayer has no effect on those who are sick.[66] However, it's hard to say how accurate these are because I don't think the power of prayer can work with people that aren't connected to the person who is sick.

What I believe is that it may be possible for family members (and others who are very close to the sick person) to be able to heal the sick person if they can open their third eyes and transfer positive energy. If you correlate what people do when they pray—focusing, thinking, shutting off the outside world—it may be possible to create positive energy to transfer to the sick person, which allows healing to occur through the release of negative energy from the sick person. This would be similar to the experience I shared above, where I connected with Alexandra and felt positive energy and love while her negative energy left her. Also, picture the end of *The Karate Kid*, when Mr. Miyagi heals Daniel's legs by rubbing his hands together to create positive energy.

That's why I think that instead of asking religious groups to pray, it should be the people who are connected to the sick individual who pray and focus positive thoughts and energy on the person that is sick. If you are not religious and don't believe in God, I don't think it needs to be a prayer to God—I think if you focus your thoughts and positive energy on the sick

ALEXANDRA'S NOTE:

I am a big believer in the power of prayer. To me, anything that enables you to express yourself—whether it's gratitude, happiness, or your fears and concerns—is prayer. As mentioned previously, I am religious and grew up going to church every Sunday. I really enjoyed the time bonding with my mother and sister, as well as the faith that there is someone up there looking out for us. Praying, for me, has always been therapeutic; if I'm having a bad day at work, I will say a prayer, and if I'm stressed because someone is sick, I'll say a prayer. I also like to pray with my children at night—I think it's a beautiful way to end the day no matter how good or bad the day was. I know Eric will never believe in the power of prayer as deeply as I do, but the fact that he is now open to it is huge to me—even if it is due to a completely different theory. I think what he believes occurs could be possible. However it happens, if it works, then it works, and that's the most important thing.

person, that may be all that is needed. If you are someone who has prayed for sick family members, I hope it helped and that your family members did get better, but think about whether your full thoughts and focus were on the sick person. If so, do you feel like your third eye could have been open, and that having it open may have transferred positive energy to help heal them?

Even if this is not the case, praying might still be a good idea, as doctors like Doogie Howser can't be everywhere.

If you believe you have experienced this before, please reach out and share your story.

Mediums

I'm not talking about the temperature of your porterhouse steak or the size of your boxers. I'm referring to the people who seem to be able to talk to the dead or see the future. Some of you reading this may have spoken to a medium during your lifetime for a variety of reasons—maybe to try to understand your future or to see if you can communicate with someone who has passed on. The concept of a medium has been around since primeval times, starting with shamans who said they could communicate with the spirit world.[67] Some debunk these people as frauds or hacks who are just playing gullible people for their hard-earned money. While it is likely there are those types out there, I do believe there are true mediums as well.

I'm sure most of you have seen the movie *Ghost* with Patrick Swayze, Whoopi Goldberg, and Demi Moore, in which Whoopi Goldberg plays a medium who is possessed by Patrick Swayze so he can talk to his wife Demi Moore after he's murdered. (If you haven't seen this movie, then go watch it. Like, *right now.*)

I'm not suggesting that this movie accurately depicts how a spirit can enter and exit a medium's body at will. However, could there be a connection that a medium is able to make with souls that have passed on? If so, is this because they are able to easily open their third eye and connect with whatever is out there?

A study conducted by scientists at the University of California and the University of San Diego looked at the brain activity of six mediums while they were trying to connect with spirits. These mediums were selected based on their "ability to report accurate and specific information about deceased individuals under blinded conditions."[68]

There is a lot of gobbledygook (yes, that is a word) in the study that I don't understand, and most of it I couldn't begin to explain, but the study concluded that "the experience of communicating with the deceased may be a distinct mental state that is not consistent with brain activity during ordinary thinking or imagination."[68]

You can take this research with a grain of salt given there were only six mediums that were studied as part of this study. However, if the research was accurate and the brain activity of these mediums differs from the brain activity of normal people, could it be possible that the third eyes of these mediums are open, which allows them to connect with those who have passed on? I don't know, but it's something to consider.

Reincarnation

Think about all the mistakes and fuck-ups we've made in this life—I know I've had a few hundred . . . thousand. Wouldn't it be great if there was the possibility that we could do it all over again—*but without those same mistakes*? How many times does the average person think, "I'll get it right in the next life"? There are several cultures and religious groups that believe in the idea of being born again, or reincarnation. Buddhists are arguably the most prominent group that believes they can be reborn in another body after dying in another, which is called "samsara."[69]

There are many stories of reincarnations throughout history, several of which are told by children who say they are another person reborn. There are two famous stories I came across while researching this.

1. The Pollock Children

     This is an interesting case from England in the 1950s. The Pollock family lost their two young daughters in a car accident (they appear to have been walking to church when a car hit them). After a year of hoping and praying for another child, the mother became pregnant. The father became convinced that they would have a pair of twins who would be their dead children reincarnated. Even though their doctor said it could not be twins, the mother gave birth to twin girls in October 1958.

Right away, the Pollocks noticed that one daughter had a white line across her forehead where one of the late daughters had a scar from a cycling injury. She also had the same birthmark on her leg that her dead sister had had. When they were four, the new daughters were able to correctly name each doll and stuffed animal that their sisters had owned. They also pointed out landmarks that they could not possibly know. For example, they believed that they had attended the school where their sisters had been going when they died. They also started talking about the car accident their late sisters died in with specific details they couldn't have known.

The memories eventually faded when the girls were five or six, but it is still an interesting case that was thoroughly investigated.[70]

2. **Shanti Devi**

Then there is the story of Shanti Devi, who was born in 1926 in Delhi, India. When she was four years old, she began telling her parents that her home wasn't in Delhi; it was ninety miles away in Mathura, where she said her husband lived. She recounted memories of being married and later dying from complications during childbirth. She described what her husband looked like (light-skinned, a wart on his cheek, reading glasses) and where his shop was located (by a local temple). Eventually, she revealed her past husband's name: Pandit Kedarnath Chaube.

As it turned out, the man existed. About eighteen months before Shanti was born, Pandit's wife, Lugdi Bai, died from complications during childbirth of her son, Navneet Lal.

Shanti's case was investigated by a number of notable people, including Ian Stevenson and Dr. K.S. Rawat (both reincarnation researchers) as well as Mahatma Gandhi. All three were struck by the fact that so many details of her story were verifiable.[71]

Life Before Life, written by Jim Tucker and Ian Stevenson, from the University of Virginia, is a really good book on reincarnations. Tucker and Stevenson recount a significant number of documented reincarnation cases with children, taking a common-sense approach in analyzing what is otherwise a highly nonsensical phenomenon. A few things from this book stood out to me:

a) Most of the children who spoke about their past lives started between the age of two and four, and they stopped talking about their past lives around age six or seven.

b) Most of the children making these statements appear to be very intelligent and creative.

c) The average time between the death of the individual and their reincarnated form being first identified by someone else was fifteen to sixteen months.

d) A good portion of the cases appeared to involve sudden, violent, or unnatural deaths.

e) Of the 1,000 cases investigated, about 200 were same-family cases, another 200 had some association with the apparent reincarnated person and the remainder were "stranger cases" where the children did not know the apparent reincarnated person.

There are several explanations given for these cases in the book, including fraud, children's fantasies, knowledge acquired through normal means, faulty memory of informants, possession, and lastly, the possibility that reincarnation actually can happen.[72]

I believe the answer may lie most closely with the possession concept. Children's brains develop in spurts called "critical periods." During these critical periods, the number of connections (synapses) between brain cells (neurons) doubles, resulting in two-year-olds having twice as many synapses as adults. The first critical period of brain development begins around age two and concludes around age seven, which is the same age range when a lot of these children experience these previous life connections.[73]

I believe it is possible that the third eyes of these children are open due to the increased brain activity, which allows them to somehow inadvertently connect with the people who have passed on and to feel like they are that person. Why those who have passed on are connecting with these children is not something I can fully explain; however, it could be that the people who passed need to say goodbye or have other unfinished business on Earth to accomplish before they move on. Is it possible that when these children have their third eyes open, these spirits can connect with them, resulting in these kids confusing that spirit's life experiences and identity as their own? Think of these kids as young mediums who don't have a way of understanding what is happening or expressing it in a way that can be fully understood by those around them.

My only explanation for why this isn't talked about more often is that parents are likely dismissive of these situations or experiences, assuming that their child just has a wild imagination—especially in Western culture, where this type of phenomenon is generally not accepted.

There are plenty of stories out there about young kids speaking to imaginary friends that we just dismiss as a product of their wild imaginations.[74] I'm sure you have seen videos on YouTube or other social media platforms where babies seem to stare at something that nobody else can see, or where kids are having conversations with people that aren't there. Maybe this isn't just "kids being kids." Maybe their perception of the world and their potential to connect with others who have passed on is greater because their brains are more active, which allows their third eyes to be open.

I'm sure you have your own opinion about whether reincarnation is real and how it happens if it is. However, I think it is hard to deny that these stories do exist and they cannot all be made up or fabricated, so in a grand and highly complex universe, the possibility that the spirits of the deceased may come back to connect to these children has to be considered.

If you have kids that you think have experienced some sort of connection to another person, whether dead or alive, please reach out. I would love to hear your stories.

Delirium

Delirium is defined as "a serious disturbance in mental abilities that results in confused thinking and reduced awareness of the environment."[75] There are a number of neurotransmitters believed to be involved in the pathogenesis of delirium, including acetylcholine, serotonin, dopamine, and gamma aminobutyric acid (GABA).[76] Essentially, a shortage of any of these chemicals may trigger delirium. There is also evidence that delirium may be caused by widespread brain dysfunction rather than localized disruption.[77] Many older people are prone to experiencing delirium.

So, what happens when you're delirious? You hallucinate, you're confused, you have changes in mood or personality, changes in sleep patterns, and difficulty concentrating. Is it possible that when you are delirious (no matter the cause), your brain functions change, which opens your third eye and allows you to connect to others?

I shared earlier how Alexandra heard a voice say "Mama, Mama" early in the morning one night when she was running a high fever, which is one of the known causes of delirium. It is certainly a possibility she was delirious when she heard this voice. I also wrote earlier about our "final connection," when our third eye is fully open as we pass on to the other side. If you look at the causes of delirium, almost all of them are serious conditions where, if I heard someone was afflicted by one of them, I would not be surprised if they passed on in relatively short order. See some of the causes below:

- brain tumors
- head trauma
- kidney or liver failure
- alcohol, medicine, or drug misuse

- certain medications, such as blood pressure medications, sleeping pills, and sedatives
- exposure to toxic substances
- extreme sleep deprivation

Anyone that has been with a loved one in the hospital when they are close to death may have experienced their loved one going through hallucinations or confusion. Is it possible that when our brain and body feel like death is coming, our third eye opens, which allows for some sort of connection to be made to others which causes hallucinations or changes in personality, which is now known as delirium?

If you have experienced delirium before, hopefully it was just due to a temporary bad fever and nothing more serious. But isn't it comforting to know that as your body senses death, it may be able to start allowing for these connections to occur until your final connection is made?

If you think you have experienced an interesting connection when you have been delirious, please reach out to describe your experience.

Paranoia

We've talked a lot about paranoia in this book, and quite honestly, who doesn't associate marijuana (or other psychedelic drugs) with paranoia? That's generally what most people think of when they think about a chronic marijuana user—*paranoia*. But what does that actually mean? I looked up the definition of paranoia and this is what I found: "[Paranoia is] a pattern of thinking that leads to irrational mistrust and suspicion of other people. It can range from mild feelings of discomfort to an intense, extremely distressing pattern of thinking that indicates a person's mental well-being is at serious risk."[78]

Yeah, I have no idea what that means either. But research shows that paranoia impacts brain activity in the amygdala, as well as in broader sensory and frontal regions.[79]

I also looked up some examples of what paranoia is:

- You think someone might steal from, hurt, or kill you.
- You feel like everyone is staring at you or talking about you.

- You think people are deliberately trying to exclude you or make you feel bad.
- You believe the government, an organization, or an individual is spying on or following you.
- You interpret certain facial gestures among others (strangers or friends) as some sort of inside joke that's all about you.
- You think people are laughing at you or whispering about you behind your back.

What if paranoia is simply a connection to negative energy while our third eye is open, which, as I noted earlier, could lead to anxiety, fear, depression, and other negative feelings? I do not know why some individuals would be more prone to connecting to negative energy than others—perhaps they just do not have the ability to stop the connections when it gets too negative and the emotions and feelings become too overwhelming for them.

Earlier, I talked about schizophrenia being associated with possessions. Paranoid schizophrenics suffer from the same symptoms as noted above, but is essentially where your mind doesn't agree with reality and delusions blur the line between what's real and what is not.[80] Similar to reincarnation, could it be that these individuals are in a constant state of connecting with others in a deep and profound way that they cannot tell what is their life and what isn't?

In general, I am not paranoid when sober, but when I am high I do become a little paranoid, more so about making sure the kids are okay and ensuring everything in our house is locked and closed—which is essentially how Alexandra behaves when she is sober. She closes the blinds in our bathroom when she is showering (our windows look over woods, so I guess she doesn't want the deer trying to peep), and she locks the doors and closes the blinds the second it becomes dark because her house was broken into when she was a young girl. As I have noted, I believe her third eye is generally open because her brain never shuts off, and for some reason she is connecting to negative energy which causes her to have fear, anxiety, and paranoia on a recurring basis.

In our experience earlier in the book, I noted how she was not paranoid when she heard the voice calling out "Mama, Mama" that one night. She noted that she had been trying to calm her paranoia recently, which she remembers trying to do that night as well, and which I hope continues going forward!

So, if paranoia is caused by your third eye opening, maybe that is why so many marijuana users become paranoid when high.

While I wish I had more suggestions on how to close your negative third eye and open your positive third eye, I think a good starting point is trying to recognize the bad thoughts as they start and try to nip them in the bud (no pun intended), and stop them right away. Punch yourself in the face (or balls, for guys), burn your finger on a candle, scream out loud as long as you can—whatever it takes to stop those feelings from manifesting. This could be applicable to anyone that has paranoia, anxiety, depression, or any other bad thoughts. Stop those feelings as quickly as you can.

If you feel this actually works for you, please reach out and describe your experience.

Dissociative Identity Disorder

If you have seen the movies *Split*, *Fight Club*, or *Me, Myself & Irene*, then you have seen a movie about someone with multiple personality disorder. Now known as Dissociative identity disorder (DID), it is essentially where one person has two or more distinct, or split, identities that have power over their behavior. Other characteristics include the inability to recall key personal information, distinct memory variations, headaches, amnesia, time loss, trances, and out-of-body experiences.[81] Some people have identities with different ages, sexual orientations, or ethnicities as well as their own postures, gestures, and distinct ways of talking. Switching between personalities can take seconds, minutes, or days. Some people with DID have said they find themselves doing things they wouldn't normally do, yet they feel they are being compelled to do it and have described this feeling as being a passenger in their body rather than the driver.

Research indicates that the cause of DID is likely a psychological response to interpersonal and environmental stresses, particularly during early childhood years when emotional neglect or abuse may interfere with personality development. What is interesting is that as many as ninety-five percent of individuals who develop dissociative disorders have recognized personal histories of recurring, overpowering, and often life-threatening disturbances or traumas at a sensitive developmental stage of childhood (usually before age six).[82] However, there are also cases where the person has experienced traumatic events during adulthood, such as war.

Given that people with DID can act like a completely different person, is it possible that the trauma these people experience alters their brain development or overall brain activity enough that their third eye is somehow open more often than others', which allows them to connect to other people who may be alive or dead? There is research showing that some patients do have alterations in their brain patterns,[83] so it is certainly a possibility that the trauma affects the brain in a way that allows their third eye to be more open than others, resulting in a deeper ability to connect. Maybe the other personalities are not inherent within the person, but are completely separate people who need to have closure in order to move on (i.e., experience the final connection) and the different personalities are really just different connections being made at different times. Think of it as the person's "miner's light" is constantly on which allows them to tap into the energies and persona of several different people who have not moved on.

They may essentially be mediums that aren't aware of their power and don't have the ability to recognize it and deal with the connections similar to how a medium will be able to.

If this is the case, the question becomes: How do you shut off that connection in order to allow all people and souls involved to move on? I don't think there is an easy answer here, because if the brain is permanently altered, this may be harder than for someone that experiences temporary paranoia or delirium.

If there are any researchers that are reading this that have done work in this space, I would love to hear from you to see what you think.

10

The Soul Thing That Is Going On

HOPEFULLY YOU FOUND THE LAST CHAPTER TO BE INTERESTING—AND, at the very least, I hope it made you think about some potential explanations for things that may not be explainable by normal scientific methods.

If you do think the third eye concept is real, and that it is possible that we can all open our third eye and connect to others, the question then becomes: What is this *thing* that we are able to connect to? Without drawing out the suspense I'm sure you have, I believe that most people would consider this connection to be a soul, a conscience, an essence, an aura, a force. At its core, it is everything that makes you *you*—your fears, your anxieties, your beliefs, your passions, whom you love, etc. There is only one you, and you are different from every other person who has ever existed or will ever exist.

Everything about you is molded into the core of what you are, which carries throughout your lifetime until you pass away. Whatever you want to call it, this "essence" has to exist on some level and in some form, though most humans cannot sense it with the traditional five senses that we currently accept we all have.

The concept of a soul is not new, as the five major world religions—Judaism, Christianity, Islam, Buddhism, and Hinduism—all believe in some version of a "self" that survives death. But these religions imagine the self's origin, journey, and destination in some different and distinctive ways.

Most Christians believe the soul enters the body at the time of conception. According to Judaism, the soul was created by God and joined to an earthly body. In Hinduism, there has never been a time when souls did not exist, and we are all bound to Samsara—the infinite cycle of birth, death, and rebirth. Like Hinduism, Buddhism accepts there was no time when we were not bound to the cycle of birth and rebirth, but it does not believe there is an eternal, unchanging "soul" that transmigrates from one life to the next. Buddhism believes there is nothing permanent in us, any more than there is any permanence in the world.

If each of us does have a soul specific to us, how is it created? Is it something innate in us, rather than a result of how we grow up, our home environment, our life experiences, who we surround ourselves with, etc.? Does our soul grow with us as we age, and is it able to change and mutate like a cell?

Ask yourself whether you would be the same person with the same concerns, beliefs, values, passions, fears, and everything else that makes you *you*, regardless of how you grew up, where you grew up, who your parents were, what ethnicity you are, who your friends are, whom you love, where you live, and whether you have kids or not.

Obviously, your life would be different if any one of the above factors was different, but would the *core you* still be the same? This may be hard to answer, but I think the answer for most people would be "yes." I have to believe that regardless of where I was born and what family I was born into, I would carry some of the below traits that make me *me*.

- curious about the natural world and the universe at large
- cares about the natural beauty of the world
- anti-organized religion and the divisive nature of it
- good work ethic
- try to go out of my way for family and friends (some people don't)
- think that most people are short-sighted and materialistic (insert social media rant here)

- not vain about my appearance (except my ridiculously huge biceps)
- want to leave the planet a better place for my kids
- enjoy traveling and experiencing what the world has to offer
- get easily frustrated with stupidity and stupid people
- curious about why people think and do what they do

I imagine that if I grew up in a different country or under different economic conditions, some of these characteristics might be slightly different, but at my core, I believe that I would still care about the same things I care about now.

So, if the soul is something that's with us from the beginning of our lives and is the core of our being, how does it get there? There are only a few theories I can think of:

1. <u>God:</u> Is there a god who is responsible for implanting a soul in every person born? I think you can guess my thoughts on this one. I guess it is possible that there is a greater being whose sole job is to create souls. (See what I did there?) Sounds like a boring job to me, but I guess it's possible. If this is the case, my next question is: How and when does God put the soul in you? Is it at conception? Do you get a starter-soul from God that is basically a template, and then it's up to you to shape your soul throughout your life? Does God choose if you get a good soul or a bad soul? *So. Many. Questions.* If you believe in God, ask yourself how God creates a soul that becomes a part of you. If God created the universe, then I can fathom that God would have the ability to create souls on a regular basis. I just don't think this is how it works.

2. <u>Some Other Higher Power:</u> If you couldn't tell already, I am what you would call agnostic. I don't believe in the traditional Judeo-Christian God, but I do believe something created this universe. Whether that's God, a higher being, simulators in a laboratory, or Elon Musk, we are all here, whether we like it or not. So, if something could create the universe, then something

must have the ability to create the core of every human and animal on our planet, along with every other organism in the universe. However, the same questions remain regarding how and when this happens—and explaining how that would happen is *way* over my head.

3. Parents: The theory that makes the most sense to me is that everyone's soul comes from their parents upon conception, almost like a starter-soul that can get shaped as we age. At the basic level, do the father's sperm and the mother's egg contain the natural ingredients to make a new soul upon conception? When I first thought of this, I realized that I had no idea where sperm and eggs come from. I imagined a sperm factory in my balls where these little swimming things were created on a nightly basis and were treated to a swim every time I had sex (sorry, Mom; my kids come from storks). Same with a woman's egg—I imagined a little chicken in a woman's ovaries that just laid an egg once a month, and *voila!*

So I started researching exactly where and how the sperm and the eggs are created. Enjoy.

1. The male's sperm: The sperm is developed in the testicles within a system of tiny tubes called the seminiferous tubules. At birth, these tubules contain simple, round cells. During puberty, testosterone and other hormones cause these cells to transform into sperm cells. Millions and millions of sperm are produced every day that are then ejaculated into a woman's vagina during intercourse. (It's ironic that I'm writing this while watching *Ghost Adventures* with my three kids lying on the bed next to me.) The sperm is produced with the influence of testosterone.

The regulation of testosterone production is controlled in order to maintain normal levels in the blood, although levels are usually highest in the morning and fall after that. The hypothalamus and the pituitary gland are important in controlling the amount of testosterone produced by the testes. In response to a gonadotrophin-releasing hormone from the hypothalamus, the pituitary gland produces a luteinizing hormone, which travels through the bloodstream to the gonads and stimulates the production and release of testosterone.[84]

Two pieces of information here were the most interesting to me: 1) The pituitary gland is important in producing or releasing testosterone, and 2) the production of testosterone is highest in the morning. Previously, I talked about how the pituitary gland has been historically connected to the third eye concept due to its location deep in the center of the brain and its connection to light. I also talked previously about how I believe that the connection to REM sleep and the witching hour is due to the fact that brain activity is highest in the morning (around 2:00–3:00 a.m.) which is when the third eye may naturally be open.

As I mentioned earlier, I do much better with visuals, so let me draw it out in a way that may help.

So, with these two facts in mind, is it possible that every man is somehow reproducing their soul on a nightly basis in their pituitary glands through the production of testosterone, which eventually turns into sperm, which then looks to attach to a woman's egg? (I envision a factory of little elves in my brain, putting pieces of my soul into little buckets that are sent down a river to the pituitary gland, which creates little testosterone seeds that hatch into sperm, all of which contain my soul.)

As I mentioned earlier, I do much better with visuals, so let me draw it out in a way that may help.

2. <u>The woman's egg cell</u>: Each woman has two ovaries, which have two main reproductive functions in the body: 1) produce oocytes (eggs) for fertilization, and 2) produce the reproductive hormones estrogen and progesterone. The function of the ovaries is controlled by a gonadotrophin-releasing hormone released from nerve cells in the hypothalamus, which send their messages to the pituitary gland to produce a luteinizing hormone and a follicle-stimulating hormone. These are carried through the bloodstream to control the menstrual cycle.[85]

Note: Similarly to the male's sperm, the female's egg is created through chemicals released by the pituitary gland and into the bloodstream.

Regardless of whether you are male or female, I think we can all agree that women's brains are **significantly** impacted by PMS, which **definitely** leads to an overall increase in brain activity (I need to be careful with what I write here). Could the menstrual cycle cause enough activity in the brain to allow a woman's third eye to open, at which point her soul is somehow reproduced through the chemicals released through the pituitary gland that eventually form the egg that also contains the woman's soul? I picture it as follows:

Research has shown that, during PMS, there is a significant increase in activity in the medial orbitofrontal cortex and that the amygdala is impacted as well, primarily by the release of estrogen.[86]

There have also been studies that suggest that women who live together synchronize their menstrual cycles, which is called "menstrual synchrony" (great band name). This has also been called the McClintock effect, named after a scientist named Martha McClintock who published a paper in *Nature* in the 1970s saying that menstrual cycle synchronization happens when the menstrual cycle onsets of two or more women become closer together in time than they were several months earlier.[87]

Now, when you think about it, how the hell does this happen? That's like me saying if I lived with a male, our jerking off schedules would synchronize just because we're living together.

Except, that is likely to happen because the average male jerks off sixty-two times a day. However, most women, as far as I'm aware, menstruate once a month (except for Alexandra, who seems to be constantly menstruating).

The current theories for this are: 1) lunar synchronization, where lunar phases drive the synchrony; 2) social affiliation, where women who are more familiar with each other naturally synchronize; and 3) pheromones cause the synchrony.[88]

Some research focuses on cells in the region of the brain called the hippocampus that generate different types of receptors for the brain chemical GABA during various phases of the menstrual cycle. These changes may affect a woman's susceptibility to anxiety, depression, and seizures.[89]

I looked up what GABA is because I thought it was a band in the 1970s (turns out that was ABBA). Here's what GABA is (stay with me here, as it gets a little technical):

a) Gamma aminobutyric acid (GABA) is a naturally-occurring amino acid that works as a neurotransmitter or chemical messenger. GABA is considered an inhibitory neurotransmitter because it blocks or inhibits certain brain signals and decreases activity in your nervous system.

b) When GABA attaches to a protein in your brain, known as a GABA receptor, it produces a calming effect and can help with feelings of anxiety, stress, and fear.

c) GABA levels are reduced across the menstrual cycle in women with PMDD (premenstrual dysphoric disorder), compared with healthy women who experience an increase in plasma GABA levels from the follicular to luteal phases.[90]

The research that noted GABA activity decreased in females who suffered PMDD versus PMS is interesting, as it suggests that during PMDD (which is a more severe form of PMS), these lower levels of GABA would likely increase brain activity.

One thing I noted from my research was that GABA is a neurotransmitter. And what do neurotransmitters do? They serve as a line connecting the brain to the body—they're *connectors*. And the more our brains are connecting, I believe the more likely our third eye is to open.

The bottom line is that I don't think I'm going out on a limb (and I'm sure every man reading this will agree) when I say that during PMS, women's brains are generally more active and all over the place. However, if hormonal changes and brain activity allow them to connect with other females they are living with, then maybe it is possible that this means their third eyes are open during menstruation.

Either way, if you can open your mind to the possibility that the third eye may have a connection to how the male and female reproductive process works, is it possible that this is how a new soul is created?

When the sperm (which includes the father's soul) meets the women's egg (which includes the mother's soul), is a new soul created that is a mix of the mother and the father? Now, this mix may contain certain characteristics of the father and certain characteristics of the mother, such as:

1. how passionate they are (though it may be passion for different things)
2. how empathetic they are
3. how sympathetic they are
4. how hard-working they are
5. how intense they are
6. what they are fearful of
7. how emotional they get (regardless of whether they show it)
8. how adventurous they are
9. how confident they naturally are
10. whether they are a natural "Type A" personality or "Type B" personality
11. whether they are prone to depression

Notice that none of these deal with physical characteristics, which are more driven by genetics, but a soul may also contain physical characteristics that transfer to our offspring. All of the characteristics of the soul of each parent come together at conception and a new soul is formed with a mix of these characteristics. The mixing may be even or uneven (60/40, 70/30, etc.) but the mixing dictates what type of soul is created. (For fun, look at the mix/match game to play with your kids later on in this book.)

ERIC'S NOTE:

I'd like to take a moment to say that when I first had this idea that the sperm and the egg could be related to soul creation, it was when I was coming up with the game to see the percentage that your kids look and act like each parent. At the time, I didn't push forward with the theory because I thought it was probably crazy. But several months later, when researching how the sperm and the egg are created within the body—and realizing that the pituitary gland is also involved in the creation of the chemicals that produce both the sperm and the egg—I had to consider whether or not my theory had something to it.

Speaking of sperm and eggs, there are also many people that believe that "spiritual sex" or "tantric sex" is a way to connect with your third eye and the souls of others. The word "tantra," which is where tantric sex comes from, means "woven together" in Sanskrit, an ancient language with Indian origins.[91] The entire idea of tantric sex is to emphasize the idea of spirituality and intimacy—essentially it is about trying to achieve heightened sensuality, connection with your partner and with their energy or spirit.

While some of you may roll your eyes when you hear about tantric sex or you may think of the people dong this as being part a nudist colony somewhere, I have to assume there are a lot of people who do practice (or try to practice) this. Naturally, all the women I have been with would say that sex with me was sacred.

It's important to recognize that during sexual stimulation, there are several chemicals that are jumping all around your body and over 30 parts of your brain are involved in an orgasm (who said men can't use their brains for anything useful!), including the amygdala, hypothalamus, and anterior cingulate cortex.[92] So with that in mind, it wouldn't be a huge stretch to think that your third eye may be open during sex as well and if you prolonged your sexual experiences, you may be able to form deeper connections to people than in any other state.

I'm going to go try this tantric sex out and let you know how it goes.......(well that was six minutes of my life I won't get back but I will keep trying).

11

This Might Get Me Sent To My Room

SO, IF OUR SOULS DO COME FROM OUR PARENTS, HOW WOULD YOU describe your own soul? Think of the things that are part of you that either come directly from your parents (nature) or from your experiences (nurture) that shape who you are. The "nature soul" comprises things that come directly from your parents and form the core of your soul; they are extremely difficult to change, though it can be done. These are similar to the eleven examples I noted in Chapter 10 (e.g. sympathy, passion, confidence, intensity, etc.). The "nurture soul" part of the equation comprises things you've experienced throughout your life that have further shaped your "nature soul" into what and who you are today.

Think of your nurture soul as your subconscious mind that is formed from all of your life experiences since you were young. This nurture soul can include some of the quirks that you exhibit on a daily basis that you have probably learned over your years but have absolutely no idea how they started and why you do them. Some of mine are: 1) I wear sandals in the shower . . . of my house; 2) I don't sleep on sheets—I have to sleep on a blanket; 3) I chew on the TV remote to calm me down; and 4) I flush the toilet before I am done peeing such that I end up flushing twice for each pee. I couldn't tell you where any of these quirks come from, but they are a part of me and likely will be until the day I have my final connection. Alexandra has a few: 1) she has to walk on the left side of me; 2) she closes the blinds when showering, even if the window faces an isolated forest; and 3) she puts the blinker on when pulling out of our driveway (the only thing on the other side of our driveway is the woods). What are some of your quirks, and why do you think you do them? Would you consider these quirks a subconscious part of your soul?

Since my youngest daughter likes to leave Play-Doh in every single room of our house, I thought a good analogy of our souls would be to picture two big pieces of Play-Doh that are different colors but are stuck together. Your nature soul is the original shape of the Play-Doh from the can, with one color coming from your father and one color coming from your mother—and when you are born, these colors are meshed together to form a new mix of the Play-Doh. As your life experiences happen, the playdough gets molded and shaped into what eventually becomes your "full soul." This full soul continues to be changed and molded as your life goes on. At some point, the Play-Doh becomes harder to mold because it's left outside in the cold ~~rain~~ (Wait, does water make Play-Doh hard? I'll be right back . . . Nope it doesn't, so ignore that statement!) and becomes more solid in nature. This is similar to when people say, "Don't bother trying to change them—they're too old." At some point, the full soul is very hard to change.

As an example, I'll use my own soul and how I inherited certain pieces of it from my parents (nature) as well as my life experiences (nurture), which molded it into my *full soul*.

I debated whether I should write this section, but the truth is that I wouldn't be fully honest with myself if I didn't elaborate on everything I've written above and how my theory correlates to my own parents. As hard as it will be to write the following, I must say that talking through it with Alexandra has been very helpful for me. I now understand my parents so much more as people—as well as the good and bad parts of them, which were likely embedded in them since they were young. Like every human on Earth, they are not perfect; they have their wonderful attributes and other attributes that drive me up the wall. However, the way their souls have been formed and shaped has influenced their relationship with one another (as well my relationship with them, of course) since I was young, so I think this is important to analyze.

Many people don't get along with their parents, don't understand their parents, or are resentful toward their parents for something that happened in their childhood. I do think it's important to step back and realize that our parents aren't going to be here forever, so trying to connect with them and understand why they are the way they are will hopefully get us to a point where we enjoy the moments we spend together, rather than spend the entire time angry or resentful toward them for something they may not be able to change.

For better or worse, marijuana was the mechanism that allowed me to realize and freely express how I feel about them and how they are as people. So, without any further ado, I wrote down the following after being high while my parents were over one night, and after coming to the realization that they just cannot change who they are (wish me luck with this):

- My Father: When I think of my father, I think of someone who was energetic during his youth, who loved sports, drinking beer, listening to music, who had a good sense of humor and was very sarcastic. He was in a fraternity in college when he met my mother. He got married relatively young (26), and my mom was likely one of only a few women he had been with before he was married. He's had his ups and downs personally and professionally. He retired a few years ago and has just been trying to enjoy retirement ever since. These days, he seems to be a man who is resigned to his role in their relationship and if he wants to avoid conflict with my mother, he needs to do whatever she wants.

  My father's life has been shaped by my mother's actions since I was a young child, mostly around religion. He certainly had a say when it came to sports, cars, and electronics, but everything else was generally dictated by my mother.

  Today, most everything he does revolves around my mom's feelings. When she gets upset because of something in the world (politics, family, religion, etc.), he feels the need to stop it as soon as possible. When she is sad, he feels sad that he can't make her happy. When she is happy, it generally involves something religious, so he goes along with the religion thing even though he doesn't seem to have any passion for it.

In general, he does not stand up for himself enough, at least not enough in my eyes. He allows himself to be dominated, and is certainly co-dependent. Sometimes, when they are having one of their arguments, I wish I could just shake him and say, "Wake up and live your life without being manipulated. If you have thoughts and feelings, state them without fear of being yelled at or put down. You have feelings too, so share them!"

He is a great dad and grandfather, and cares about his family very much. He always provided for us and took an interest in what we were doing, which I believe was part of him from the very beginning. Now, he loves playing with my kids and would play with them for days if he could.

He is very passionate about new gadgets, electronics, and cars, and has always had a great work ethic. He has a great sense of humor and is very sarcastic, which I think he uses to connect to those he cares about, which is very similar to what I do when I'm trying to connect.

- My Mother: When I think of my mother, I think of someone who genuinely cares for her family and wants us all to be happy and together as much as possible. She had a successful career, raised three kids, and was heavily involved in her synagogue. She is trying to enjoy retirement now as best she knows how (generally by filling up her calendar so she doesn't have a second to relax). She is still very committed to helping at her temple and finds higher meaning in volunteering wherever she can.

  The best way to describe my mother is to think about Marie Barone from *Everybody Loves Raymond*. If you have never seen the show, either you don't have a television or you've been living under a rock (I don't know where that expression came from, but it's literally the worst expression I've ever heard). In the show, Marie Barone is the grandmother from across the street who loves her family. However, there is always a self-serving undertone to her actions and her thoughts (e.g., bringing over food because her daughter-in-law's food is not good, or suggesting a cleaning service because she thinks the house is a mess, etc.).

My mother is like that with most of the people she cares about: my father, her children, and her grandchildren. I don't know if she does it on purpose, or if she just thinks she's doing the "right thing," but it's certainly a form of manipulation. For us, it mostly involves religion, ensuring our socks match, and a clean house, among other things.

My mother grew up with religion and tradition, and I believe it stuck with her because she needed a sense of belonging to something and being accepted by other people—and religion was the easiest way to get that. She thinks it's her duty to have her kids and her grandkids follow in the ways of her traditions, and worries she'll be perceived as a failure if she doesn't fulfill that duty.

She is a very good person at heart and wants to do right and help out, but she just doesn't know how to turn off her brain. (Luckily, she now has a medical marijuana card that she can use to help her relax.)

But whether she knows it or not, her anxiety and emotional manipulation have taken their toll on me as a person. Much like my father, this has caused me to walk on eggshells around her in terms of what I say and how I say it, because anything I say wrong could trigger an emotional meltdown that could last for hours or days. It has been like that since I was a kid and has continued through my adulthood. Due to this, I have bent to her will when it comes to certain things, primarily around religion and religious holidays, as well as other sensitive topics like politics, COVID-19, or anything else that could cause controversy. When I do say something she doesn't like, she gets upset, depressed, and generally negative.

I don't think she does any of this to cause heartache or anger; I think that this is just part of who she is (and has been since she was young) and that she doesn't know any other way to be.

Sometimes, I wish I could just shake her and say, "Stop treating everyone as if you know everything that is right for us! We are our own people and can make our own decisions without your help. It's okay for people to think differently than you without you being offended; that's part of life. Just because we don't do what you want us to do doesn't make us bad people, or make us mean, or suggest that we love you less."

The following are the parts of my full soul that I believe come from my father:

• <u>The need to be funny to gain acceptance</u>: My father has always found a way to be funny and sarcastic in order to get people to like him. I believe this is a strong part of my nurture soul, and something he probably learned from his mother. I am definitely the same way and enjoy making people laugh (though you may disagree after reading this book).

• <u>The need to make people happy</u>: Whether it's making my kids happy by buying video games, doing good work, or making Alexandra happy by doing nice things for her, I have a strong need to make people happy or make people smile. I believe my dad has always felt like he wanted to make people happy, whether it was buying me cars, paying for college, or going to temple with my mother when he probably has no real interest in going. He loves to make his grandkids happy by playing with them every time he sees them. We are very similar in that way, and I believe this is part of my nature soul.

• <u>The desire to travel the world</u>: I know deep down inside, if he had the option, he would buy an RV and travel the United States or sell his house and travel around the world. He has done some traveling but hasn't been able to as much as he wants, either because my mother didn't want to, or more recently because of the COVID-19 pandemic. He enjoys going places and experiencing new things, as do I. I believe this came from his upbringing and is more part of the nurture component of his soul that I also picked up on during my childhood

- Problem solver and researcher: You give my dad something to figure out or research and he's your man. He's a problem solver—always has been. Even when it was putting a piece of furniture or something large together that took him the entire day, he saw it through. Guess you could say he was stubborn like that. I certainly inherited that part of him. I'm leaning toward this being a part of the nature component of my full soul, as I know plenty of people that just do not have it in them to try to figure things out. I guess it's also possible that some people learn this based on experiences with their parents as well, but I think the desire to want to figure it out on your own is more natural than nurture.

The following are the parts of my full soul that I believe came from my mother:

- The need to get things done right away: She needs to settle things sooner rather than letting them drag on, and I am generally the same way. If something needs to be done, I do it and don't procrastinate. Apparently, the opposite of procrastination is anticipation, so I guess we are both anticipators. This is a big piece of my nature soul.

- Impatience: If there are things that I don't get answers to right away or I can't get settled right away, I get very impatient/ unsettled. If I am doing a project and I can't get answers from someone helping me, I start losing my mind. She is the same way with organizing and trying to get things finalized—she needs answers yesterday, even if the thing she is organizing is ten years down the road. I believe this is also part of my nature soul and likely was passed down from my grandparents.

- Volunteering: She likes to do volunteer work, as do I. It makes me feel good to give back to others, as it does for her. I also think this is part of the nurture component of our souls, and it is something I am very proud of.

- Craving attention and acceptance from others: You could say this is the biggest part of our nature souls—the need for acceptance by peers, friends, and family members. I am generally the same way. I always feel good when people want to hang out with me and show that they want to be my friend. Furthermore, there are times when I do crave being with people other than my family in order to feel like I am accepted. This need for attention has led to some of the more questionable decisions in my life, and is something I still have to work hard to push down. For my mother, most of her life decisions and life actions tend to be geared toward being socially involved and part of a group, which primarily has been her temple/synagogue.

- Yearning for more meaning to life: Her search for meaning is through religion; mine is through some of the things I write in this book. Either way, we both seem to have tried to find deeper meaning in our lives, which I think is beautiful. She and I just went different ways when it came to achieving this goal, and that is okay. I am not suggesting either method is better than the other, as what's important is that we both feel we have achieved that deeper meaning. I think this piece is somewhat learned (the nurture component of our full souls) and was something we may have picked up from our families when we were younger.

- Verbal and emotional manipulation: I understand this may come across as harsh in terms of the characterization. However, in my relationship with Alexandra, I have come to realize that I have been manipulative and controlling in how I speak to her (I'm sure she'll have some thoughts on this). Whether my mother will ever admit it or not, she does the same thing, through either her words or her emotional reactions. While I tend to yell and try to be "manly" to get someone to agree with me, she tends to get sad or depressed to try to get what she wants. I equate it to my three-year-old daughter getting upset and pouting until she gets what she wants. I am not saying that my mother acts like a three-year-old, but that she uses a similar method for getting what she wants. I don't know if she was born with this trait or if this was something she learned during her youth—I have never had that kind of conversation with her. Either way, it became part of her full soul and it is now very hard for her to change.

As you can see from the above characteristics, I feel like I am more like my mother than my father in many ways relating to my soul. The traits that come from my parents are very hard to change in terms of how I am as a person. I have gotten better at reacting to some of these traits over the years, and even more recently, through the writing and observations in this book. However, the most overwhelming and destructive feature that seems to come from my mother is the need to control and manipulate, which modified my nature soul into what it was as a grown up. Like her, I don't think I was born as a manipulator, but it was learned behavior from my youth. I am not happy I am like this, but the reality is that it became part of me and very hard for me *not* to manipulate, especially with Alexandra.

The point of sharing all of this is to show that there are certain parts of my parents' souls that are hard for them to change, just like there are parts of all of us that are hard to change. Anxiety, depression, manipulation, passion, fear, stress—these things are part of our souls. In order to even try to change these things, you need to recognize them and then work hard to change them. I'm sure if my brothers did the same exercise, they would find characteristics about them that come from my mother and my father (albeit in different proportions than myself).

When I look at my own relationship with Alexandra, it's clear that my experiences when I was young helped to shape my nurture soul to a point where my actions and reactions in my past and current relationships were caused by a desire to not be manipulated or dominated the way my father was in his relationship with my mother. This resulted in me manipulating others because I promised myself I would never allow what was happening to my dad to happen to me; I would always be in control of my relationships and be in control of how I was being treated. If someone didn't want to be with me, then I would say, "Okay, bye-bye. I'm in control here!" This is probably why I am so stubborn. As a result of that, I have always been the one that dominated and manipulated, and it nearly led Alexandra and me to separate many, many times. I have to work *hard* to not do that with her, because my subconscious reaction is to be manipulative and controlling, and it is hard to not give into that instinct.

While I am not necessarily blaming my parents for how I interact with others, the reality is I feel that had I grown up in a different environment, I may not have become a manipulator later in my life.

My experiences with cannabis and talking about this with Alexandra have made me realize how I act and have allowed me to try to change, more so because I don't want my kids to be like this—where they think there must be someone who is manipulated and someone who manipulates. I don't want them to have to choose between the two. They should be able to see two equals in a relationship, where both people make decisions and respect each other. It is not easy for me to change, but I am trying, and that's all anyone can ask. I wish everyone (including my parents) could be aware of themselves and try to change for the better, because life is just too fucking short to spend it angry and resentful.

ALEXANDRA'S NOTE:

I know how difficult it was for Eric to write down his feelings above. It has taken me a long time to understand and accept the dynamics between him and his parents, since I grew up in a much different environment with affectionate, loud, warm family members who were always in your business, but in a good way. My mother has always been my number one supporter, and she would do anything for her grandchildren.

From what I have seen, I would have to agree with Eric's assessment of his parents. Eric's comparison of his mother to the grandmother from *Everyone Loves Raymond* is really funny and quite accurate. I won't pretend to understand all the various factors that drive her involvement with religion; however, I have always been respectful of her beliefs. It does appear that her life revolved around Judaism and their temple, as it is an important community setting for her. As Eric mentioned, his need to never be like his dad made him become the one who had to dominate. It has taken a while for Eric to get to the point where he understands me when I say that he is acting just like his mother in that he's being controlling and very one-sided.

However, I can't fully put into words the major changes I have seen in him, especially with his ability to understand where his inherent issues come from and how to try to change them. He is more patient, understanding, communicative, and happier. All of these have translated to a more consistent state of peacefulness and happiness. I am not saying marijuana will do this for everybody; I can only state how it has positively impacted him in the past twelve to eighteen months.

12

I'm Getting To My Climax

WHILE THE QUESTION OF WHETHER WE HAVE A SOUL OR NOT IS NOT something I can prove one way or the other, I think it's worth it to ask yourself whether you think you have a soul and, if so, what that would mean for you. It is certainly possible that our souls don't exist, and we all just vanish into nothing when we die—but that's a boring concept, isn't it?

The concept of having a soul that is ours and ours alone leads to some interesting questions that really get to the heart of discovering who we are and where we came from.

Are we part of something greater? Something we can't comprehend, at least at this point in our existence?

If our souls do exist and are somehow designed to reproduce when our third eye is open, is that proof of some sort of intelligent design? You can call this intelligent design a creator, God, a supernatural force, the CEO of the simulation company that created this universe we think we live in (I'll give more of my thoughts on simulation later in the book), or something else that we can't even comprehend.

The bottom line is that if our souls do exist, and if they can be passed on through reproduction, something must have designed it to happen this way. There is a theory that has been around since the early 1990s that states that the universe and its inhabitants could not have evolved by the "blind chance" set forth in Darwinism. This theory argues that there are holes in the theory of evolution and claims that these holes scientifically prove the presence of an "intelligent designer" in nature. It does not state that God is the intelligent designer; it only states that there is clear evidence in nature of intelligent design. The designer could be God, but it could also be some other supernatural force or an extraterrestrial race.[93]

So, the question is: If this intelligent design isn't God, what or who is it? The possibilities really do boggle the mind and help make the stupid shit we go through on a daily basis fairly unimportant.

Was there a first soul?

At some point, there had to have been a "first soul." This is part of a larger discussion about the origin of life as we know it. However, if you do believe in souls and that our souls are created from our parents, then there had to be an original father of the soul (I'm not talking about Sam Cooke, but you should look him up anyway). If you believe in evolution, does that mean that everything that came before us—monkeys, birds, dinosaurs, fish, amoebas, microbes—had a soul? Or is the development of a soul connected to the complexity of the organisms on Earth, meaning that the first soul appeared in something that more closely resembled humans? So, who or what was the first soul?

If you don't have children, does your soul not continue on?

I don't think this is the case. I believe that if you don't have children, it just means you are not involved in the creation of a new soul. The creation of a new soul doesn't have anything to do with how your soul continues on when you die. Your soul may disperse to people to whom you were close in life, including any children, family, and friends (I will talk more about this shortly).

Can our souls change?

If our souls are created through our parents, does that mean our souls are set in stone, or can they adapt based on our life experiences? You know, that whole "nature versus nurture" argument. Like I noted earlier, I believe that our souls may develop and change but that at some point, our souls are more or less set in stone. I think that the ways in which our soul is reflected in our actions, beliefs, and characteristics during our lifetime may change, but we are who we are, and there are very few things that can impact our core self. Later, I will talk about how I think a soul can be damaged, but that doesn't change the basic nature of what our souls are. I will give you two examples of what I mean:

a) **Passion:** We all know people who are more passionate than others. We may be born with a passion for something, even if we don't know what that passion is early on. This passion may change over someone's lifetime. Whether they choose to take advantage of that passion is another question, but someone who is passionate will always be passionate.

b) **Creativity and intelligence:** We all know people who seem to have a different level of creativity and different level of intelligence than others. This doesn't make them better or worse as a person, it just makes them who they are. Some people just have the ability to be creative or solve a problem that very few people can. I believe that these characteristics are part of someone's soul—you're born with them, and they will never change during your lifetime. Again, where that creativity and intelligence is used is up to the individual person.

Would this change your view on abortion or physician-assisted suicide?

If you were to believe that a soul is created at conception, would that make you more pro-choice or pro-life? Does it even matter? If we all have souls that go to the same place after we die, is it relevant whether that soul gets to that place sooner or later? I readily admit that this is a difficult topic, and I am not looking to get into an ethical debate with anyone about the topic of abortion. However, would it comfort people to know that an aborted fetus does move on somewhere, just like the rest of us? There are stories about women who feel a connection to their unborn child while they are in the womb. Obviously, this could be due to the physical connection they have while the fetus is there, but could their souls be connected as well? Or would the fact that an unborn fetus has a soul at conception make you more pro-life because they are truly a "human being" once conceived? Obviously, you have to make up your own mind on that issue, regardless of where you stand.

The same is true for physician-assisted suicide. Some of you may know the story of Dr. Kevorkian (and if you don't, go watch the movie *You Don't Know Jack* with Al Pacino—*hoo-ah*) and his role in assisted suicides in the 1980s and 1990s.[94] Would it comfort the families of those who are impacted by this to know that someone's soul does move on and that they were possibly directly touched by that person's soul after death? Only those who have been through something like this can answer that question, but with the amount of pain, suffering, and agony some patients and families go through while facing the death of themselves or a loved one, I would imagine it would be comforting to know that there is a soul and it can (and should) achieve a positive final connection before moving on.

For dying Americans, the average cost of one month of hospital care is over $30,000, and over half of that for one month of hospice care.[95] This doesn't even include the emotional toll that it takes on relatives, parents, kids, and other friends and close relationships to the individual, which can last for years and years after the death. Would it not be easier—and more human(e)—to facilitate whoever is dying in achieving a positive and warm final connection so they can move on to whatever is beyond this life on Earth? I never understood the desire for most people to want their relatives to live as a shell of their former selves, relying on tubes and needles and doctors to keep them alive for a matter of weeks or months. While I certainly understand the pain of potentially having to decide whether to end someone's life, the reality is that we need to think about what is in the patient's best interest.

If you can be comforted by the idea that this person has a soul, would it not make for a more peaceful and positive experience for all?

I know it's hard to think about, but if we are so easily able to enjoy and embrace a person's life, we should also be able to embrace a person's death—and realize that death is not the end. It's the beginning of something new.

I have told my family that if I am ever in a situation like that—if the suffering for the rest of my life will be greater than or equal to the pleasure for the rest of my life—I want to pull the plug. I can embrace death in a positive way, full of warmth and dignity. Plus, I don't want some hot nurse wiping my ass for me as I drool all over her hair and mumble "I'm horny" into her back with half a hard-on.

Can our souls be hurt?

We've all heard the phrase "their soul is hurting" in reference to someone who has been hurt or who has lost a loved one recently. But can a soul *actually* be hurt? If a soul is a living thing, then it's fathomable that it could be damaged or suppressed due to life events. Going back to passion, I am sure you have also heard the phrase: "They lost their passion for life." This usually happens to somebody after they have experienced something truly terrible. This doesn't mean they stop being a passionate person at their core; they just temporarily feel like they don't care about life. With help, whether it's therapy or better life circumstances, that passion can return. I think the people who die while their soul is still hurting are the ones who can't move on and stick around to resolve whatever was hurting their soul prior to death, similar to Alexandra's ex-boyfriend.

I feel like my oldest son's soul was hurt when Alexandra and I separated many years back under less-than-ideal circumstances. While we did eventually get back together, when Alexandra and I fight now, I know he gets worried that we're going to separate again. He'll never say it or show it, but he needs that reassurance that everything is going to be okay. That's just part of him now, and it may always be, unless he really tries to change it. He needs reassurance.

So now, every time Alexandra and I are in a good mood or a good place, he is happy. We can hear it in his voice when he is happy. It raises a bar. While nothing is guaranteed, I hope we continue to have good moments so that he continues to feel reassured.

Do we have soulmates?

The concept of a romantic soulmate—someone who completes us and is destined to be our other half—has been around forever. We've been told since we were young that we need to find our soulmate in order to be happy in life. Most men vomit at that thought, and most women swoon because they think it is their life goal to find a soulmate, especially after watching *Jerry Maguire*. ("You complete me." Yech!)

So, in order to find happiness, we *must* find the *one* person who is our other half and then, if we're lucky, spend the rest of our natural lives with them. But when you think about this concept, how likely is it really that any of us will end up with our true soulmate? How many people on Earth really find that special someone? How the hell do we know if the person we have found is actually our soulmate or if our soulmate is still out there? I'm sure many of us feel like we've ended up with the "right" person, but it's not like there is a soulmate meter that we can carry around with us to figure out who our soulmate is.

There are many more questions relating to this concept:

1. **Do we each have one soulmate we need to meet in order to achieve eternal happiness?**

    I find this highly unlikely. For one thing, the number of variables that would have to be met in order to find and fall in love with your soulmate in the short time we all have on this planet—with how many *billions* of people are currently alive—is astronomical to the point of being impossible. Think about it—if you're born into a family in the United States and you don't travel, and your soulmate is a person in Asia who also doesn't travel (because you're soulmates, right?), are you ever going to meet that person? Hell no. Your soulmate would likely have to be born in the same general geographic area as you and have similar socio-economic conditions as you. Before planes, trains, and automobiles, your soulmate would have needed to exist within a geographic area of less than 500 miles in order for you to be able to meet them. These days, people do travel across the globe more often, but it would still literally be like finding a needle in a haystack the size of planet Earth.

2. **Is something guiding our decisions in order to put us in a position to meet our soulmate?**

If we do have only one soulmate, you would think that whatever created our souls would at least give us a fighting chance at finding them. In reality, most humans have maybe fifty years to find their soulmate, given the fact that the average human lives to around seventy-five and most of us aren't concerned with finding our soulmate until maybe our mid-twenties. Are the important life decisions we make being guided by divine intervention? And if so, are these decisions guided with the intention of helping us find our soulmate?

There's a show I recently watched called *The One* that is about a genetic test Person A could take to find out who their soulmate is (Person B). The only way it would fully work, though, is if Person B took the test as well, which would reveal Person A as their soulmate. The concept of the show is that our DNA is somehow able to help accomplish this feat. However, outside of this type of technology, I am not aware of any way that you can find your soulmate. I know certain dating apps proclaim to be able to help do this, but I find it hard to believe that the questions they ask about height, weight, and one's favorite pet will lead you to your one perfect life match.

3. **Are family members automatically our soulmates because we are created by the same souls?**

It would make sense that if a new soul is created upon the combination of two separate souls, that brothers and sisters (and even half-brothers and half-sisters) would automatically be soulmates, as they would share the same source of their souls. I can't tell you how many times I've said the exact same thing as my brothers at the exact same time (even while sober, not just while high)—things that if it happened once, you would chalk it up to a coincidence, but when it happens frequently, you start to wonder if there's more to it. Alexandra has experienced the same thing. She seems to be able to sense things with her siblings and her parents on a consistent basis. Maybe this happens because her third eye is open more than mine, which allows these connections to occur with our siblings and family on a consistent level. There's also the study into how/why twins are more connected than most people. Sometimes, one twin experiences a sensation of something that's happening to the other, such as emotional distress or physical pain.[96] Again, this could be the fact that they grow up in similar environments and are naturally closer than most siblings, but could it also be that they have the ability to connect to each other's souls much easier than most siblings and most people in general?

4. **Are we all soulmates?**

Given the potential that some force may have initially created the first soul, we have to admit there is a possibility that we all came from the same place and that we are all connected and are naturally soulmates. What this "force" is, I have no idea, but I think it's comforting to think that we are all connected in some way, that we are all mates at the basic level.

5. **If we are all soulmates, is getting high the easiest way to connect to other souls?**

I believe so (or maybe that's just my excuse to get high). I think it is a possibility that can easily be tested using the steps I outlined earlier in the book. If marijuana doesn't work for someone, there could be other ways to connect, like meditation, yoga, or some other natural way we haven't found yet.

This is another rather difficult topic for me to comment on, as my views on the soul are probably a bit more spiritual than Eric's. However, I did feel it important to respond. As a Catholic, I was taught that we are essentially made up of three things: body, spirit, and soul. God creates each unique soul with the human procreation of each new body. I won't get into the differences between spirit and soul; however, Catholics generally believe the soul is what makes you, well, you. Soul, or anima in Latin, refers to the animating principle of a thing; it is what makes something alive. I grew up learning that our soul is either enriched or damaged with the decisions we make throughout life. We also believe that the soul is immortal and when you pass—or go through your "final connection" as Eric calls it—your soul leaves your body and goes to be judged before God. To put it simply, if you were a good person and lived a good life, you would go to heaven. If you didn't live your life well, you would either go to purgatory or to hell. This has always resonated with me because I feel that even if bad people get away with things in this life, they won't in the next. That may seem childish to some, but it does give me a sense of comfort.

The notion of soulmates has never really sat well with me, even as a child. Perhaps it is because my parents divorced when I was six, but who knows. In any case, I think I've been blessed with several "soulmates." I've often referred to my sister and mother as my soulmates because of the strong connection and bond we share with each other. At times in my life, I've referred to my two childhood best friends as my soulmates as well. I think someone with whom you share a strong connection can be your soulmate. However, I do agree with Eric that the concept of having just one soulmate seems to be far-fetched.

13

Dispersing Theory (No, It's Not A Heavy Metal Band)

WHAT HAPPENS WHEN WE DIE? THIS IS ONE OF THE BIGGEST QUESTIONS we have as human beings. Some people think we head up to the pearly gates of heaven to beg for entry so we can see our loved ones again. Some people think we can go to hell to suffer for eternity for our sins (if there really is a hell, I may be in trouble). Others think we just go back to the same place we were before we were born—*nothingness.*

I personally would love it to be like the movie *Defending Your Life,* in which Albert Brooks and Meryl Streep spend purgatory watching clips of their lives while attorneys and judges debate whether they should move on to heaven or go back to Earth to try to "right their wrongs." All the while, they eat whatever they want, have sex with whomever they want, and go to the "Past Lives Pavilion" to see who they were in prior lives. It would certainly be a great way to spend purgatory.

However, as wonderful as that sounds, that is not what I think happens when we die. While high, one of the more intense visions I had was about what happens when we pass on (this was on the night when I had my first out-of-body experience).

As I mentioned earlier, I believe our soul has other souls that are near or around us, like planets to a sun. Some souls are closer to us and easier to connect to, and others are far away and harder to connect to. My vision was that when we die, our soul leaves our bodies and all of our energy disperses into the other souls around us, similar to a sun exploding and its remnants disbursing to the planets rotating around it. Those closest to us—our family and friends—would likely be the ones who receive more of our soul than others. However, I think there is a possibility that random people can also receive part of our souls. I'm calling this my "soul-dispersing theory," and I think it's as good of a theory as any out there!

Basically, what I think happens is that when you die, a little bit of you becomes part of someone else, maybe temporarily or maybe permanently. It would be nice to think that you become a part of others after you die, hopefully changing them in a good way.

Scientists have tried to research whether the soul can be measured when someone dies. Some parapsychologists have attempted to establish, by scientific experiment, whether a soul can separate from the body, especially at death. In 1901, Duncan MacDougall conducted an experiment in which he made weight measurements of patients as they died. He claimed that there was weight loss of varying amounts at the time of death; he concluded the soul weighed 21 grams, based on measurements of a single patient while discarding conflicting results.[97]

The physicist Robert L. Park has written that MacDougall's experiments "are not regarded today as having any scientific merit,"[98] and the psychologist Bruce Hood wrote that "because the weight loss was not reliable or replicable, his findings were unscientific."[99]

In 1911, MacDougall tried photographing the soul the moment it left the body and performed a dozen experiments in which he photographed "a light resembling that of the interstellar ether" in or around patients' skulls at the moments they died.[100]

While these findings were dismissed by the scientific community as unreliable, MacDougall's work continues to resonate with people not because of what he found (or failed to find), but because of what he suggested and wanted to prove: *that souls exist.*

Physicist Sean M. Carroll has written that the idea of a soul is incompatible with quantum field theory (QFT). He writes that, for a soul to exist, "Not only is new physics required, but dramatically new physics. Within QFT, there can't be a new collection of 'spirit particles' and 'spirit forces' that interact with our regular atoms, because we would have detected them in existing experiments."[101]

What's interesting about this theory is that it doesn't incorporate the chance that these "spirit particles," as he calls them, are already part of us from the time we are conceived. It almost seems the universe has designed a way to hide the existence of the soul from us (like a cheat code hidden in a video game).

If a soul does leave a body at the time of the death, is there a way to prove it? Possibly, but maybe not through measurements as we typically think of them—weight, visual evidence, etc. Maybe the way to prove the soul exists is to see what happens to people who are close to someone soon after that individual dies. Do the people around them feel something different around the time of death? Do they feel like the deceased person's soul is part of them or maybe part of someone they are close to?

I'll give you an example. There is a story about Amanda Kloots, who is the widow of Nick Cordero, a Broadway star who died of COVID-19 in 2020. The story involves her two-year-old son, and she explained how she was with her young son one day, shortly after Nick Cordero passed, and she felt her son's energy shift and he eventually started touching her face and staring at her. Eventually he pulled her face to him and kissed her for a few minutes before she felt his energy shift again and went back to being more like his normal self.[103]

I think that her experience (and that of others who have felt something like this) are real and brings up an interesting way to determine whether the soul exists.

If the soul does disperse after death, is there a way to study how those close to the person who died are affected in the minutes, days, weeks, and months after the person passes away? How they are affected could be shown in many ways, including:

- physical changes (e.g., a baby acting like their father, as in the example above)
- dreams/nightmares about the deceased person (which I discussed earlier)
- feelings of comfort, as if the deceased person is part of them somehow
- feelings of a presence that was not there before (not a scary presence, just a feeling that someone/something is there)

These feelings may be temporary as the soul passes through, or they may be more enduring if the soul attaches to the person and does not leave for a while because they have something they want to try to communicate before they move on.

If the soul passes through others, does the last thought or feeling of the deceased person result in how this manifests in others around them? In the example above of Amanda Kloots, was the last thought of her husband to hug and kiss his wife, which manifested in his soul passing through their son, resulting in the son hugging and kissing her?

Of course, there is nothing to suggest that these feelings are always good or comforting. There are many cultures that talk about how the sins of prior generations are paid back by future generations through the genetic passing down of guilt and bad feelings. Naturally, most of the organized religions of the world associate this process with Satan and demons. However, what if this process actually does occur, but more through the dispersing of souls after death that attach to future generations?

Alexandra has told me about how her family believes that sinful or "evil" family members who've died will prey on current family members and make things worse for those who are living. She gives the example of the fear of her house being broken into (she is paranoid about our house being broken into) and says that the fear she experiences on a consistent basis is made worse by evil souls who want her to suffer.

Regardless, if our souls do disperse upon death, then maybe we can be comforted by the fact that a piece of us remains in the universe forever, either attached to loved ones or others.

THE SOUL CONCLUSION

Whew! I'm tired from all of that, and I appreciate you getting through that with me. I will say that none of this has been easy to write or summarize in a way that makes sense. I certainly understand that the concept of a soul is likely one that will be pure theory and faith until there are scientific methods that can somehow prove it exists.

However, in a world where millions and millions of people believe in a god they have never met, never heard, and never seen, yet form their deepest spiritual beliefs based on the concept of faith in a book written by humans thousands of years ago, why would this be any different? Would it be a huge leap to believe that not only do we have souls, but that we can connect to other souls, and our souls do continue on in some form after we die?

People use the terms "soul searching" and "soul awakening" all the time, usually in reference to a traumatic life event after which someone needs to "find themselves." I think this journey with marijuana has led me down rabbit holes I never expected to go down and has made me feel things I never expected to feel. Have I found my soul? Has my soul been awakened? I am not sure, but I do know that I feel more connected to everything and more at ease than at any prior time in my life. I hope that others can experience the same after reading this book. We are on this planet for the blink of an eye, so why not try to spend that blink making true, deep connections with those around us and finding some peace with ourselves and our purpose?

For those who believe in organized religion, more power to you. I know the sense of love, family, warmth, and comfort is a good thing, and I don't take away from religion for being able to give that to people. It's just not for me. For me, the thought of something greater that allows us all to be connected gives *me* comfort and warmth, and the experiences and visions I have had are enough to comfort me for the rest of my life here on Earth. When I die, if I'm wrong, I guess I'll come back and haunt you all to tell you everything in this book is bullshit and that you should get on your knees and memorize every word in the Book of Genesis.

And if you think my soul-dispersing theory above is weird, just wait for what's next—simulation theory.

14

This Whole Book Might Not Be Real

HANG WITH ME FOR A LITTLE LONGER, AND ONCE WE'RE THROUGH this, we'll move on to some fun stuff that may or may not make your mind explode.

We've all likely played with simulations at some point. From the video game *The Sims* to flight simulators, to choose-your-own-adventure books, there are plenty of times when we have enjoyed engaging with a simulated existence. And, of course, there are movies—like *The Matrix*, *The Truman Show*, or even *Groundhog Day*—that portray life as some sort of a simulation.

So the question on everyone's lips—their chapped lips (*Groundhog Day*, anyone?)—is: Are we living in a simulation? It's a question more and more people are asking. Some of the smartest people in the world—Elon Musk, Neil DeGrasse Tyson, and philosopher Nick Bostrom, to name a few[104]—have stated on the record that we might be or likely are. But what does that even mean?

The theory that we are living in a simulation is mind-numbing. If true, it makes all the decisions we make in life moot and pointless. Who cares if I get fired or lose money or cheat on someone? It's all a game, anyway, so I might as well enjoy life as much as possible!

I'm not going to try to conclude whether we are living in a simulation or not, because there is no way to prove it. Maybe someday we'll be able to scientifically prove whether we are or not, but that day is not today.

But for now, we can ask ourselves several questions:

1. What would living in a simulation actually mean?
2. Am I living in in my own simulation, in which everything around me is just for me—like my own little made-up world?
3. Is everyone I know part of my simulation, or are they sharing it with me? Are we all just being watched together to see how our lives turn out collectively?
4. Do other simulations exist for other people? If so, will I ever be able to see what those are like? Maybe other people get a simulation like *Avatar* or *Star Wars*, with some human and some alien beings. If that is the case, I would like to ask my simulators for a trade please.

Before I get into some more questions about simulations, I'd like to share a few more of the experiences I've had while high that led to me thinking about whether I really am in a simulation. (This is also the last time I'll say that I know all these experiences could just be the chemicals in my brain mixing and matching—because *I know*.) None of these thoughts are proof that we are living in a simulation, they're just observations I've had while high that made me think we could be.

The Movie Reel

There have been multiple times when I've felt like my brain was spinning like a movie reel, VHS tape (some of you may have to look that up), or a projector. I envision my thoughts coming into my brain, being recorded, and then flowing out of my brain. One time, while high, I was taking a shower (I'm not sure if that's relevant; I just want to set the scene.) and I remember having the thought that our minds are like a movie reel, and then I moved on from that movie reel thought to other thoughts, including: 1) Alexandra Daddario is a great actress;

2) my fantasy football team sucks, and; 3) oops, I need to get the dog some more food.

Maybe ten seconds later, I remember thinking, "I can't remember what I was just thinking, but I want to go back to that thought." When I did that, I could feel my brain rewinding, so to speak, so that I could actually remember what it was I'd been thinking earlier. I went backward from *oops, I need to get the dog some more food*, to *my fantasy football team sucks*, to *Alexandra Daddario is a great actress*, until, eventually, I got back to the movie reel thought. This reversal probably happened in a sixty-second span, and it was a very vivid visual that I had of my brain rewinding or moving backward, similar to an old movie reel.

Even a few months later, as I write this, I can recall the feeling of the initial "movie reel" thought slipping away, and having to really stop my brain and focus in order to back up, thought-by-thought, and get to the original thought again. I don't experience this sensation often, but it definitely stuck with me enough that I wrote it down when it happened.

Someone Is Watching!

I have felt like someone is watching—or even *making*—my decisions on a consistent basis. Think of the games *The Oregon Trail* or *SimCity* (for those of you too young to know what the hell I'm talking about, look them up—they were both great games).

The entire point of the game is to make decisions as you move from the eastern part of the United States out to Oregon along the Oregon Trail. Each one of the decisions you make has a consequence attached to it—you broke your wagon, you lost a child, your family starved to death, etc. The goal was to make it to Oregon with as many children and wives as possible (just kidding about the wives).

Similarly, I have felt like someone or something is watching me and recording every single one of my decisions to lump into some large database, which then analyzes my decisions and the related consequences.

For example, Alexandra never picks stuff up off the floor, and I *hate* it because I spend all my time picking stuff up off the floor. But what leads to the decision to pick something up or not? There *has* to be something, either in our brain or elsewhere, that says either "pick it up" or "don't pick it up." One decision leads to one version of the future (me being annoyed at her for not picking it up), and one decision leads to another version of the future (me not being annoyed at her for picking it up).

As another example, there is a funny episode of *Frasier* called "Sliding Frasiers" with the following premise: Frasier is supposed to go to a speed-dating event and asks his radio show producer if he should wear a suit or a sweater, remarking that the slightest decision can have far-reaching effects. Then the viewer is shown what would have happened in each circumstance: 1) wearing the suit, he is knocked to the floor at a local coffee shop by a cute girl named Monica, and they hit it off, while his radio producer meets a handsome coworker named Mike; and 2) wearing the sweater, Mike is the one knocked to the floor by Monica, and Frasier goes to the speed-dating event, which ends up being a disaster.

Here are a few visual explanations of my visions that may make it easier to understand what I have felt:

1. Think of driving down a road. Every five minutes, you come to a fork in the road. If you go right, it leads to one destination, and if you go left, it leads to another destination. As it relates to our lives, these "forks in the road" go on for your entire life and relate to every decision you or I have made or will ever make. Billions and billions of forks that all lead to a different outcome for our lives.

2. Think of the game *Plinko* from *The Price is Right* or "the wall" on the gameshow *The Wall.* Whether those chips or balls go just one space to the left or right decides the eventual outcome of the game of our lives. Think of it as one of these walls, but with billions and billions of decisions that need to be made in the "Game of Eric."

3. A funnier, more lighthearted visual is the movie *Labyrinth,* in which every decision that the character played by Jennifer Connelly (I love you) makes brings her closer or takes her farther away from rescuing her little brother, Toby, who was

stolen from his crib by a creepy-looking David Bowie, taken to another world, and hidden in a castle. (You have no idea how scary the Fireys were in that movie to a six-year-old.) If you haven't seen this movie, go watch it, because it's great.

Glitch in the Matrix

One time, I had a short but intense experience where I felt a "glitch." Everything that was happening right then and there (I was talking to Alexandra and my daughter in the kitchen of my house one night) seemed to stop for a second or two and then start up again. Afterward, I distinctly remember thinking about Alexandra and my three-year-old daughter and having the thought, "This isn't real, and you guys aren't real," which made me pretty sad. It felt like I was in *The Truman Show*, when Jim Carey's character realizes that everyone around him is being fake and nobody has any real feelings for him. It felt like everything Alexandra and my kids do is predetermined and that their actions are deliberate in order to make me react a certain way. Though it was a short experience, it was very vivid for me. I did tell Alexandra this after I felt this happen and she proceeded to slap me in the face hard, which does lead me to believe she is, in fact, real.

Again, these experiences do not happen very often—maybe one percent of the times I have gotten high—but they have been very vivid and consistent with the fact that I felt like someone or something was watching my life, and that my decisions were either being monitored or being made for me.

So, what if we are in a simulation?

If we are in a simulation, then okay, I'm game. It means everything in life is out of control, and it's nice to think that every stupid decision you make really doesn't matter.

But if someone or something is watching us make our own decisions for record-keeping purposes or statistical analysis, who are they and why are they doing that?

The following are some of the possibilities I have thought of.

1. **Statistical analysis for longer life**

    Could there be a human (or alien) population that created a simulation to record our decisions in order to research which patterns lead to living the longest life possible? These decisions could involve eating habits, drinking habits, sleeping habits, sexual behavior, video game playing habits, and countless others that lead to certain humans living longer than others. Is every one of our decisions fed into some supercomputer for analysis?

    This could be true, but I have to imagine that any race or species that can create a simulation of this magnitude would be able to create medicines and healthcare procedures to allow their population to live pretty damn long—if not forever. So, I'm not sure how much I believe in this possibility.

    However, it leads to the question of whether it's possible that humans would, at some point in the future, have the ability to run a complex simulation. If you aren't familiar with Moore's Law, it basically implies that computers, machines that run on computers, and computing power all become smaller, faster, and cheaper with time, as transistors on integrated circuits become more efficient. According to expert opinion, Moore's Law is estimated to end sometime in the 2030s, if it's not already ended.[104] What this means is that computers are projected to reach their limits in the 2030s because transistors will be unable to operate within smaller circuits at increasingly higher temperatures. This is because cooling the transistors will require more energy than the amount of energy that passes through the transistor itself.

    Now, as an accountant, I have absolutely no idea what half of this means. However, what I can deduce is that computing power will reach a limit at some point in the future. If this theory is right and the ability of computing power to advance is limited, then it's likely that the idea of a simulation run by humans is not possible. However, if this theory is wrong and the ability to create better, faster, more able supercomputers is not limited because of some factor we are not yet aware of, then a simulation may be possible as well. Several large companies continue to develop additional ways to create advancements in chip (what's that?) technology.

So, if the theory is wrong, what would prevent humans from eventually creating a supercomputer that could run a simulation strong enough to replicate life as we know it?

2. **Squid Game?**

Maybe our simulations are similar to the concept of the show *Squid Game*, in which rich people bet money on who will survive a series of games. The end result of those games is the deaths of the losing contestants who willingly entered the games in order to win the ultimate prize—the equivalent of $40 million. Maybe our simulators are placing bets on who will live the longest based on decisions we make in life. If that's the case, they shouldn't put money on me—I'm not living much past fifty-five at this pace.

3. **Contest**

Maybe there is some sort of contest where each simulator has to get their subject (me) to realize the human race is just a simulation in order to win a prize. If that's the case, then you win, my simulator friend—please tell me the prize is a vacation to somewhere nice, as I could really use it.

It's like that game at the boardwalk or country fair where you shoot water down the hole to get your horse to the finish line first in order to win a prize. The more accurate you are, the more likely your horse will get to the finish line first. Maybe my simulator was the most accurate with their decision-making that they got me to the "finish line" first and now the game is over. (The question is: What happens to me now? If this theory is correct, shouldn't I have been "offed" like a character in *The Sopranos*?)

As a side note, when I wrote the line about the simulator potentially winning the game now, I felt an intense sensation in the center of my forehead, three hours after I took 15 mg of edibles. It could have been signs of a stroke, but I hope it was just my simulator buzzing me to tell me I was dead on.

Whatever the case may be, there would have to be some end goal to the simulation, some way to win—unless whoever is simulating our world is content to watch us forever.

So, if there is a simulation, what types of decisions are made for us, and how does it work?

For those of you unfamiliar with the butterfly effect (the theory, not the movie), Wikipedia defines it as the following:

> In chaos theory, the butterfly effect is the sensitive dependence on initial conditions in which a small change in one state of a deterministic nonlinear system can result in large differences in a later state.
>
> The term is closely associated with the work of mathematician and meteorologist Edward Lorenz. He noted that the butterfly effect is derived from the metaphorical example of the details of a tornado (the exact time of formation, the exact path taken) being influenced by minor perturbations, such as a distant butterfly flapping its wings several weeks earlier . . .
>
> The phrase refers to the idea that a butterfly's wings might create tiny changes in the atmosphere that may ultimately alter the path of a tornado or delay, accelerate, or even prevent the occurrence of a tornado in another location . . . The flapping wing represents a small change in the initial condition of the **system**, which cascades to large-scale alterations of events. Had the butterfly not flapped its wings, the trajectory of the **system** might have been vastly different.[105]

What if this "system" noted above is the simulation, and whatever/whoever created the system is responsible for deciding everything you do during your life?

Below are just a few of the decisions that a simulator would have to make over the course of your life that might dictate either how long you live or whether you end up realizing you're in a simulation (depending on what the end goal of the simulation is from those noted above). Of course, there are billions of decisions that are made over the course of someone's life.

- Food

  Do our simulators have to make decisions that weigh the short-term happiness of food that tastes delicious but that is bad for us against the long-term benefits of being healthy? A few decisions may be:

  - Chicken parmesan sandwich or a salad for lunch?
  - Eat that fifth slice of pizza knowing it will likely give you diarrhea later or stick with the just the four slices?
  - Drink a bottle of water or enjoy the sweet, sugary wonderfulness of a soda?
  - Do you go for the deliciousness of a molten lava cake with vanilla ice cream or the fruit cup with all that weird water in the bottom?
  - Do you hop on the fad of a two-day fast or not?

- Love

  Do our simulators have to make decisions regarding who we are attracted to and how bold or shy we are? For example:

  - Do you like big boobs or small boobs, light eyes or dark eyes, big butts or little butts, tall or short, etc.?
  - Are you gay, straight, bisexual, trans, asexual, or somewhere in between?
  - Are you bold or shy when it comes to approaching someone you're attracted to?

- Do you write an email to your friend of five years to tell her you love her or not?
- Do you buy your significant other something expensive even though they might not like it, or something cheaper but of more sentimental value to them?
- Do you decide to leave your partner after realizing you're miserable, or do you stay with them because you think it's best for the kids?

- Education and Work

  Do our simulators have to make decisions about whether we enjoy learning, how much we are influenced by money, if we care about work/life balance or not, etc.?

  - How hard do you want to study in school?
  - Do you care about grades?
  - What type of knowledge do you yearn for as a kid?
  - Do you want to stay after class to learn more from the teacher or go play with your friends?
  - Do you decide to leave a company you've worked at for years for a job that pays less but that you enjoy more?
  - Do you want to work hard for a promotion or work less to stay at the same level you are now because it means you can spend more time with your family?
  - Do you want to work for another few years to get a good bonus or retire early and travel the world?

- Personal Preferences and Hobbies

  - Do you keep a condom with you or risk unprotected sex?
  - Do you want kids? If so, how many kids do you want?
  - Do you accept religion or question everything about it?
  - Do you stay in, have a glass of wine, and go to bed at 10:00 p.m. or go out with your friends until 4:00 a.m. and feel exhausted the next day?

- Do you decide to stay sober or experiment with alcohol, marijuana, or other drugs?
- And, of course, do you pick stuff up off the floor or not?

Now, there are multiple questions that come into play here, none of which I have the answers to (shocking):

- Would the simulators simulate every living being on Earth? Are they simulating butterflies, lantern flies-bugs, fruit flies, and dogs? Or are they just simulating humans?
- When do they start simulating us? Is it while we're in the womb, when we're a baby? Or is it at whatever point we start making decisions that impact our lives (e.g., when we can crawl)?
- Are they making decisions all the time, or are there times they turn autopilot on and let us make the decisions on our own? I think autopilot would be for when we're getting ready for bed or peeing or something else that doesn't impact how long we live. I would imagine whether I should take a shit or not is not a decision that needs to be made for me and would impact how my life ends. But certainly, the decision whether or not to eat the entire box of strawberry cheesecake that Alexandra came home with could have an impact on my life in terms of higher cholesterol. Maybe the simulators are like airplane pilots who are just responsible for getting the plane off the ground, landing it, and stepping in when there's turbulence and guiding the plane out of it as safely as possible. Of course, the plane is our life, and the turbulence could be a hairy situation during which the decisions made could result in a different outcome of our lives.
- Why make the decisions they're making? What would be the objective of them stepping in to decide for us? Is it purely to make decisions that allow us to live the longest? Let's go back to the earlier example of why I pick stuff off the floor. Why do I make the decision to pick something off the floor? The main reason I can think of is because I hate everything about clutter on the floor: 1) the way it looks; 2) the fact that people leave

clutter on the floor all the time; 3) the fact that no one bothers to take the time to pick something up off the floor; and 4) the fact that I have to waste my time to clean it up when I could be doing something more fun, like killing fruit flies. All of these things literally make my blood pressure increase just at the thought of them. So, is the decision to clean this off the floor being made to reduce my heart rate and blood pressure in order to make me hopefully live longer? I can tell you that if I didn't clean the clutter, I would be thinking about it all day, and the entire time I'd be thinking about it, my heart rate, blood pressure, and stress levels would be higher than normal, which I assume can't be good for me.

- Is our subconscious mind what the simulators monitor? At a high level, our subconscious mind stores and retrieves data and makes sure that we respond exactly how we are programmed to respond.[106] When you think of it, you don't really have any control over your subconscious, especially as you get older— you do things without thinking about them (unless you train yourself to change). Is this subconscious what the simulators are monitoring and tracking to see how we process our life experiences? If I was simulating humans, I would certainly want to understand how humans are at a subconscious level.

However, none of this explains at all why people die young, either of natural causes or otherwise. Maybe the simulators step in to make decisions, or maybe there is some randomness to our deaths and there are certain things that can't be stopped by their decisions. (I'm not looking to create an explanation why awful things like pediatric cancer or suicide in teenagers happen. There are awful things that people experience on this planet, whether simulated or not. If anyone reading this has experienced any of these awful things, you have my sincerest condolences. These are just theories, so please don't take them as anything more than that.)

Can I prove any of this? Of course not—it's not like my simulator is checking in from time to time through his little headset, saying, "Hey, you! I'm sorry I helped you make that awful decision last night that will completely ruin your marriage, get you fired, nearly maimed, and tortured by your ex-best friend, and potentially put in prison for life. Sorry, but I have to do it for the simulation." I wish I did have something like that to fall back on for some of my life decisions, but I don't.

All of our experiences are based on the notion that this universe works in a certain way that's based on things we, as a human race, have learned since the time we were able to learn. We think we understand how the universe was created, but there are still a lot of things we don't understand, such as whether our universe is the only universe or is just one of many universes.

If the universe as we understand it was created 13.8 billion years ago, that means humans have been around for a micro-second of time compared to the age of the entire universe (humans have been around for 0.002 percent of the age of the universe, to be exact). The time our brains have been able to learn and understand the universe is a fraction of that—roughly 5,000 years, which brings the number down to 0.0004 percent.

But consider what we have been able to do in that small fraction of time. We invented the stone tool, we invented the photograph, we invented the saxophone, we learned to drive, we learned to fly, we flew to the moon, we invented the Internet (or did Al Gore do that?), we invented the cellphone, we sent spacecraft to Mars, we started developing AI robots, and most recently, we invented TikTok. **We have advanced technologically to the point that, if you extract where we have gotten to in a short amount of time, then hundreds or thousands of years from now, humans may be able to create simulations real enough to trick the subjects into thinking they're not living in one.**

All I'm saying is that I don't see how a simulation theory is any more unlikely than the idea of a dude sitting up in heaven, answering prayers and deciding which college football team should win this week. As far as I'm aware, outside of a book written by humans thousands of years ago claiming people saw and talked to God, no one has proven God exists. Maybe Jesus will return to Earth to cleanse it and complete the First Resurrection. I'm just saying, I'm willing to bet my right pinky that doesn't happen, at least in my lifetime. Anyone want to take me up on that bet?

I know it can be a sobering and sad thought that the decisions we make aren't real, the people we love aren't real, and the sights we see and the smells we smell aren't real (some smells from my kids and dog *shouldn't* be real). I don't want to think about it either, but it should certainly be considered as a possibility.

Do I think we are a simulation? That's hard to say, as everything I've experienced in life has definitely felt real and not driven by someone or something else. I also find it hard to believe that whatever or who-ever created the simulation would need to do so, as they are probably advanced enough to conquer the universe, so why waste time creating a simulation to watch us? I'm not sure what the cost versus benefit of creating that simulation would be.

I also keep coming back to the thought that since I'm writing that I think I am in a simulation, then whoever is watching me would likely shut me off and end my simulation. As far as I can tell, that hasn't hap-pened yet.

However, if we are living in a simulation, I just have one request: For whoever or whatever is doing the decision-making, please make some better decisions that get me laid more, get me more sleep, and get me more and better food. Also, I'm sorry for what you had to see this morning.

15

Yep

ENOUGH OF THE SERIOUS STUFF! EVERYTHING I WROTE PRIOR TO THIS was a trip for me to write, so I'm happy to finally get to this section of interesting thoughts I've had while high relating to a variety of topics. I called this chapter "Yep" because I really have no succinct way to explain and summarize what I wrote in this chapter. These are literally thoughts and concepts I came up with while high and have absolutely no connection to each other.

Some of these topics may be considered sensitive—please realize that I don't mean to offend, anger, delegitimize, or piss on anyone who disagrees with me. These are my thoughts and observations and mine alone.

Seriously, though, if you got through everything else I wrote, I don't think you're going to be terribly offended by what I write below. If I'm wrong about that, the Devil made me do it, I swear.

MY THOUGHTS ON THE CONCEPT OF GOD

Okay, now it's time to talk about God. I get it that it's a touchy subject, because we're all sensitive, emotional beings who like to think we are right about everything (including myself).

I am not going to pretend I have all the answers; I'm smart enough to realize I don't, and I can readily admit that I could be wrong. As you can probably tell, I am not a religious (in the true meaning of the word) person. I do not subscribe to any of the major religions. I've just never bought into it—that there's an imaginary man in the sky we have to pray to in order to be saved when we die. Yeah, not for me.

It makes sense that human beings want comfort and a sense that their lives mean something. They want to believe that if they follow all the rules they have been taught since they could barely walk, there will be a reward for them when they die—a lovely place commonly referred to as heaven. I get it. It's nice to feel all warm and tingly inside while believing in something greater than ourselves.

However, there has been research that argues that the human brain is pre-wired to believe in some form of higher being. The below is an excerpt from *The Independent* from 2009.

> A belief in God is deeply embedded in the human brain, which is programmed for religious experiences, according to a study that analyses why religion is a universal human feature that has encompassed all cultures throughout history. Scientists searching for the neural "God spot," which is supposed to control religious belief, believe that there is not just one but several areas of the brain that form the biological foundations of religious belief.
>
> The researchers said their findings support the idea that the brain has evolved to be sensitive to any form of belief that improves the chances of survival, which could explain why a belief in God and the supernatural became so widespread in human evolutionary history.[107]

While I believe that most human beings lack common sense and reason when it comes to this subject, I don't think anyone who believes in the traditional Judeo-Christian/Muslim god is stupid. I just think they have failed to ask enough questions about their beliefs in a god to determine if it really makes sense that a god, as they perceive it, could actually exist.

I am sure some of you have heard of Occam's Razor, which essentially says that "all else being equal, the simplest answer is probably the right one."

In 2010, Richard Swinburne, a Christian philosopher, noted that "God is the simplest explanation for the universe, because God is a single thing."[108] But is that accurate? Would intelligent creation be more likely than the current theory of the Big Bang? That is for you to think about.

For most people, their religious beliefs come from their parents. They are born into a family that believe in a certain set of religious beliefs and are raised at a very young age to follow those same beliefs—for example, the concept of God, heaven, and hell, as well as traditions that come with those beliefs (e.g., baptism, Bar Mitzvahs, religious holidays, etc.).

Some people, like myself, question those beliefs as just lunacy. How could Earth only be only 5,000 years old? How could there be different places people go when they die? I'm not even getting into the stories of the Bible and how utterly ridiculous they are. I do not follow the Bible's every word and believe that everything documented by humans approximately 2,000 years ago is the "truth." For those of you that do, we're just never going to see third eye to third eye.

For me, the "truth" about a topic is something that has been factually proven through some scientific means and testing (sights, sounds, observations, etc.). So, the truth about Judaism and Christianity could not have come from humans thousands of years ago who relayed stories down through the generations to eventually be written in a book. Admittedly, some of the Hebrew Bible is more about how people should live and the legal requirements of the times, and the New Testament is more stories about Jesus and people's commitment to Jesus. However, for the "truth" about a topic as large and important as religion and God to come from a book that was written by humans who had no concept of how the universe worked and thought lightning was created by God to strike down nonbelievers, that just doesn't fly with me.

Organized religion certainly has a lot of good things associated with it—such as family, tradition, charity, good deeds, sense of community, support during a tragedy, and the concept of right and wrong—but those things can also occur without religion.

Growing up in a Jewish household with a fairly religious, traditional mother and a less-concerned Jewish father, I was exposed to the rules of Judaism early on. I remember thinking to myself, "These rules are so stupid." For those unfamiliar with Judaism, here are some of the rules I'm referring to.

- You can't eat pork.
- You can't eat shellfish.
- You can't mix dairy and cheese.
- You have to have separate cutlery for meat and dairy.
- You cannot make or worship idols (not sure if this applies to *American Idol* or not).
- Only men can wear a *yarmulke* in temple. (However, it should be noted this rule has been updated in recent years to allow women to wear *yarmulkes*. I wonder if God approved of that rule change?)
- You have to become an accountant, lawyer, doctor, or Hollywood producer. (At least I followed that one.)
- You have to go to temple every Friday night and then not work from Friday evening through Saturday evening, only to go back to temple Sunday morning for services and bagels with lox and cream cheese.
- You have to marry a Jewish girl (or at least someone who looks Jewish). While this is not an official rule, it's similar to NBA players putting their hands up every time they commit a foul— no one says they have to officially do it, but it's widely accepted as what you have to do.
- You must have three beautiful Jewish children who will have a bar/bat mitzvah and follow the rules noted above. (Didn't follow this one, either.)

However, it must be said that there are millions of people who do follow these rules, do not question them, and lead very happy lives (and not just for Judaism, but all religions). I have plenty of friends who I am sure believe in God, follow religious tradition, and are none the worse for wear. So, for those of you who do as well, you have my respect and best wishes.

When I went to college, I heard some people say that Jewish people were evil and would go to hell (which was ironic because I was living in a dorm that was already hell on earth, as there was no sex, no alcohol, and no drugs allowed, even though it was *college*). Either way, that reinforced my belief that organized religion was divisive and served very little purpose for me on this planet. It only got worse from there, as I was further exposed to the way religion weaves its way into social issues (e.g., gay marriage, abortion, healthcare, and politics in general).

However, just because I don't believe in organized religion doesn't mean that I don't believe in a higher power. Call me agnostic, I guess, but I think it's a bit naïve to think there isn't another power that created the universe, whether it's the Big Bang or something else. Hell, I think we'll eventually find out there are multiple universes out there, so clearly *something* had to create this design.

So, there are a lot of questions I have had since I was young. These questions are noted below and generally apply to any monotheistic religion (for the purposes of the write-up, I am assigning a sex to God as a male, but if God does exist, it *has* to be a woman).

1. **Where is God?**

    Most major religions believe that God is in heaven, which is traditionally in the sky. In fact, the words for heaven or heavens in both Hebrew (*shamayim*) and Greek (*ouranos*)[109] can also be translated as "sky."

    But how does that actually work? How high up is God? Is God even in this plane of existence, or does he reside in another plane that we can't see? If so, how does he interact with us humans who are in a different plane? If heaven does exist, it would likely be in a different plane that none of us can see until we die. If that's the case, how could any human have ever heard or seen God unless they were just tripping out of their minds?

I guess it's possible God can move between different planes to chat with us here on Earth, but it's been over 2,000 years since I'm aware of that last happening so what is he waiting for? You would think at some point, he would cross-over and have a discussion with *someone* about what is going on these days.

2. **What sustains God?**

How does God keep living? Can God breathe or is he sustained by some other chemical in the universe that he supposedly created? If God is a sentient being, I would imagine he needs energy to survive. Is he eating Chick-fil-A every day? Does he have a steady supply of 5-Hour Energy available to keep him going? I am being facetious, but as far as we know, everything in this universe needs energy to survive, so how does God sustain? God created the entire universe in six days and on the seventh day, he had to rest. This implies he used energy to create the stars, planets, oceans, land, forests, and animals of this planet and, because of all that energy disbursement, he was exhausted and needed some shut eye. So how did God recuperate during this seventh day to regenerate the energy needed to continue being God?

3. **What does God do all day and night?**

Is he just chilling up there, watching all of us go about our day (even when we go to the bathroom)? It's got to be exhausting to be God every second of every day when you think of his responsibilities. I hope he at least has a tablet or an executive assistant to manage all his supposed tasks:

   a. Intervening in our lives on a daily basis.
   b. Having detailed discussions with people about whether they're allowed into heaven, and then welcoming them in if they are.
   c. Listening to our prayers—literally billions and billions of them in a single day—all in different languages, asking for different things at the same time. Some people

write them down, some people think them, some people speak them, some people sing them. How does God manage all that?

d. Heals sickness. That means God has the ability to change our biology and the chemicals within our bodies. Essentially, God is the combination of Doogie Howser, every character on *Scrubs*, Meredith Grey, Hawkeye Pierce from *M*A*S*H*, Bones McCoy from *Star Trek,* and Dr. House. Why do we even need doctors at all? God's got your back. I guess I'm just confused why some people still die from cancer, heart attacks, strokes, diabetes, or any other illness if God can heal. Most religious people will say it is God's will or part of God's plan to let someone die. Okay—if that's the case, what is God basing his decision on to heal or not heal?

e. Changes hearts. I'm not quite sure what this means, but I guess God can change how we think about life or how we feel about it.

f. Protects us. Somehow, God has the ability to protect certain people and not others. Not quite sure how this works—maybe God can predict what will happen and change some evil person's heart to prevent some catastrophe. I guess God was busy during the Revolutionary War, the Civil War, WWI, the Holocaust, WWII, the Korean War, the Vietnam War, the Gulf War, 9/11, every school shooting over the past century, as well as any of the other battles and wars that have befallen humanity since its existence. Is that God's will?

g. Develops wisdom. Somehow, after all of the above, God can help people develop wisdom. I thought that's why we all went to college and spent $100,000 on eight semesters of learning. Turns out I was wrong—God provides this for free! I imagine this is a different type of wisdom than book smarts.

4. **How does God decide which prayers are granted and which prayers are not?**

    You've all watched sporting events where you have fans, players and coaches from both teams with their hands folded and eyes closed, praying to God for the next base hit, strikeout, touchdown, interception, or overtime goal for their team. How does God decide which team he wants to win? Does God have a fantasy team, or does he decide who wins based on a coinflip?

    Again, I am being facetious, but if you assume that half of the world's population is religious, half of those people pray daily, and half of those prayers include a wish, that would amount to one billion prayers a day that have some sort of wish included. How many of those wishes do you think come to fruition? I can't imagine it's a large percentage. There are also a lot of wishes that don't come true, so how does God decide this? If there's a decision-making process involved, does that mean God has a brain to make these decisions? If God does have a brain, what created God's brain? Which leads me to my next question . . .

5. **Has God been around forever or does God have an age?**

    Unfortunately, the Bible claims Earth was only created between 5,000 and 6,000 years ago,[110] but makes no mention as to the age of the universe. But, theoretically, God has existed for a finite period of time. If God did exist before our universe was created, then where was he? What other universe did he exist in? If God hasn't existed forever, then who or what created God? Clearly something had to come together to make God. Who are God's parents? If God has been around forever, but just created Earth 5,000 years ago, what was he doing prior to creating Earth (I really hope he was just hanging out and getting high).

6. **If God created the planet, why did he include things that kill us?**

    God literally created things on this planet that are designed to destroy us. Earthquakes, tornados, hurricanes, fires, floods, drought, excessive heat, excessive cold, tigers, mosquitos, and Liam Neeson. If he created these things to kill us, that's a pretty messed up thing for God to do, don't you think? Why would this all-loving God create things designed to kill us? Personally, I would much prefer having a world that just has sunflowers, butterflies, and Golden Doodles.

7.   **How does God not have the ability to stop bad things from happening?**

So, how can a god that exhausted so much energy to create the heavens and Earth in six days not bother to create new crops for the starving children in Africa or stop a tornado from forming and killing hundreds of people in Kansas, including children? Does he not have that power? If he does, does it mean he chooses not to use that power to stop tragedies from happening? If so, again, that's pretty messed up of God. Some religious people argue that children suffer because of "original sin," but you tell me what kind of sense that makes.

8.   **Why did God create animals that serve only as consumption for other beings on the same planet?**

Billions of animals are raised in horrible conditions, with short life spans, so us humans can have the Number 6 Happy Meal at our local McDonald's. This killing also involves baby animals who haven't yet experienced life. Seems like God could have just made us vegetarians. It would be pretty messed up of God to create animals that are meant to be consumed by either humans or other animals. I know some people argue that it's "free will," but it's not really. A great white shark is designed to eat that tuna fish as it goes by. I admit, I do eat some meat and fish, however, I have greatly reduced my meat intake over the past several years and am none the worse for wear.

If you are religious and believe in a god, feel free to send me your responses to the above questions, because I'm generally curious what you believe and what you think makes sense to you. Maybe there are answers to these questions that are based on common sense and reality, and I just haven't heard them yet.

THE TEST TO COMPARE SIBLINGS TO PARENTS: COMBINING SOULS AT BIRTH

I wrote earlier about my theory that our souls come from our parents. I think, if that's the case, that each output of that "mixing together of souls" produces a slightly different version of a new soul, which manifests itself through a combination of physical and non-physical characteristics. (Like how apple pies may look and taste different even if made by the same person just because of slightly different amounts of each ingredient.)

So, I have a fun game you can play to test what mixture of soul you might be from your parents' souls.

Think of your parents, as individuals, and consider what makes your mom your mom and your dad your dad. This can be both physical and non-physical traits, characteristics, mannerisms, fears, anxieties, passions, etc. Of course, this assumes that you know your mom and dad enough to comment on the questions below. This can be done whether they are still alive or not, and you should involve siblings when possible so that there's no bias involved.

1. Who would you say you look like more—your mom or your dad? Or are you a good 50/50 split of each of them? If you look like one parent more than the other, write down what percentage you look like that parent versus the other and put that to the side.
2. Who would you say you're more like from a nonphysical perspective? For help, you can ask yourself the following questions. Really think them through and enlist the help of a sibling or someone who knows you and your parents well. Afterward, write down the split between your mom and dad in terms of who you are more like.
   a) Are they passionate about certain things (does not need to be the same things) like you are?
   b) Who has more similar personality traits to you (sympathetic, empathetic, depressed, anxious, etc.)?
   c) Who reacts similarly to you to different things (crying, outburst, impartial, etc.)?

d) In general, are they impulsive or restrained in terms of their reactions?

e) Do they get angry easily or not?

f) Are they a planner or not? For example, do they always need to know what they're doing and where they're going?

g) Are there other things at their core and your core that make you closer to one parent compared to the other?

h) Write down the split between your mom and dad in terms of who you are more alike.

3. See if the percentages are close to each other for both the physical and non-physical traits. They may not be perfectly aligned, but see if they generally swing in favor of one parent or the other. Make sure you don't force it; it should be a collaborative agreement between you and your siblings (assuming you have some and you still talk to each other).

4. I tried this with Alexandra in terms of how my brothers and I aligned with my parents, and it generally worked out that there was a correlation physically and non-physically to one of our parents.

If you have children, you can do this same exercise to see if these splits of physical and non-physical traits are the same. It will be difficult if you have younger children, especially if they are still learning to talk or interact with others, but it's still fun.

You can use the below table as an example. Notice how Child 1 and Child 2 are much more like one parent, while Child 3 is more of a blend between the two parents.

Child	Physical Traits		Non-physical Traits		Total		Percentage	
	Mom	Dad	Mom	Dad	Mom	Dad	Mom	Dad
1	75	25	65	35	140	60	70%	30%
2	20	80	35	65	55	145	27%	73%
3	50	50	55	45	105	95	53%	47%

If this generally holds up for your family, ask yourselves what it means. Does it mean that when our souls are created by our parents, we get a certain percentage of physical and non-physical traits from each parent, which means we really are more like one parent than the other? If so, what factors drive that percentage in favor of one parent versus the other?

EVERYONE SHOULD PLAN THEIR OWN FUNERAL

Think about every funeral you've ever been to. What type of experience was it for you (besides sad)? Did you come away thinking, "Wow, that funeral really celebrated that person's life!" Probably not. It was likely a mixture of your standard religious prayers, relatives sharing what type of person the deceased was from their point of view, and maybe a funny story or two. Then you went to the cemetery and then got some lunch at someone's house. I know that sounds awful, but when you break it down, that's generally what happens.

Wouldn't it be great if, instead of other people talking at your funeral, you wrote out what you wanted to say and had somebody else read it on your behalf? You would get to say everything you always wanted to say and essentially "let it out." At that point, you're not there, so offend whomever you want to offend and profess your love for others. I'm sure there may be some things better left unsaid, but you get my point.

So, with that in mind, here is how I would plan my own funeral:

1. I want my funeral at 7:00 a.m. I want to test who really cared about me and see how early they are willing to get up for me. Everyone who is invited but doesn't show up needs to donate $50 to an environmental organization of their choice. I would also offer the funeral live-streamed to help people make their decision.

2. Everyone who does show up must wear some Devils hockey gear. Hopefully by the time I croak, the Devils will be competitive again and people will be proud to wear something with a Devils logo on it.

3. I will have a fund set aside to cover everyone's ride sharing costs for the funeral because . . .

4. Everyone needs to show up with some liquor or weed. I want my funeral to be a party. Even if you don't do liquor or weed, I want you to bring some for everyone else who does.

5. When everyone is there and the funeral is ready to begin, I want to play four songs: "Wings for Marie – Part 2" by Tool, "I and Love and You" by The Avett Brothers, "When My Time Comes" by Dawes, and "No One's Gonna Love You" by Band of Horses. If you've never heard these songs, go listen to them and tell me they're not great songs for a funeral, especially if you're drunk or high by that point.

6. Once the songs are over, someone will read my letter, which will go as follows:

Thank you for coming to my funeral. I know it was probably a drag getting up at the butt-crack of dawn, so to show my love and appreciation for you, I want everyone to either do a shot or pop an edible right now. Let's all relax a little bit, shall we?

Thank you for also wearing Devils gear, especially for anyone that is a Rangers or Islanders fan—however, I didn't know a ton of Islanders fans and tried to avoid associating with any known Rangers fans, so hopefully there are not a lot of you in the crowd. But if there are, I do appreciate you wearing the gear of the one true hockey team in the tri-state area.

Also, I hope you appreciated those songs by Tool, The Avett Brothers, Dawes and Band of Horses. I sincerely hope you enjoyed them as much as I have throughout my life. Music was very important to me, and I found comfort and joy in listening to this type of music. Sure, I had to sit through some awful music for my kids and tried to get into whatever they were listening to, but at the end of the day, rock and alternative music was what I connected with the most. Tool, Deftones, The Avett Brothers, Cold War Kids, Radiohead, 311, Sevendust, Soundgarden, Smashing Pumpkins, Dawes, The Head and the Heart, Dave Matthews Band, Delta Spirit, Silversun Pickups, Alice In Chains, BTS, and Bone Thugs-N-Harmony—those were the bands that I turned to the most.

For those of you that couldn't make it and are watching on livestream, I appreciate you donating to the environmental organization of your choice. There are a lot of good ones out there that do a lot of good work to try to save the one planet we have. I know most of you probably don't care about environmental causes, but you should. There's nothing weak or uncool about caring about the environment. I recycled, donated to environmental organizations, drove an electric car, had solar panels on my house, and voted for politicians that professed to care about the environment. And I was likely the most masculine person you knew. Please care about the environment going forward; we all need to do our part.

For those of you who are here and knew me professionally, thank you for coming. I tried my best to do good work and be the best accountant I could be. I gave up several vacations, baseball games, karate tournaments, and personal time with my family to take on work responsibilities. I wasn't perfect, but I hope you appreciated that I tried my hardest to deliver.

For those of you who knew me personally, I am grateful for your friendship. There were several "friends" I had that I lost along the way, mostly for pretty stupid reasons. All I can say is that I tried to be a good friend, to be generous with my time and my efforts to help people out. Some people realized that, some didn't, and that's okay. I quickly realized that I can't please everyone and all anyone can do is try to be a good friend. Some will stick with you throughout and some won't. To those that stuck with me— thank you. You meant more to me than you'll ever know.

I truly hope there are a few tears in the room at this point because, damn it, there should be. For everyone who is drinking, please take another shot of something. My preference would be whiskey, but tequila will do. Just please, for the love of everything holy, no vodka. If anyone here is drinking vodka, I may throw up in my coffin.

For those of you smoking weed or doing edibles, do a little more. I have pizza coming in about thirty minutes—two Brooklyn pies, two baked zitis, two whites, two chicken parms, a cheese tortellini alfredo pizza, and ten plains. I also have some ice cream and warm chocolate lava cake coming as well. Now I'm hungry just thinking about all that while writing this out.

Anyway, on to my family. To my kids—I'm sorry I'm dead, but don't worry, I will still try to haunt you most of the time. (Except when you're having sex. When you do have sex, please wear protection because who knows if abortion will be legal in the United States for much longer and you don't want to have to deal with that, or STDs—not fun.) Thank you for being my kids. I know you didn't have a choice in the matter, and I only believe two of you may actually be my genetic children, but I raised all of you, and it was the honor of my life to be your dad. You made me so proud every day with what you accomplished and the type of people you've become. Never forget to be there for each other and to support each other always. You will all make mistakes in life, and there is nothing wrong with that, but be there and support each other when you do. That is your role from now on—please do it for me.

To my brothers—thank you for always being there for me and my family. They loved you like you were their brothers too, and I hope you find happiness in the rest of your life.

To my parents—if you are still alive, I hope you remember who I was as a person. Even though you tried very hard to mess me up, I was a happy person when I died, so I hope that gives you some comfort. If you're dead, then I'm sure I am joining you wherever we all go when we die.

To Alexandra—thank you and goodbye.

To anyone I didn't mention—you must not have been that important to me, but please do another shot or take an edible in my name.

To all of you—be kind to the planet and to each other. Also, please, I beg you, buy my book Higher Connections: Observations of a Certified Public Pothead *. My family will need the royalties.*

Now go enjoy some pizza and lava cake and enjoy your buzz or high. You're welcome.

For the record, this is absolutely how I would say goodbye to Alexandra, and she would absolutely be laughing when she heard it.

ALEXANDRA'S NOTE:

Eric is right; I would be laughing, but at the same time thinking, "This motherfucker . . ."

WHICH DECADE OF YOUR LIFE
IS THE BEST TO DIE IN?

We all want to live forever (or at least long enough to see aliens finally visit Earth). But, unless you're Tom Brady, none of us are likely to live forever. As the saying goes, there are only a few things in life that are certain, and those would be: 1) federal income taxes; 2) state income taxes; 3) local taxes; 4) county taxes; 5) municipal taxes; 6) sales tax; 7) credit card fees; 8) excise taxes; 9) gift taxes; 10) estate taxes; 11) property taxes; 12) gas tax; 13) utility taxes; 14) GST; 15) HST; 16) SHT; and, finally, 17) death.

So, when death does finally come, as it will for us all, what is the best decade of your life in which to kick the bucket? I've rated each decade, starting with your twenties (because anything earlier than that is just not good) on a scale of 1 to 10 (1 being the worst, 10 being the best) based on how favorable it would be to die in that decade.

Please note these ratings are based on my life experiences and may be different for others, so feel free to create your own scale. Remember, this is all in fun, so let's not overcomplicate things.

Twenties = 2/10

Dying in this decade of your life would generally suck, for obvious reasons:

1. You've barely lived your life at this point.
2. Hopefully, you graduated high school and went to the college of your dreams, somewhat far away from your parents. You lived your life in college as a free man or woman and took advantage of everything college has to offer. You immediately got a cushy new job at twenty-three and have a long career ahead of you.
3. You're able to go to bars, get wasted, and go home at 3:00 a.m., because why not? You're in your twenties!
4. You have no responsibilities, no children, and no husband or wife (unless you grew up in the Midwest or Southern part of the United States, in which case you likely have been married and have six kids by the time you're in your twenties).

5. You can go out on weekends with your friends, you can go to whatever concerts you want, and you can go on vacation wherever and with whomever you want.

6. You're excited to start your career and actually care about getting to work on time and staying late because your career is the only thing that matters.

7. You hopefully earn a decent living, at least enough to impress your friends and the hot young people you meet. You can go back to your college and impress your friends with all the money you have earned when you buy a round of shots for twenty people and all you have to fork out is a ten-dollar bill.

8. You can have sex multiple times a day, with multiple people, and not blink an eye. You're ready and open to whatever life brings you from a sexual standpoint.

9. You can generally eat and drink whatever you want without worrying about gaining weight or being too hungover to function the next day.

The only reason this is a 2/10 and not a 1/10 is because, if you die in your twenties, it's likely not from natural causes. It's likely from doing something you should only do in your twenties, such as: 1) overdosing on cocaine laced with fentanyl while doing a line off of two naked girls you met earlier in the night; 2) climbing a tower at a concert trying to get a better view of your favorite band and falling to the ground because you've been drinking beer for two days straight, doing mushrooms for three days straight, and you haven't slept in four days; or 3) dying from your parachute not opening while jumping out of a plane at 40,000 feet. Otherwise, your twenties is a pretty crappy decade to die in.

Thirties = 1/10

This is my pick for the worst decade to die in for mostly obvious reasons, such as:

1. You've likely hit several peaks in your life in terms of looks, money, freedom, self-worth, and the number of weddings you'll attend.

2. If you've done things right, you've been able to pay off your student loans and have started saving money for retirement.

3. You're advancing in your career to the point where you can see yourself reaching the pinnacle of whatever career you're in, which is when the money will really start rolling in.

4. You've been through your twenties and have taken full advantage of the single life, but you've now settled down, are in a committed relationship, or are married to your significant other and have either started a family or are trying to start a family.

5. You have hopefully saved up enough to put a down payment on a nice starter house, preferably near your friends, and can finally build that koi pond you've always dreamed of.

6. You drive a nice, state-of-the-art car that will hopefully be big enough for your young family going forward.

7. Your siblings and friends are all starting to have kids, and you've accepted the fact that your life, as you've known it, is effectively over—no vacations, no concerts, no more going out to bars and clubs whenever you want to. All of that is generally over, and you've accepted it.

8. If you have young kids, you and your significant other are tired, but still find time to have sex three to four times a month, and you both still generally look like you did in your mid- to late twenties.

9. You can generally still eat and drink what you want. However, you've started to drink less overall because hangovers are awful, and you just can't recover the same way you could in your twenties. You've started experimenting with edibles and have realized how much better it makes you feel than alcohol.

And then—boom! Something happens to you, and you're dead. Similar to your twenties, the cause is likely not a natural death (unless you have eaten barbeque as your daily meal for the past twenty years). It's usually something stupid, like getting run over by a dump truck as you cross the street while looking at your phone, or drowning in the ocean because you thought you could do a night swim across the bay like you did in college. It's never anything cool or interesting; it's just sad and still in the "damn-that-should-never-happen-to-anyone" category.

The one "good" thing about dying in your thirties is that you'll always be remembered as a "loving spouse and parent" who loved their family unconditionally and did fun things with them on a weekly basis. Other than that, this is the worst decade in which to go.

Forties = 4/10

Now, for full disclosure, I am in my forties as I write this. So, while I wanted to give this a 6/10, a small part of my brain (maybe my simulator) said, "Give it a 4/10 instead, dummy, or else we'll kill you now." So, to play it safe, my rating is a 4/10. Here are the primary reasons why this is a mixed-bag decade to die in:

1. You're likely at or near your earnings peak—which is great because you can afford things you've never been able to afford before, but awful because your significant other keeps nagging you to redo the bathroom, kitchen, study, and attic and take trips around the world. All of this generally leaves you with nothing left over for the new car that just came out that you've wanted for two years.

2. You've been able to see parts of the world you always wanted to see—during family vacations or traveling for work. You realize there are a lot of places nicer than the United States and start thinking about whether you'd be able to retire overseas somewhere.

3. You're at the height of your looks. You're still able to work out and stay in shape while also able to afford nice clothes, so you can still look good with clothes on and clothes off. You know you only have a few good years left of people calling you handsome. If you're a man, hopefully, you still have most of your hair, and it's mostly not gray. If you're a woman, hopefully you're still able to get that long, flowing hair you had in your twenties and thirties.

4. Your kids are likely older and can take care of themselves to the point that you just need to make sure they're alive every once in a while. Although, you still likely have to drive your kids to seventy different things during the weekdays, as well as another 900 things during the weekend.

5. You are starting to go out again on weekends with your significant other and friends. You can start thinking about seeing concerts again, going out to nice dinners (while paying a babysitter $55 an hour to sit at your house on their phone the whole time taking selfies of themselves while you are constantly wondering if your children are alive), and maybe taking a short weekend getaway to the Caribbean, or somewhere else warm and isolated.

6. With any luck, your parents are still alive so they can see what you have (hopefully) accomplished in your life, and they may also help with babysitting your kids so you don't have to pay $55 an hour for a babysitter.

7. If you're still married, you're likely happy with your significant other and are fine with spending the rest of your life with them.

8. If you're divorced, then you hopefully have enough money to attract a young, beautiful specimen who just wants a sugar daddy or a sugar mamma.

9. You realize that you're at or past mid-life at this point, and you're starting to wind down in your life, which is somewhat depressing.

All in all, you have a lot going for you in your forties. However, there are some good things about dying in your forties that make it not such a terrible decade to die in.

1. You've hopefully made it to several of the goals you wanted to achieve in terms of your career, family, and what values are important to you. So, there aren't really many more goals you're hoping to achieve. In reality, the forties are about sustaining what you have until you can retire and live your ultimate life.

2. If you're a man, you're likely looking your best and still have most of your hair without many wrinkles. When people look at you, they still see a good-looking, middle-aged man. If you die in your forties, no one has to see you start to look bad—no wrinkles, no hair loss, no back fat, and no dry mouth. You're at your physical peak, and that's how people will remember you. Your penis likely starts to malfunction, and you have to take little blue pills to get an erection in order to get ready for the once-a-month sex you're having (unless you're divorced and actually getting action). Luckily, you still have enough energy to take care of things on your own, but you realize your sexual abilities are starting to wane and that it's just going to get worse.

3. If you're a woman, you're likely having to think about Botox or plastic surgery to keep things where they were when you were younger. This can get expensive and comes with risk, but may beat the alternative of just letting gravity do its thing.

4. You've had to start changing your diet and start eating things like green smoothies, cauliflower pizza, and avocado toast, as opposed to chicken parm, pizza, and crumb cake every day. It sucks, and you realize this will be your diet going forward, and it will only get worse as you age and your cholesterol increases.

5. You may die of natural causes in your forties and it's generally around the age when people stop saying, "Oh, that's just way too young to die." People are more concerned about your young family you left behind and start focusing on them pretty soon after you're gone.

Because of that, I'm giving this a 4/10, even though I think it should be a 6/10, because you've done a lot in life, are still able to function, and it's not embarrassing to die in your forties.

Fifties = 5/10

I'm giving this decade a 5/10. It's not the greatest decade to die in, but it's also not that bad of a decade to die in. Here are the cons:

1. You've done a lot in your career and have made it to the absolute top of where you always wanted to be. You're also likely earning the most money you will in your career.

2. You're close to retirement and can start envisioning what you want to do during retirement.

3. With the kids grown up, you have more time to volunteer or participate on some boards, which gets you recognized in your community and well known in professional and personal circles.

4. Your kids are hopefully through college, and you don't have to worry about funding any more tuition payments. You'll maybe have to fund a couple weddings, but you'll cross that bridge when needed, because hopefully your kids are smart enough to marry into money.

5. You go out to nice dinners and events with your significant other and with friends. You have a great social life and are able to see your friends for athletic and social events as you want to.

6. You see your kids often enough because they still live either in your house after graduating college or close enough that you see them a few times a month.

7. You can still have sex. It's not great or emotional, but it gets you through the day for the ten days a year you still have it.

8. If you're married, you likely still love your significant other and, now that the kids are out of the house (hopefully), you're able to reconnect with them and remember why you fell in love with them in the first place.

9. If you're divorced, you are likely able to date sophisticated younger men or women who don't have kids, or older men or women who are looking for freedom and a second chance at love. You can vacation whenever and wherever you want with them.

10. You have found a new diet that is both tasty and healthy. Maybe you can even afford a private chef to make healthy and delicious meals for you.

11. You still have your memory, both short-term and long-term.

12. Overall, your life is good and you're looking forward to retirement.

Now, why your fifties is an okay decade to die in compared to most others is similar to why your forties is an okay decade to die in compared to most others: Things likely start to go downhill after your fifties—physically, mentally, and sexually—so dying in your fifties isn't that bad. Again, it saves you the pain of having to see yourself decline as you get into your sixties and seventies. So, overall, I went with a 5/10.

Sixties = 3/10

This decade is a 3/10. It's right up there with the worst decades to die in. Here are the pros of dying in your sixties:

1. You're old enough that dying in this decade is not that embarrassing. When people hear you died in your sixties, they'll think, "Yeah, that's okay; they probably had a good life."
2. You've likely died of something relatively quickly, like a heart attack or stroke. Which may be painful, but you're likely knocked unconscious from the pain, so you aren't conscious for your last breath. Maybe you've died from a heart attack after a romantic session with your new, hot, thirty-year-old wife before the life insurance policies were formally executed, denying her the millions she was supposed to get.
3. You've seen your kids grow up, get married, potentially start having a family of their own, which is satisfying.
4. Maybe you've started outliving some of the people you didn't get along with in high school. You'll never admit it, but every time you see a death notice for one of those people, a small grin spreads across your face. You feel bad for their family but then remember the time in the eighth grade when they pushed you into your locker in front of the girl you'd had a crush on since the fifth grade. You mutter quietly, "I guess there is a god," and move on with your day.

Here are the cons of dying in your sixties:

1. You're free! After forty plus years of working, you've finally achieved the ultimate bliss—retirement. You've worked hard

and have done a lot of things you're proud of, and this is what you've been working for your entire life.

2. You're still physically able to play sports with your friends and family (not necessarily on the professional level but enough to say you were a stud in high school).

3. You have the use of most of your mental capacities, although it's sometimes tough to remember the names of people you knew twenty, thirty, forty years ago. You know it's getting worse, but it's not to the point that people notice when they're talking with you.

4. If you were smart and saved, you have plenty of money and can take trips around the world with your friends and family as you desire, especially now that you've retired.

5. You eat good food, you drink good wine, and you hopefully take good edibles on a periodic but consistent basis.

6. It feels like this decade is your chance at a second life to do whatever it is you wanted to do that you couldn't while you were working for so long.

For the sole reason that this is the decade of your retirement, it's the worst one to die in. To me, it would feel like a punch in the gut to die in my sixties. It in no way compares to dying in your seventies.

Seventies = 9/10

This decade is right up there with the best decades to die in. Here are the pros of dying in this decade:

1. You've lived a good life at this point. You have seen your family change—some dying, some being born. It gets harder to see them and keep up with their energy.

2. You're not able to drive as well anymore, so your kids suggest getting a driver to help out.

3. You've been able to travel since your sixties and have visited places you've dreamed of visiting since your childhood. Recently, it's become harder to travel to these new places due to a knee, hip, or elbow replacement.

4. You've eaten great foods and great wines, but recently your sense of taste has decreased to the point that you wonder how much longer it will last.
5. You're starting to hurt all over because of a variety of issues. The number of doctors you have to visit on a weekly basis has increased, as have the medications you've been prescribed.
6. You're constantly constipated and need to chug Ex-Lax to be able to take a proper number two.
7. If your significant other is still alive, it may be tough to care for them as well. Maybe they have medical issues that aren't yet to the point where you need help at home, but it is definitely to the point that taking care of them is getting harder to do by yourself.
8. If your significant other is not alive, you're likely alone most of the time because it takes too much energy to date someone new. You are too tired and depressed to go out most of the time.
9. It gets harder to think about how much time you have left, and you become happy just to wake up each day.

Here are the cons of dying in this decade:

1. Your seventies are still considered somewhat young, especially as medical advances are more able to prolong our lives.
2. You still want to see your grandkids grow up, and you want to potentially have great-grandkids.
3. You still enjoy life, even though it's harder to feel good about your body and mind.
4. Maybe you just started a new hobby or something else you've always wanted to do and are looking forward to doing that for as long as possible.

Other than the four above, I can't think of any more cons of dying in your seventies. It's the age when most people likely think they've accomplished a lot and are okay with dying. They're likely tired physically and mentally, and they are resigned to death coming sooner rather than later and are at peace with it. Sure, most folks would like to keep going for as long as they are physically and mentally able to, but the seventies is a weird decade in which that may or may not happen. For these reasons, your seventies is a good decade to go—Lucky Sevens, if possible.

Eighties = 8/10

This decade is a pretty good decade to go in, mostly because not many folks get out of their eighties. The pros of dying in this decade of your life are:

1. You can start bragging that you made it to your eighties even though you smoked, drank, and ate red meat your entire life.

2. Your long-term memory is gone but your short-term memory is fine, which is okay, because most of the people you knew longest are dead anyway.

3. If you're a man, you likely have a home service maid named Helga, who is twenty-eight, from Sweden, and has to give you a sponge bath every week—which is fine because your short-term memory is still working well enough.

4. If you're a woman, maybe your granddaughter brings over her new twenty-five-year-old boyfriend that reminds you of a crush you had in college and brings a smile to your face.

5. You're mostly still able to do things, with some help. You can see plays, movies, sporting events, and concerts if you'd like. You may need a cane or wheelchair to go, but at least it gets you out of the house.

6. You look forward to the simplest things, like a visit from your family, or watching your favorite program on TV.

7. You no longer have to worry about taking a shit since you now have a colostomy bag constantly attached to you.

8. Your cause of death is almost certainly going to be natural—no shame, no amusing story when you die. You're *expected* to kick the bucket at this point. If you're lucky, you'll go in your sleep or while banging your seventy-year-old girlfriend or boyfriend from down the hall.

The main cons of dying in this decade are:

1. This has got to be a miserable decade to live in, which is the biggest con for me. You're probably alone, hurting, and not all mentally there.
2. You have family, but they may not see you much anymore. They'll come by once in a while, but it's not as frequent.
3. Maybe you had a goal of getting to one hundred so you could be on the local news.

Overall, if I had a choice, I'd rather just go in my seventies and not have to deal with the pain of the eighties, like peeing and getting out of bed. But overall, if you can make it to your eighties in fairly good health, it's a pretty good decade to go in.

Nineties = 5/10

The reality is that if you make it to your nineties, it really doesn't matter if it's a good decade to go in or not—you won't feel it or remember it, anyway. If you're able to make it to your nineties, God bless you, and I hope you have lived a great life.

One Hundreds – Not Rated

My brain isn't able to process what it's like to get to your hundreds. I can't imagine it's good, but you'd be pretty famous for making it to one hundred. Though you may not be aware you're famous and made it to one hundred, your family would, and your legacy would live on for a long time. Give me that piece of it, but the rest of it must be awful.

I hope that section was fun for you. I hope I die somewhere between seventy-six and eighty-two. That feels like the right age, when I can look back and say, "Yeah, that seems about right."

HOW THE TYPICAL MALE FEELS
EACH DAY OF THE WEEK

Caveats:

1. This summary is mostly for young men who have a nine-to-five job, either single or with a girlfriend.
2. This assumes you're not in prison, as I can only imagine what your average days are like there.
3. This does not apply to anyone with children—especially children who play sports, do music, take dance class or any other activity that involves transporting them somewhere else. Kids' activities dominate your thoughts, moods, diets, and daily exhaustion levels in a way that nothing else in life does. But you do it for your kids—or so you can watch other parents try to live vicariously through their children, which is pathetic and hilarious to watch.

Monday

Your life blows. No matter how old you are, whether you're married or single, whether you're hot, ugly, small, tall, fat, skinny, or LGBTQIA (or whatever it is by the time this book comes out), your life is at the lowest point ever. There is literally nothing to look forward to. You force yourself up around 6:30 a.m. to go to the gym, after staying up too late to watch Sunday Night Football the night before. You have a shit workout at the gym, and then you head to work, hopefully by 9:00 a.m. Work blows. You have no idea how you're going to muster the energy to get through the week. You somehow get through work, get home at 6:00 p.m., and pop in some leftover pizza and Chinese food. Even though you should go to bed, you stay up to watch Monday Night Football in order to see some second-string running back hopefully get at least 5.7 points so you can win one fantasy league, but not more than 7.1 points so you don't lose in another league (you know who you are). Hopefully the game ends by 11:00 p.m. and you pass out by 11:30 p.m., happy that your guy got 5.9 points because of a last-minute garbage play that got him 22 yards.

Tuesday

You wake up at 6:00 a.m. to go to the gym but end up saying, "Fuck it," and snooze until 7:00 a.m. Your life still blows, but you don't feel as bad as you did yesterday, mostly because of your fantasy wins. You definitely regret downing the leftover pizza and Chinese food, and spend the next twenty-five minutes thanking God for triple-ply toilet paper and strong plumbing. The workday is equal to Monday, as you have not yet reached Hump Day. You get home, realize you should get your ass to the gym, and enjoy a healthy meal. You generally feel better about life after your good shit in the morning, your workout, and your healthy meal. It's a nice evening of catching up on your shows on Cable DVR/HBO/HBO Max/Paramount TV/Netflix/Hulu/Roku/Amazon Prime/Apple TV/Showtime/Starz/Cinemax/whatever streaming service has launched since this was written. After feeling good that you caught up with two of your favorite shows, you go to bed around 12:30 am.

Wednesday

You feel tired from staying up too late the night before but are happy with the decision you made. You have a pretty good day at work, as you only had to hear fifteen people say, "Hey, man! It's Hump Day!" Generally, by Wednesday afternoon, you can finally see the light at the end of the workweek tunnel. After some coercion, you decide to go out and celebrate fifteen-cent wing night at Applebee's, along with two-dollar Miller Lites and two orders of riblets. After the two orders of riblets, fifteen Miller Lites, and watching your favorite hockey team lose in overtime, you go home, put on *Temptation Island* to see if Becky and Rob stay together or break up (you definitely think they're going to break up, but something inside you really wants them to stay together). After confirming that Becky and Rob do leave the island together, the show throws you a curveball and tells you that they have since broken up. Your stomach appears to be as upset as you are, and you realize that the riblets and fifteen Miller Lites need to find a new home. After crying and shitting for fifteen minutes, you pass out around 1:00 a.m., off to dream of Thirsty Thursday.

Thursday

You wake up at 7:00 a.m., somewhat rested, but your ass is still reeling from the night before. You feel gross, so you take an extra-long shower, cursing yourself for not getting up to go to the gym. Since you'll be seeing your significant other tonight, you shave your nether regions (every little bit helps) and ensure there's no remaining riblet sauce on you. You head to work, thinking about whether you should start Defense A or Defense B for Thursday Night Football. Then you respond to the 500 text messages you ignored from your significant other the night before. As you're three-quarters of the way through your response to her, you catch a glimpse of a twenty-something walking to work in a short skirt and tight blouse on the sidewalk next to you. All you hear is your automatic collision alert going off as you realize you're about to rear-end a Mustang (and not in a good way). Thank God for technology as you stop just short of hitting the Mustang (don't text and drive). You finally get to work and commiserate with your buddies to see who feels the worst after last night. After a generally awful workday, you get ready to meet your significant other for happy hour with her friends. You force yourself to enjoy happy hour with her friends, try to stay clear of anything beer related, and think about getting home to catch the last hour of Thursday Night Football. You finally get out of the happy hour, head to your house with your significant other, and plop down on the couch to watch football. After twenty-five actual minutes and two football minutes, your significant other comes out in the see-through lingerie she bought two days ago. The rest of the night is a mix of fluids, disappointment, crying, and sleep.

Friday

You wake up at 6:15 a.m. because your significant other's drool is running down your naked chest, and you try to remember who was crying the night before and why. Doesn't matter. You get up, realize you need about three cups of coffee, check for any weird stains on your side of the bed, and get ready for work. You kiss your significant other goodbye and tell her you'll see her tomorrow. You head to work actually looking forward to getting there because the sooner you get there, the sooner you can get out, since none of your bosses are actually in the office. You get to work, respond to the phrase, "Thank God it's Friday!" by saying, "Your God or mine?" and get to your desk, where you start planning for your boozy lunch. Boozy lunch starts around 11:30 a.m. and ends around 2:00 p.m. You check your emails to see if there's anything that absolutely can't wait until Monday and respond if there is. By 4:00 p.m., you're starting to plan your escape. With any luck, you're out of work by 4:30 p.m. and on your way to the sweet, sweet weekend. You're feeling great, and there's nothing in the world that could ruin this high for you. After seeing the significant other last night at happy hour and drinking on Wednesday night, you're ready for a relaxing Friday night involving an edible, your favorite pizza, and watching *Diners, Drive-ins and Dives* until you pass out at 11:00 p.m. Friday night is the one night that stirs all human emotions: 1) exhausted from a long week; 2) relieved the prior week is over; 3) content with your decision to not go out and just have a nice night in with a pizza; 4) stressed about meeting your significant other's friends for dinner Saturday night; and 5) happy you don't have to leave your house until Saturday afternoon.

Saturday

What a blessed morning. There is nothing more pure, more beautiful, more awesome, or more fulfilling than waking up at 9:00 a.m. on a Saturday morning with nothing to do but go to the gym, go food shopping, and meeting up with your significant other in the evening for dinner. The world is yours for the taking. You have a nice breakfast, go do a long workout, go food shopping, head to your favorite deli to flirt with the girl who takes your order, head home to watch some college football, take a nap around 4:00 p.m., wake up around 5:00 p.m., and start getting ready to meet your significant other for dinner. You have a nice dinner with her and her friends, stay out drinking until 12:30 a.m., go home, have wild, drunken sex, and watch reruns of *Everybody Loves Raymond*. Saturday is a good day and a good night, and you're generally on top of the world. Why can't every day be Saturday you ask yourself as you drift off to sleep at 2:30 am.

Sunday

Eh, Sunday. It starts out as a fine day. You wake up at 8:30 a.m. with a partial hangover and get breakfast with the significant other. If she doesn't go home after, you figure out what you want to do with the rest of your day—run errands, hang out with her, hang out with friends, see your family, or watch your favorite sport on TV. In the fall, Sunday is dedicated to football, and more specifically fantasy football. Your entire mood for the day is dependent on what some third-string wide receiver on the Jacksonville Jaguars does or doesn't do. Sunday really should be a relaxing day—it's still the weekend—but in the back of your mind is the fact that tomorrow is Monday, when you have to start the entire shit week all over again. As the day goes on, you feel your mood getting worse and worse. By dinner time, you want to call your boss and tell him you've quit, so you don't have to put yourself through another awful week at work. Sunday night gets a little better, as there is usually something good on TV that you look forward to watching. But by 11:30 p.m., you realize you need to cry yourself to sleep in order to wake up on Monday and that your life blows.

RANKING THE BEST COMBINATION OF PLEASURE AND RELIEF

One day while high, I wondered what the majority of people would say their most pleasurable and relieving experience was in their life. I got to thinking that there are five main experiences that cause pleasure and relief: 1) eating; 2) orgasming; 3) peeing; 4) pooping; and 5) blowing your nose.

So, I decided to rank the five items below in terms of the one that gives you the best combination of pleasure and relief:

1. The best pee of your life
2. The best shit of your life
3. The best meal of your life
4. The best nose blow of your life
5. The best orgasm of your life

So without further ado, here is the ranking from least to most:

5) The best nose blow of your life.

Yes, it feels awesome to get a huge wad of snot out of your nose, especially when you can feel it dripping down your nose and into your mouth. A nice tissue, napkin, or spare receipt should always be something you keep in your pocket in case of an emergency, especially on a windy day in New York City. Spending twenty seconds dumping sixteen ounces of snot into a nice, warm tissue is a lovely feeling. It's something I have to do fairly often when I get one of my famous colds. But the reality is, if you absolutely need to, you can just shoot a nice snot rocket, regardless of where you are or who you're around. It's really the only one of these five things you can do regardless of who is around you.

4) The best orgasm of your life.

Hear me out on this one. Most of us, on average, masturbate or have sex three to four times a week. Hopefully, you're orgasming every time (I know that's a given for the women I've been with). For other men, I can't really speak to whether their women are orgasming every time. But, for the purposes of this ranking, I have assumed that everyone is orgasming three to four times a week. For most of us, an orgasm is an orgasm. (I hear there are ways for women to have more intense orgasms, but that's never happened to me, so what do I know?) The point is, the difference between a regular orgasm and the best orgasm of your life isn't that much (at least mine aren't). Maybe yours are because you're having sex with Alexandra Daddario or Eric Bana, but for most of us, we're lucky to snag a six or a seven. If you can snag a nine or a ten, I would think this ranking goes up to third on this list, maybe second. But I ranked it fourth and if you don't agree with me, you can blow me (hopefully to the point of orgasming).

3) The best pee of your life.

Yes, we all pee all the time. But you can't tell me there are many things better than when you finally get off a six-hour flight from Newark to LA (which was delayed getting out of Newark because a cockroach was

204 | ERIC & ALEXANDRA RIGHT

blocking the runway and you were stuck in a window seat next to two large bodybuilders who were asleep the entire flight and there was no way you were waking them up) and you finally hit the restroom in the LA airport and spend the next ten minutes letting every last drop of urine out of your bladder. You thank the piss gods that your bladder was strong enough to hold it the entire flight without pissing your pants, and you curse your stupidity for not booking an aisle seat. The only reason this is not ranked first or second for me is because if you absolutely had to, you could generally find somewhere to piss so that it doesn't build up to the point that you piss your pants.

I've certainly let myself pee into enough water bottles while sitting in the Lincoln Tunnel at 1:00 a.m. wondering where everyone is going. The only problem with that is hoping you have another water bottle in case you spill over. If worse comes to absolute worst, you could probably just go in your pants and hope that no one notices or that you have a towel nearby to try to dry it off before interacting with humans who can see your crotch. This entire scenario is obviously different for women, who may have to get a little more creative.

2) The best meal of your life.

The best meal of my life was in Ravello, Italy on a nice, warm, summer evening. Alexandra and I were on vacation in Italy, traveling through Venice, Florence, Tuscany, Rome, and the Amalfi Coast. I had some good pizzas in the other cities, and they were all delicious and so different from most pizzas in the United States. Fresh, simple, sweet, chewy, and otherwise wonderful. But this pizza in Ravello blew them all away. And it was so simple—ricotta-stuffed crust with tomato sauce, basil, and mozzarella in the middle. So simple, but it was like nothing I had ever tasted before. I told Alexandra that if I died right after that meal, I was good and content with dying at that point. Now, for others, it may be caviar, seafood, steak, pasta, fruit, or even the perfect glass of wine. But just think of that time you had the best food of your life and how you felt in that moment. Maybe this doesn't cause any relief, but the amount of pleasure involved in the best meal of your life catapults this up to second for me.

1) The best poop of your life.

Pound for shitty pound, nothing makes me appreciate more where I am in life than a fantastic poop. At some point in the future, I'll be doing this into a bucket, or have a tube hooked up to my insides while some hot nurse scrubs my crotch with a loofah, so I have to enjoy each poop while I can still take them by myself. The reason this is ranked first is due to the awesome combination of relief and pleasure that comes with this type of poop.

Think about the time you had some bad shrimp scampi, raw seafood, or something else that disagreed with you, and how the gurgling in your stomach started almost right away. It could also come from being poisoned or drugged, which just means there's something awesome going on in your life that someone would do this to you (*Wedding Crashers* and *Dumb and Dumber* come to mind). The only thing on your mind from the moment your tummy starts gurgling is finding a toilet and getting every last drop of evil out through your bottom.

Unlike peeing or blowing your nose, this type of bodily fluid can generally only be relieved in a toilet with enough toilet paper to supply a household of five for a week (and triple-ply is always a nice touch). You can never, *ever* go in your pants. You also cannot go outside, as you're generally left with nothing to wipe the remnants away. So, the only option is to find a toilet as soon as possible, and nothing else matters—not your significant other, not your kids, not your boss, not work, not your dignity. You will make up an excuse about your kid hitting his head on a table in order to jump off a Zoom meeting for fifteen minutes in order to deal with the aliens inside your bowels. You may risk a firing from a boss who is expecting you to join a call, and you have no way of notifying him you'll be late because you couldn't finish typing the email to tell him you'll be late before you had to run to the toilet.

If you're fortunate enough to find a nice, warm toilet with an ample amount of toilet paper, and you've done your "duty," you can't tell me you don't see doves flying in the air and the sun shining through the bathroom walls. The world is right again.

Thus, the best shit of your life is firmly in place as my first choice, and I dare you to tell me I'm wrong.

THE STORY OF ANDY, HOW AND WHO

[Andy walks up to How]

Andy: Hey.. nice to meet you. How are you?

How: Am I what?

Andy: What? How are you today?

How: That's the worst English I've ever heard in my life. Am I to-day? What the fuck are you saying?

Andy: Are you thick?

How: Are you fucking serious? If you are insinuating that I am attracted to you in any way shape or form, and because of that insane attraction, my penis is now thick, you're just crazy...Are you hitting on me?

Andy: Um ok...I don't know what that means since I just met you but how can I not show you I'm not attracted to you?

How: Wait, is that a double negative?

Andy: Good question; I know who would know that answer.

How: Maybe – let's go ask him, he's right across the street.

Andy: Who? I meant my old high school English teacher who is now my drug dealer and I was about to call him for a resupply. Where are you taking me?

How: Just follow me

[Andy and How Walk to Who's House]

How: Hey

Who: Hey..whos' your friend?

How: I mean I guess I would consider you a friend

Andy: I think he was talking about me?

How: Who?

Andy: Um yeah….that guy (Andy points to Who).

Who: Are you talking to me? You call me "that guy"? How dare you..….

How: Dare I what?

Andy: How dare me? How dare you!

Who: How dares everyone, that's what he fucking does.

How: I admit I had a gambling problem but that stopped years ago. Anyways, this guy had a question for you about double negatives.

Andy: I don't even remember what we were talking about. I think you were insinuating something about how you thought I was attracted to you.

How: I know – you asked if I was getting thick around you.

Who: You were thick around him?

Andy: Who?

Who: What? Don't rope me into your little love dispute.

Andy: Roping who into what?

Who: Dude – seriously – what the fuck is your problem? I haven't been into what since college – and that was one drunken night and it was a mistake.

Andy: Am I tripping? What the fuck is happening?

Who: "What the fuck" – ha – yeah, that was his nickname for a while. I've been suppressing those memories for a while, but it was a fun night.

How: Dude – I had no idea. I met what a few years ago and one thing led to another and we ended up dating for a few years.

Andy: You met what?

How: Yeah – we met and hit it off instantly – I miss him, but it wasn't meant to be.

Andy: Ok – I need to get out of here – how I have dealt with you two this long is beyond me.

How: Well don't blame me man – you came up to me and introduced yourself to me.

Andy: Sorry dude, I thought you were nice and attractive.

How: Well – thanks man – you too.

Andy: How did you pronounce your name?

How: How

Andy: Yes – that's what I'm asking.

How: Yes – how

Andy (looking at who) – Who does this guy think he is?

Who: Think he is what?

How: Stop talking about what already!

Who: Sorry man – I can't help it – he was hot.

Andy: Alright – I'm done – I'm going inside and taking my clothes off - who wants to join me?

Who: Don't presume I want to join you.

Andy: How would I know if you didn't?

How: Um what? I'm going inside if who doesn't want to.

Who: Fine – I got nothing else going on today.

Andy: I need to lay off the edibles

As Andy goes inside, How and Who look at each other, give each other a high five and proceed to head inside for what turns out to be the greatest night of their lives.

THE ENVIRONMENT

I care about the environment – there I said it. I'm a tree-hugging Libtard and am not afraid to admit that I care about maintaining and protecting the (literally) one and only planet we all inhabit. However, I am not happy to point out the fact that the human race has completely and utterly demolished, destroyed, deforested, de-ozoned, over-plasticked and changed the planet over the past 200 years to the point where there are serious consequences for most of the people living here.

Most people assume you have to either be for the environment or for economic growth but that couldn't be farther from the truth. I am all for economic investments in things that are good for the planet (or at least less bad): renewable energy, electric cars, eco-tourism and the like.

Some of the people I have met that seem to care more for the economy than protecting the environment claim to be religious. To those of you that believe in a God, let me ask you a simple question – this God of yours – did he/she/it create this planet *purely* to have the human race go ahead and destroy it?

Did God just say – "here's a toy called Earth, please go ahead and destroy every aspect of the beauty and wonder that I put here for your own narcissism and economic benefit"? God theoretically created humanity in a beautiful garden called Eden that many of us would now consider "*paradise*".

Would anyone reading this really consider the Earth paradise right now? Yes, there are certain parts of the planet that would be considered "paradise", mostly because they have been protected so that humans couldn't destroy absolutely everything in order to build the next trampoline park or strip mall. However, even under some of those places we consider paradise, there are stories of overfishing, over-pollution, damaged coral reefs and plastic waste all over the oceans.

Now with ice melting, the poles will likely be the next destination for humans to make their mark to extract natural resources and destroy most of the natural beauty that will show itself once the poles are ice-free.

We are all facing a world that is more polluted, hotter, less diverse and beautiful with more and more chemicals being put into our bodies from pretty much everything we consume. At this rate, I'm shocked half of us don't have some form of cancer from the variety of products we have consumed throughout our lives.

If caring about the environment, climate change, pollution and plastic waste makes me a Tree Hugger than find me some trees to fuck. I drive a solar car, have solar panels on my house, recycle everything I can (including plastic bags), donate to environmental organizations and keep my house at a balmy 65 in the winter and summer. I am trying to do my part. Is it enough to offset what is happening in India, China and other third-world countries? Absolutely not.

Yet, the reality is we cannot even agree on the basics like whether temperatures are actually increasing or not and whether human activities are having *any* influence on the climate. There are bloggers and news personalities that jump up and down calling climate change a "hoax" and say that either:

1. Temperature stations are rigged,
2. The Earth has always warmed and cooled,
3. Scientists gathering the data are funded by left-leaning organizations
4. The sun is in a solar maximum,
5. Scientists have been saying the same thing since the 1970's and nothing has changed
6. Al Gore takes private planes everywhere

While some of these points may be somewhat valid (Al Gore probably does take private planes), it doesn't change the *facts* that are available, either from satellite observations or ice core data that shows definitive proof of how the climate is changing at an unprecedented rate right now. [112]

If you don't believe the data or think everything is a hoax, then just do me a favor – without anyone around - close your eyes, turn off the TV, forget whether you are a conservative or liberal (I know this may be impossible to do – just try) and answer this simple question:

> *Compared to when you were young, do you think it is hotter now than it was when you were growing up? Are you getting less snow in the winter? Do you still have leaves on the trees while Trick-or-Treating? Are flowers blooming earlier now than they did? Is fox mating season earlier than it used to be (if you've never heard a fox during mating season, it's a real interesting sound that makes you wonder whether you should call the guys from Ghost Adventures)*

Without the pressure of revealing your answer, I can guarantee a majority of you reading this would say it is more likely than not that it is hotter in general now than it was when you grew up.

If there is one thing we *should* all be able to agree on, it is something that we can use our senses available to us in order to understand, appreciate and respect. We can see, touch, feel, smell and hear nature every day. Do we really want the beauty that remains on this planet to disappear forever – because it is happening and there is a window to protect what remains for future generations. Our five basic senses do not lie to us:

1. **Seeing** – we can all watch the news about wildfires, floods, hurricanes, and extreme temperatures around the world. We can all walk outside our doors or turn on the television and see the pollution of our skies, the dead fish from oil spills or the statistics that document the impacts we are having on temperature, CO2 emissions and diversity. There should not be any disagreement about the one thing each of us should be able to do: see. We can (and should) also all go to a national park and see the absolutely beauty of the trees, mountains, rivers and wildlife that exist on our planet. We can all marvel at the beauty of leaves blooming, flowers blossoming and wildlife mating. People hunt, fish and hike for a reason – it's visually beautiful to do so – whether you are a Republican, Democrat, Catholic, Buddhist or agnostic. We can *all* appreciate the visual beauty of nature.

2. **Hearing** – going outside in the morning or at night and listening to the crickets chirping, the birds singing, the trees blowing and the sound of *absolutely nothing else* is one of the most peaceful, calming and best experiences you can have as a human.

3. **Smelling** – whether it is the smells of fresh wood burning at a campfire in the forest, the smell of a field of flowers after a spring shower, or the smell of fresh bear shit, there is nothing that sticks in your mind quite like the smells of nature. If you have never been camping in the woods or taken a hike in a national park, you must do so. There are very few things as cleansing and rewarding like being outside in nature, closing your eyes and just inhaling the beauty of the world. Unless

you're with someone that hasn't showered in a few days – then, you may want to go alone.

4. **Touching** – whether it is gripping the trigger of a shotgun on a hunting trip, feeling a cold beer can next to a campfire, gripping your paddle tight on a whitewater trip down a river, or grabbing your fishing pole on the way to your fly fishing trip, the beauty of nature is also expressed through the things we bring with us into nature.

5. **Tasting** – whether it is baked beans on a camping excursion, fresh salmon at a five-star restaurant or a brisket sandwich at the local pub, everything we taste on this planet comes from something grown, raised, picked or caught in the wild or raised within nature. If this planet is not treated well, everything from our food supply to our own health is going to be negatively impacted by the continued degradation of the planet. I don't know you, but I LOVE to eat and want to continue eating as much and as frequently as I can for the rest of my life. But I won't do that at the expense of the overall health of the planet, so if it means paying a little bit more for healthier and more sustainable products, then so be it. Consider it my down payment to future generations.

Libtards and Repugnicans should be able to read #1 - #5 above and be able to say that at the very least, we can all agree we want a healthy, beautiful and functional planet for our kids and grandkids to enjoy as much as our generation and past generations. If we can't even say that, then what are we doing here?

We shouldn't be afraid to say we care about this planet and for those of you that do enjoy making fun of those that care – ask yourself why you do this? What does this say about yourself? Do you really want another strip mall being put up versus an area where people can enjoy nature? Will that really make your neighborhood a better place?

We also shouldn't be afraid to elect people that *will* put the environment in the same view as economic growth. We all want to do well economically but I hope it is not at the cost of the overall health of the planet going forward.

If we all do our part to actually work to remove the labels about who should care about this planet, I am hoping we can all find a way to agree on what is happening and work to find cost-effective and long lasting solutions to mitigate the problem rather than continue to use typical catchphrases and jargon used to support both sides.

I apologize if this came off as a rant, but it is an important subject for me and one I try to weave into my daily life, sober or high.

16

If There is a Hell, Here's a Preview of What Sends Me There

THE BELOW ARE SOME MORE HUMOROUS OBSERVATIONS I'VE HAD while high. Some are observations about being high, while others are random questions and thoughts I have had while high. Some are pretty gross, and I apologize in advance for this—but, as I have learned from a very young age, everybody poops, everybody pees, and everybody has sex (hopefully).

These observations were funny in my head when I wrote them down and that's all that matters. I am sure that some of these are probably the stupidest things you will ever read. Either way, I hope you enjoy the below, and again, I apologize in advance for what you are about to read. They are in no particular order because I was too lazy to go back and reorganize them.

- Being high is the only time when your biggest problems in life are how long it takes to wipe your ass and how much of a pain in the ass it's going to be to get out of bed and go downstairs to get more water.

- Being high is the only time when *Jurassic World: Fallen Kingdom* is the greatest movie in the world and Chris Pratt is the greatest actor in the world.

- Being high is the only time when you can watch *The NeverEnding Story* and realize that the large, alien dog is the creepiest thing you've ever seen.

- Being high is the only time when you can watch *Jeopardy!* and think that you're the smartest person in the world because the question is "This is the Mouse whose name begins with the Letter M and currently owns multiple homes in Orlando, Florida, California, Tokyo, China, and Paris," and your answer is "Mighty!"

- The theme song for *The Walking Dead* is honestly the coolest thing to listen to while you're high—you can't keep your eyes off the screen!

- The best song to listen to while high is Hoobastank's "Running Away"—the words blow your mind.

- Being high is the only time when you try to calculate the ratio of funny lines to serious lines on *Diners, Drive-Ins and Dives*. For the record, I calculated a ratio of roughly three funny lines for every one serious line.

- Being high is the only time when you catch awful edits, horrible cuts, and terrible inconsistencies in movies and get mad at yourself for not spotting them the hundreds of times you watched the movie before (*Swingers* is a big culprit here). It's truly amazing how many movies have awful consistency in them. I guess when you're high, this type of stuff really bothers you.

- Being high is the only time when you realize that if your dog could spend its life chasing rabbits, humping your leg, and literally smelling, licking, and eating anything it possibly can (including dog shit, human shit, human urine, human vomit, dog vomit, dog urine, deer urine, deer shit, and frogs), it would be the happiest thing on the planet.

- When I was younger and watched *Forest Gump* for the first time and saw how long he lasted with Jenny in bed, I was like, "Really!? That's how long you have to have sex for? Damn—I better practice." And practice I did.

- My mom really is the best texter I know. She's always first to respond—morning, noon, or night—and always has something smart to say, even if she uses the word "enuf" far too often. Half of my friends I won't hear back from for a week, and the other half have me blocked. I should text them my mom's number to show them how a true friend should respond.

- Do me a favor—find two people having a conversation in sign language on YouTube, put it on mute, and try to figure out what the hell they're saying. I guarantee that you will have one of the best laughs you've had in a while. I am not trying to offend anyone that is deaf, but it is still pretty funny. You can also find "Sign Language Interpreter WAP" on YouTube; it's pretty funny as well.

- If you live in a city and live in a high-rise, do you ever watch people across the street from you and wonder what they're talking about? I'm sure people think their conversation is pretty mundane, like, "What's on Netflix right now?" or "Guess who I ran into at the supermarket!" when what's really being discussed is more like, "Do you want the dominatrix to come over at 9:30 or 9:45?" or "So, I decided to take the head out of the freezer today—I figured we could defrost it and serve it with some of the eel cum we have stored in the closet."

- Speaking of cities, there should be nothing that freaks people out more than the steam coming out of the streets of a major city. I'm sure there is a completely rational explanation for it—it's a vent for gas, it's the exhaust of the subway below, it's the devil taking a steam bath—but when I see steam, I think of fire, and when I think of fire, I think of explosions. Yet, people walk by these steam vents on a daily basis with nary a worry. Does this not bother anyone else?

- Speaking of being freaked out, there is nothing that freaks you out more while high than riding an elevator. Recently, I was high while staying in a hotel, and I kept pushing the button for my floor, but it wouldn't work. I spent ten minutes pushing the button before I realized that I was forgetting to swipe my key card against the stupid black thing on the elevator. Once I got it started, I became convinced I was either falling up or falling down to my death. The elevator was shaking, I was on the floor crying, and I'm pretty sure I shit my pants. Then, finally, the ding of the elevator rang, the doors opened to my floor, and I rolled onto the fourth floor.

- Being high is a *great* time to have a conversation with a three-year-old, because they truly are one of the most fascinating things ever. I was having a conversation with my three-year-old, sitting outside one night while on vacation, and we started talking about space and the stars. I was hearing all sorts of things come out of her mouth: "It's your eye, right there." "The babyship is going home." "I want to go on the babyship to go fly in the black sky." "The big spaceship went to the supermarket." At one point, she started saying, "The babyships are coming," and I got so freaked out that I called Neil deGrasse Tyson and the Space Force to warn them of an incoming invasion.

- I was high when I learned what a "Rick Roll" was, and it blew my mind. I was watching TV with my eleven-year-old, and this is how it went down:

  Son: Do you know the song, "Never Gonna Give You Up"?
  Me: Nope. Never heard of it.

Son: Okay, well here's a good joke: knock-knock.

Me: Who's there?

Son: Never.

Me: Never who?

Son: *Never gonna give you up, never gonna let you down, never gonna run around and desert you. Never gonna make you cry, never gonna say goodbye, never gonna tell a lie and hurt you.*

Me: That was amazing. Where did you learn that?

Son: I saw it on the Internet. It's called a Rick Roll.

Yep. That's apparently a thing now, and I couldn't be prouder of my son for knowing it.

- Being high is the only time when you can sit there and laugh hysterically about the walk you and your dog had this morning in a wooded park, with no one around, in which the following happened: 1) she smelled, ate, and eventually got the liquidy shit of some animal all over her legs; 2) she proceeded to run around me in circles, brushing up on my legs to try to get the liquidy shit off of her; 3) after concluding her runs around me, she proceeded to vomit the liquidy animal shit all over my socks and shoes; 4) after seeing the liquidy animal shit eaten by my dog and now all over my legs, along with the vomit on my socks and shoes, I proceeded to dry heave and eventually vomit on my dog's back and the ground; 5) as I vomited pretty loudly, it ended up scaring a local flock of birds in the nearby bushes; 6) seeing the flock of birds, my dog decided to chase after them while I am bent over from getting the last bits of nastiness out of my body; 7) as she starts to chase them, she knocks me right over into the mix of liquidy animal shit, dog vomit, and now human vomit. Luckily, I landed on my side, but unfortunately, some of it got into my pockets—which contained my car key, cell phone, and Chapstick; and 8) finally, I am able to chase down my precious pet in a few minutes, grab the leash, and get her back to my car, where I open all windows, start the car, and hightail it home to take the longest shower of my life. As I get home, Alexandra looks at me and asks, "What the hell happened to you, and what is that god awful smell?" to which I still have the wit to respond, "You should see the other guy." (For the record, seven of the eight things above actually happened to me; I'll let you decide which one didn't.)

- Being high is the only time you can accidentally cut yourself on your finger, go to get some antibiotic ointment and a Band-Aid, put the ointment and the Band-Aid on your finger, and forty-five minutes later, realize that you put it on the wrong finger and have been bleeding all over your couch.

- Speaking of my dog, here are the top reasons I believe she follows me everywhere I go, day or night:

  o She wants to play.
  o She wants to pee or poop outside.
  o She wants me to go outside to pee while I'm high so she can lick my pee, get high, eat Cheetos, and talk with me about third eyes and souls.
  o She wants to go for a long walk to eat liquid animal shit.
  o She is sexually attracted to me and wants to have my half-stud/half-dog babies (this is definitely happening when she is in heat).
  o She wants me to give her another tater tot from Sonic, even though the last time I gave her one was six months ago.

  As much as I want to believe my dog just wants to play, I truly believe that dogs are simple-minded beings with only one thing on their minds—Sonic. (Those tater tots *are* delicious!)

- You can't tell me that doing subtitles for live TV isn't the hardest job you could have. Imagine the pressure on these folks during a presidential press conference, when the president is at a cement factory in Ohio talking to the owner about the cement truck he just emptied into their warehouse lot to demonstrate new, US-built technology. He says, "Today, I shot a load of cement into this lad's backyard," and you, as a professional subtitle writer, accidentally type, "Today, I shot a load of semen into this lad's backside." Pay these subtitle writers properly!

- Speaking of the opposite of the hardest job in the world, you can't tell me that news anchors aren't the greatest people in the world. No other breed of human would be able to report on a story about an eighteen-month-old girl in critical condition at a local hospital after her father committed a murder-suicide against her mother, followed by her grandmother breaking her hip while trying to call 911 and then dying twelve hours later, and then, three seconds after that harrowing story, have the ability to turn to the camera with a big, white, perfect news-anchor smile and say, "Thanks for the report, Stacy. Coming up, Mike is here with a look at this weekend's weather, and I hear that we finally have a beautiful stretch of weather coming up! We should all take our kids out to the beach on Mother's Day and have a great day with Mom and Grandma." The news then cuts to Mike, who's standing on the beach somewhere while Hurricane "Oldest White Name On Record" lashes him with 150 mph winds, a sixteen-foot storm surge, and sideways rain (yes there are hurricanes in May). Mike then proceeds to say, "I'm not sure what to say, Meghan. Not sure why people can't simply download an app to look up what the fucking weather is going to be like this Mother's Day . . . I'm out of here."

- Is there anything worse than when your favorite mixed drink is done slightly wrong? Maybe just one ingredient is missing, or there's a disproportionate amount of one juice compared to the other. Then you debate whether you should say something to the bartender. In the end, you end up drinking it—even though it costs you $15—because you're worried the bartender is going to spit in the next one they make you. Then you're pissed and switch to a crappy light beer to save your money. Before you know it, it's 3:00 a.m. and you've had sixteen light beers. The moral of the story is: send the drink back, risk the spit (especially if it's a hot bartender, because isn't your ultimate goal to swap spit with a hot girl that looks like a bartender anyways?), enjoy a proper tasting drink, and avoid the sixteen light beers.

- Speaking of beer, being high is when I discovered Madison Beer. For those of you who don't know Madison Beer, look her up. For those of you who may be seeing Madison Beer in the future, Google "Madison Beer August 2021" (hopefully pictures of the University of Wisconsin bars don't pop up from August 2021—if they do, you still may get some very good pictures but not any as good as the real Madison Beer). I dare you to yell at me for spending twelve hours researching her and finding out how to get backstage to meet her at her next concert. I'm still working on that (just kidding any police authorities reading this).

- I enjoy taking dumps at night, letting the dog into the bathroom, and then shutting the door so she can relish in all my glory. I wait to see how long it takes her to start clawing on the door to be let out. Depending on what I've eaten, it can take between six and nine seconds for her to reach this limit. I am honored to have that effect on her.

- What two words in any language have more of an impact than "I'm pregnant"? They bring out pretty much every emotion you can think of: surprise, happiness, sadness, anger, doubt, envy, horror. There's the additional emotion of rage that can also be triggered by the phrase "But it's not yours—I had a threesome with your brother and your best friend, so I still need to figure out whose it is."

- Cuddling with your kids is one of the greatest things in life. I don't care if you're the most macho dude on the planet with no ability to generate emotions of any kind other than the occasional grunt. If these guys cuddled with their young kids, they would think the same thing. The reason is simple: It's fleeting—you know there's a limit to how long your kids are going to choose to cuddle with you. If it were up to most parents, I'm sure they would cuddle or hug their kids as long as they lived, and I imagine that if it were normal or accepted, most kids would never stop cuddling with their parents. Maybe it's why a lot of people cuddle up with their parents when their parents are close to death. It's a great, warm, peaceful feeling when you cuddle with your kids; it helps each party feel more connected to each other. However, for whatever reason, society doesn't allow for adult cuddling to be seen as normal, so we forgave that a long time ago. It's likely seen as weak for children to admit they're so attached or dependent on their parents. However, Japan has cuddling cafes, Canada has cuddling rooms and there are apps that purely exist to find platonic cuddlers. Maybe we all just need to cuddle to solve the world's problems.

- Want to see one of the creepiest TV characters that I assume has never been talked about? Watch Everybody Loves Raymond—Season 2, Episode 23, "The Garage Sale." Around the sixteen-minute mark, when Deborah and Raymond are talking about having another kid, look at the guy in the background who is eavesdropping on the conversation. Tell me he's not one of the creepiest TV characters you've ever seen. First, there's the way he looks at them and stares at them after saying, "Oh, I wasn't listening." Then, there's his height (he's shorter than Deborah by at least three inches), and the way he's got his shirt tucked in and his pants pulled up to his belly button. Not to mention that he's skinny as all hell and is fiddling with a long wire connected to some old TV or something. Maybe it's just because I was high, but I watched that scene and got freaked the hell out.

- I've realized there is nothing I hate more in this life than crushed ice. Not traffic, not constipation, not avocados, not flan, and not monkfish (look those creepy motherfuckers up and tell me they're not the ugliest thing you've ever seen on this planet). Crushed ice could be the worst invention ever. Who thought up this horrible idea? There had to be someone in the history of ice-making who was thumbing themselves in the ass one night and said, "I got it! I have the idea that is going to make this company thousands. We're going to give people options with their ice—cubed or crushed! People love options! Brilliant!" The only potential time someone should ever get crushed ice is when they're sipping on a straight-up glass of Everclear 190 and need to water down the drink over the course of ten minutes. If not, what is the point of it? You can't have it in your drink because you half choke every time you take a sip. You're not going to use it to cool down your wife's nether regions. You're not going to use it to fill up a cooler for the big tailgate. The only thing I've ever seen people get crushed ice for is to eat it. For all of you people who eat crushed ice, I just have one question: WHY ARE YOU EATING CRUSHED ICE? It just turns into water two seconds after you put it into your mouth. If you're looking for water, just drink water. No one likes the sound of it—CRUNCH, CRUNCH, CRUNCH, CRUNCH, CRUNCH—and the noise is constant, because every chip of ice is like a single atom of water. So, to get your body properly hydrated, you need to chew on 6,000 chips over the course of ninety minutes. If you want to crunch something, go put a few paint chips in your mouth and do it until you pass out from lead poisoning (not to the point of death, but to the point where you lose feeling in your penis for the rest of your life). Whew. I feel better. Now I gotta go switch the ice cube option on my refrigerator from cubed to crushed so I can enjoy a nice drink tonight.

- Don't ever deal with cockroaches, whitefishes, or water bugs when high. I'm not going to get into why, because there's just too much. But if there is even the slightest possibility you will be seeing a cockroach in the next sixty minutes (if smoking) or eight hours (if doing an edible), put the bong or gummy bag away and order a glass of wine. You and your future nightmares will be glad you did.

- When you're high, do not try to learn a dual washer/dryer for the first time. I made that mistake, and I'm pretty sure I ended up putting the detergent in the lint trap and the fabric softener in the bleach hole (great porn name, by the way). And don't even get me started with how to start the damn thing.

- One time I was high, I saw an email come in and out of my inbox (grow up). I thought I was seeing things because I was high, but the next day, the email came through as quarantined. I have to say, seeing an email come into your box and then disappear is one of the most confusing things I have ever seen. However, I have to think that if I'd been sober, it would have been equally as confusing.

- <u>Have you ever tried to write something in Word in a font that is underlined? Try it and tell me it's not the most uncomfortably awkward and annoying thing EVER</u> .

- As a father, there is no prouder moment than when your three-year-old girl looks at you with a loving smile (one that could light up even the heart of a narcissistic, diabolical, evil, crotchety old man), holds that smile for ten seconds and then, she lets out the loudest, most magnificent, most perfectly timed fart. It makes you realize that love is truly thicker than flatulence.

- But seriously, my proudest moment as a man (which also happened to be while I was high) was when I was peeing in my bathroom and my three-year-old daughter, runs in from the other side of the house, points to my penis, and says, "Ew, Daddy, your pee-pee is so big." Naturally, I said, "Yes, honey, it is. Thank you for pointing that out. Can you go tell that to Mommy?"

- I'm not saying the movies *Vacation* and *Pitch Perfect* are going to go down in history as the best comedies of all time, but there are some seriously funny moments in both of those movies. I dare you to watch these movies without laughing out loud (even if you only are laughing out loud on the inside). Plus, if Alexandra Daddario and I don't work out, Anna Kendrick is my backup person to leave my Alexandra for.

- I was thinking of moving to Mississippi, but then I watched the movie *A Time to Kill* and I realized that apparently no one in the entire state has air conditioning. Seriously, watch that movie and focus on how sweaty these people are in most of the scenes. I get that it's humid in the south, but you would think that at least some of these buildings would have air conditioning.

- Speaking of sweating, I have been high while sitting at hotel swimming pools and I realized that few things make me laugh more than when I see people sitting in a pool up to their waist (with or without a drink in their hands) that get pissed when kids or other people swim by them or jump into the water near them and get them wet. What exactly are you pissed off about? You're in a fucking pool—expect to get wet and stop getting angry when someone (especially a five- or six-year-old kid) has the gall to splash water on you while literally half your body is wet.

- Watching my dog say hello to dogs she's meeting for the first time is hilarious to me. As any dog owner knows, it generally consists of: 1) sniffing noses for five to ten seconds (anything longer is generally taken as a declaration of war); 2) each dog backing away for a period of another five to ten seconds to reset their emotions; and 3) if one dog is interested in furthering the conversation, another ten- to fifteen-second ass-sniffing process begins, until one of the owners pulls their dog away, ruining its hopes and dreams for another day. Imagine if humans did this? Picture yourself walking down the street and then seeing some attractive individual of the opposite sex. You work up the courage to say hi, they say hi back, and then you both get down on all fours to start sniffing each other's ass while asking where you're from and what do you for a living. That would be just great on a nice, hot, humid day in New York City, when both people have just gotten off the non-air-conditioned subway after not showering for forty-eight hours. Yum.

- I love baseball. What other sport still needs coaches to send signals to players using 400 different combinations of pointing, patting, tapping, clapping, and crotch grabbing? You would think that if the NFL can transmit plays to quarterbacks, baseball coaches could just say "steal" into an earpiece in the baserunner's ear. I guess this is just a way to keep the third-base coach employed, because really, what exactly would you say they do here? (Office Space, anyone?)

- Speaking of 400 different combinations, do you ever watch professional athletes celebrate an amazing play with combinations of high-fives, low-fives, pats, claps, pounds, and hip bumps while jumping in the air? Do you ever wonder when they get the time to practice these and how they practice them? Do they just spend time looking in the mirror at their houses, practicing their moves? They're always perfectly synchronized, and they never mess up!

- Why do sports players need so much practice? That's literally like saying an accountant needs to practice on his calculator before doing a tax return or a porn star needs to masturbate six times a day in order to get ready for the big porn shoot. What are these players doing? You've literally been doing this sport for 75 percent of your life, shouldn't you know how to shoot a basket, score a goal, or hit a ball? I get that practice makes perfect, but come on! You should know your craft at this point.

- There is nothing funnier to me than hearing an announcer on TV summarize what two NFL dudes are talking about in a heated conversation on the sideline. I heard one guy say, after a blown coverage led to a touchdown by the other team, "These guys are over there talking about what went wrong, and they're saying, 'Player X, you got to get deep and have vision.'" I'm like, that is definitely not what they are saying on the sideline. I would write what I think they were actually saying, but I don't want to get in trouble with the "PC Police."

- Speaking of sports, I have an idea for how to better the overall sports experience in this country. I am sick of watching the most physically gifted athletes play sports. These athletes make millions playing a game, mostly because they were born with the physical gifts necessary to succeed. I propose reversing that trend through the creation of sports leagues involving the average American. I'll call it the AASL ("S" is for your favorite sport). This would involve average guys (and gals) in their twenties, thirties, and forties playing the sport they love, having it televised, and having fantasy leagues to support the league. Who wouldn't want to watch thirty-five-year-old dads playing football? Imagine a guy trying to run fifty yards and being too winded to get to the endzone. There would be some great prop bets: How many heart attacks will this game feature? How many people will throw up on a teammate? Will anyone's belly completely fall out of their uniform? And the best part about these leagues? No practicing. Let the players figure it out in real time. The reality is that if you involve fantasy and gambling, the AASL is bound to succeed.

- One time—while I was high, of course—my three-year-old daughter and I were pretend fighting (don't judge me, she calls it "fighting hands") in bed. While we were doing that, my dog got up on the bench in front of our bed and looked at us like "What are you doing, and can I join?" At one point, I flipped my daughter over on her stomach and, as she got up on all fours in front of me with her butt in the air, she said, "Daddy, I want to do doggie." I probably laughed for ten minutes after that and then realized I'm going to need therapy for the next fifteen years to get that statement out of my head. No boyfriends until she's in a nursing home.

- Only when I am high would the answer to the following question be: "Titanic":

    "Hey Dad, should we watch the movie "*Titanic*" or something called "The Boobytrap on the Campus of Munch my Hole University"?

- Only when I am high would I be happy to explain to my 12 year old what the term "munch" means.

- Maybe this is because I'm high, but go watch the Alice in Chains *MTV Unplugged* videos online and tell me that the two singers don't have one of the best harmonies of any band in history. I have to imagine that if Layne Staley hadn't spiraled into drugs and his eventual suicide, Alice in Chains could have been one of the biggest bands of all time.

- If you haven't watched the video of Danny Carey (of the band Tool) playing the drums to "Pneuma" live, then you haven't lived. Please look up that video and tell me he's not the best drummer of all time. If you can think of a better drummer, please send me his name (excluding Mike Portnoy and the guy from the movie *Whiplash*—assuming the last scene actually happened the way the movie portrayed it).

- If I was the toothpaste or mouthwash industries, I would be 150% behind legalizing cannabis. When I am high, I brush my teeth and do mouthwash after every single time I eat something. In a normal session, that can be anywhere between 5 and 122 times. I have gone through a half a tube of toothpaste in one night because I was eating something every thirteen minutes. And I am generally not consuming large quantities of food each time—I am more likely to eat a sprinkle off some ice cream than an entire ice cream cone. But even if I just eat a sprinkle, I am upstairs ten minutes later brushing my teeth like I just ate out some ninety-five-year-old great-grandmother. It doesn't matter—I have to get my teeth clean. Seriously, if anyone from those two industries is reading, I am totally open to a sponsorship opportunity. We'll call it the *"How to Get Your Teeth and Gums Highly Clean"* campaign and include tips on how often to brush and mouthwash per mg of edible consumed in order to maintain pristine mouth cleanliness while high. It's a slam dunk.

- What is your FOMORT? For those of you who don't know what FOMORT is, it stands for Fear of Missing Out Response Time. The easiest way to determine your FOMORT is to put your smartphone down and time how long it takes until you have the desire or need to pick it up again to check your messages or social media feeds or to see what has changed in the world since the last time you looked at your phone. I would venture to guess that most people's FOMORT is under sixty seconds—maybe even under thirty seconds. I have spent time watching people in airports, train stations, and just out and about, and most people seem to be able to be without their phones for between thirty to sixty seconds. I have seen people put their phone away only to take it out ten seconds later, use it for thirty seconds, put it away for ten seconds, and then repeat that pattern for a few minutes. It is fascinating to me. My FOMORT is around one to two minutes, but I have trained my brain to not worry about what news story, message, email, Tweet, or score alert I am missing out on. It is not easy, but I hope you can train yourself to increase your FOMORT and put the phone down for longer periods of time. I guarantee that you are not missing out on anything important—absolutely *nothing* important has changed in the world during the time your phone is in your pocket. Unless it's an update on the *Higher Connections* podcast.

- If you are a girl who wants to end a relationship with a guy but don't know how, I have the perfect solution for you. After taking a dump, forget to get that last wipe in that really cleans everything out of your butthole. Let that little bit of remaining goodness waft in your panties for a while and then proceed to have sex with your guy. Guaranteed, he will be out of your life in a matter of hours. Unless, of course, he is into that sort of thing—in which case, good luck to you.

- Have you ever thought about the fact that you are just a walking skeleton? Look at the picture below—that's you, that's me, that's everyone you knew, everyone you know, everyone you love or will ever love, everyone you hate or will ever hate, and everyone you have had sex with (yes, there's a category for skeleton porn, but it's not what you think—it's people having sex in a grave- yard). We are all going to turn into that when we die (unless you are cremated, of course).

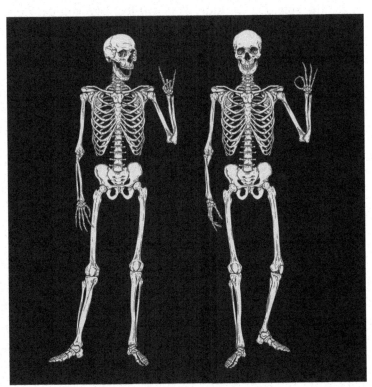

- Getting old is great. The best part of getting old is waking up in the morning and having your first thought of the day *not* be: 1) It's good to be alive; 2) I love my kids so much; or 3) I'm really not looking forward to my two-hour commute to work and the fifteen awful meetings I have. Nope. My first thought on most days is: Will I be able to poop today? Seriously, there are days when I'll exercise, get eight hours of sleep, eat nothing but pears, strawberries, avocados, apples, raspberries, bananas, carrots, beets, broccoli, artichokes, brussels sprouts, lentils, and kidney beans (those are all high in fiber), and still not be able to drop one. There are other days when I'll eat pasta, white bread, cereal, a stack of pancakes, four egg-and-cheese sandwiches, and two pounds of mashed potatoes, and I'm running for the toilet like Jeff Daniels in *Dumb and Dumber.* Luckily, these days I am like Jeff Daniels and am able to get one out each night. But you can't tell me that when you are constipated, there's a better feeling than getting something out, even if it's a nugget the size of a ladybug. You still feel like you gave birth to the biggest dump of all time.

- A few random thoughts about the gym:

  1. I have come to realize that there is no one I trust more in life than the people who wash towels at my gym. Every time I go to the gym—between working out, the sauna, and taking a shower—I am wrapping myself in about four towels. I see the types of people that go to the gym, and I see how disgusting they are, so I really hope these folks who do the laundry at the gym are using some sort of deep-cleaning detergent.
  2. I don't understand people who walk around the gym locker room without sandals. I see guys just walking in their bare feet, and it literally sends shivers up my spine. Look at the locker room floor of a gym next time you're in one—besides the huge number of pubes and other hairs on the floor, I can only imagine what bodily fluids

and body parts are scattered on the floor too. Yet guys will just walk around like it's no big thing. *Gross.*

3. I recently saw a story of a lady who got upset at a guy for staring at her at the gym. You can look up the story, but here's the basic fact pattern:

   a. She is apparently a personal trainer and a "TikTok personality"—whatever that is.
   b. She was herself doing exercises, presumably for social media purposes.
   c. She was wearing one of those tight outfits that a lot of women wear (you know the ones).
   d. While she was recording, she realized some guy was "checking her out."
   e. She proceeded to call the guy out for checking her out.
   f. Apparently, the guy didn't stop staring at her, even after her husband came over to lift weights with her.[112]

You can form your own thoughts on this story, but I think it says a lot about where we are with society today. Can you imagine this happening twenty years ago, ten years ago, or even five years ago? An attractive woman who wears skimpy outfits to the gym is appalled that a guy is staring at her while she is recording herself to get attention and likes on TikTok?

I get that there are some creeps out there, but when you break this down, this lady was upset because some guy was doing *exactly* what she was trying to get millions of other people to do—stare at her while she works out. In the meantime, she has now embarrassed this guy, causing unknown consequences for him.

A lot of people praised her for "standing up to the man." You want to stand up to someone, how about you stand up for yourself and don't give in to the need to constantly post on social media about how awesome you are for being able to get to the gym eighteen times a week? I get it, you're in great physical shape—congratulations. How about you work on your mental fitness and don't get upset when people look at you at the gym? If you want to get TikTok views, do the workouts in your own home where no one can stare at you. And don't tell me you're upset about the attention this drew—it likely got you a million followers on social media, which is *exactly* what you were looking for.

There are millions of people who go to the gym just to stare at themselves in the mirror. I go to the gym to relieve stress, not to compare the size of my biceps to the guy next to me. It goes back to the point that we are so consumed with staring outwards that no one looks inward anymore at who they are as a person. That's why I think we are generally lost as a society.

CONCLUSION

SO, FOR THE ONE PERSON LEFT STICKING WITH ME THROUGH MY RAMbling thoughts on marijuana, my experiences, the benefits, and all of my observations while high, all I can say is: Thank you! Thank you for reading about my journey, which has been very rewarding and freeing for me. I never thought I would have the guts to write down some of my thoughts on these subjects, but it has been fun.

Everyone knows that marijuana and other drugs are psychoactive (mind-altering), but I'm not sure many people have really stopped to think about what that means and whether we can expand our knowledge by having our minds altered, even if temporarily. When high, are we really able to see things happening in this universe that we can't when sober? Are we able to connect to each other in a profound way? Are we able to have life-altering visions and experiences that can give us comfort about our life and what happens when our lives—as we know them—are finished? These are some of the biggest questions humankind has ever posed. What if we could find some of the answers simply by getting high?

I'm in my forties, so at this point, what am I scared of? I could find out I have cancer tomorrow and be told I have six years to live. I was just reading an article about someone who got ALS and was dead within a year, so I'm willing to take the risk. Am I condoning smoking seven days a week, starting when you're eighteen? Absolutely not. As with most things in life, marijuana needs to be consumed in moderation at an age where you can responsibly understand what you're putting into your body. However, I certainly think there are worse things in the world than getting high once in a while, especially in this day and age, with stress and anxiety levels at an all-time high.

I understand there were some thoughts and theories in this book that are definitely "out there." But remember that some of the theories we take for granted now were questioned and even ridiculed when they were first proposed:

1. Earth not being flat
2. The sun, not Earth, being the center of the galaxy
3. Darwinism/Evolution
4. Gravity
5. General relativity
6. Global warming caused by humans (yes, it's happening, and yes, it's caused by us—accept it and try to find solutions)

All of these theories were eventually proven to be true (or, in the case of #6, 95 percent proven as of the time of this writing).

I truly hope that you've found some benefits in what I have written, especially regarding trying to form deeper and more meaningful connections. The goal is to experience more profound connections than what you have been able to so far in your life. Remember, don't force them. If you train yourself to recognize these connections, they should start to come more naturally for you. If they do, please share these with others in your life (and me too!) and think about the benefits for you and the people you connect with.

Of course, everything I have written could turn out to be a whole, big "Nothing Burger" (damn it, I'm hungry again). I am okay with that—I'm a big boy who can handle the likelihood that my experiences were *my* experiences alone. I've accepted the possibility, but I would rather share my experiences and see if others can achieve the same results than be scared of what people will think. Maybe like people who are born with bigger noses, bigger muscles, and bigger (r)ears, I've been blessed with a bigger third eye that allows me to connect with those around me in an awesome way. However, if you keep an open mind and are open to the possibility of these connections, it can be a fun trip. I hope you enjoy the ride and make some deep and meaningful connections to those close to you in your life.

If you have enjoyed reading, please email me at higherconnec-tionsnow@gmail.com and check out our podcast, *Higher Connections*, where Alexandra and I will continue discussing the experiences we have while under the influence of marijuana. Hope to see you there and stay connected!

ACKNOWLEDGEMENTS

I WANTED TO TAKE SOME TIME TO THANK EVERYONE WHO HELPED shape this book into what it is. Being a first-time writer, I had no idea what went into a book, but it certainly took the effort of many—including my family and Alexandra's family, who helped ensure the messages were clear.

A special thank you to Alexandra's sister, my brothers, and Alexandra, of course, for taking the time to read and include their commentary and thoughts.

Another thank you to Alexandra for going through this journey with me. I don't know where we will be in twenty years, but this was a special journey to go through, and there is no one else that I would have chosen to go through it with.

ALEXANDRA'S NOTE:

Aw—love you!

NOTES

1   Brooke Bobb, "Bad Vibes, Be Gone: How to Energetically Clear Your Space with Sage," *Vogue*, August 22, 2016, https://www.vogue.com/article/sage-ho w-to-cleanse-energy-home-office-smudging.

2   Laura Smith, "How a Racist Hate-Monger Masterminded America's War on Drugs," *Timeline*, February 28, 2018, https://timeline.com/harry-anslinge r-racist-war-on-drugs-prison-industrial-complex-fb5cbc281189.

3   Amy Tikkanen, "Why Is Marijuana Illegal in the US?" *Encyclopedia Britannica*, accessed August 2021, https://www.britannica.com/story/why-i s-marijuana-illegal-in-the-us.

4   "The Truth about Marijuana – International Statistics" | Foundation for A Drug-Free World, accessed March 2022, https://www.drugfreeworld.org/ drugfacts/marijuana/international-statistics.html.

5   "Map of Marijuana Legality by State" | DISA Global Solutions, accessed March 2022, https://disa.com/map-of-marijuana-legality-by-state.

6   "Marijuana Arrests By The Numbers" | ACLU, accessed March 2022, https:// www.aclu.org/gallery/marijuana-arrests-numbers.

7   "Marijuana Arrests Fall Precipitously Nationwide in 2020" *Norml*, September 27, 2021, https://norml.org/blog/2021/09/27/marijuana-arrests-fall-precip- itously-nationwide-in-2020/.

8   "Mediterranean diet for heart health" | Mayo Clinic, July 23, 2021, https:// www.mayoclinic.org/healthy-lifestyle/nutrition-and-healthy-eating/ in-depth/mediterranean-diet/art-20047801.

9   Katherine Margengo, LDN, R.D. and Jamie Smith, "What to Know about Vegan Diets," *Medical News Today*, April 27, 2020, https://www.medicalnew- stoday.com/articles/149636.

10 John Bowden, "Americans Drink about 2.3 Gallons of Alcohol a Year: Study," *The Hill*, January 14, 2020, https://thehill.com/policy/healthcare/4782 35-americans-drink-about-23-gallons-of-alcohol-a-year-study.

11 "Alcohol Facts and Statistics | National Institute On Alcohol Abuse and Alcoholism (NIAAA)," *National Institute on Alcohol Abuse and Alcoholism,*

2021, https://www.niaaa.nih.gov/publications/brochures-and-fact-sheets/alcohol-facts-and-statistics.

[12] Andrei Ionescu, "Small Amounts of Alcohol Have Big Impacts on Brain Health," *Earth.Com,* November 27, 2021, https://www.earth.com/news/small-amounts-of-alcohol-have-big-impacts-on-brain-health/.

[13] "Diseases and Death," *Centers for Disease Control and Prevention,* accessed August 2021, https://www.cdc.gov/tobacco/data_statistics/fact_sheets/fast_facts.

[14] "Is Eating Too Much Red Meat Bad For You?" *Scripps Health*, 2020, https://www.scripps.org/news_items/4258-is-red-meat-bad-for-you.

[15] Stephanie Watson, "*How Bad For You Are Fried Foods?*" Nourish by WebMD, June 22, 2017, https://www.webmd.com/diet/news/20170622/how-bad-for-you-are-fried-foods#:~:text=Fried%20foods%20are%20high%20in,2%20diabetes%20and%20heart%20disease.

[16] Mary Jane Brown, PhD, "Should You Avoid Fish Because of Mercury?" *Healthline*, September 14, 2018, https://www.healthline.com/nutrition/mercury-content-of-fish.

[17] Neha Pathak, MD, "Air Pollution Kills as Many People as Cigarettes," *WebMD*, October 25, 2019, https://www.webmd.com/lung/news/20191008/air-pollution-kills-as-many-people-as-cigarettes.

[18] Juli Fraga, "How Living in a City Can Mess with Your Mental Health," *Healthline*, February 25, 2019, https://www.healthline.com/health/mental-health/living-in-a-city.

[19] Julia Jacobo, "Teens Spend More than 7 hours On Screens for Entertainment a Day: Report," *ABC News,* October 29, 2019, https://abcnews.go.com/US/teens-spend-hours-screens-entertainment-day-report/story?id=66607555.

[20] Isaac Stanley-Becker, "'Horns' Are Growing on Young People's Skulls. Phone Use is to Blame, Research Suggests," *Washington Post*, June 25, 2019, https://www.washingtonpost.com/nation/2019/06/20/horns-are-growing-young-peoples-skulls-phone-use-is-blame-research-suggests/.

[21] Tim Newman, "What's to Know About Gambling Addiction?" *Medical News Today,* June 19, 2018, https://www.medicalnewstoday.com/articles/15929#:~:text=Problem%20gambling%20is%20harmful%20to,feelings%20of%20despondency%20and%20helplessness.

[22] Carolyn Crist, "Synthetic Chemical in Consumer Products Linked to Early Death, Study Says," *WebMD*, October 12, 2021, https://www.webmd.com/a-to-z-guides/news/20211012/snythetic-chemical-consumer-products-linked-early-death-study.

[23] "*20 Health Benefits of Cannabis That Everyone Should Know*," Medical Cannabis Network, July 22, 2019, https://www.healtheuropa.eu/health-benefits-of-cannabis/92499/.

24 Karen Schmidt, "Cannabis Use Disorder May Be Linked to Growing Number of Heart Attacks in Younger Adults," *www.Heart.org*, November 8, 2021, https://www.heart.org/en/news/2021/11/08/cannabis-use-disorder-may-be-linked-to-growing-number-of-heart-attacks-in-younger-adults.

25 "Marijuana and Heart Health: What you Need to Know," Harvard Health Publishing website https://www.health.harvard.edu/heart-health/marijuana-and-heart-health-what-you-need-to-know. January 29, 2022.

26 *"What Are Marijuana's Effects on Lung Health?"* National Institute on Drug Abuse website., https://nida.nih.gov/publications/research-reports/marijuana/what-are-marijuanas-effects-lung-health. April 13, 2021 Accessed February 28, 2022.

27 *"The Influence of Marijuana on Physiologic Processes and Exercise,"* Physiopedia website. Accessed February 28, 2022, https://www.physio-pedia.com/The_influence_of_marijuana_on_physiologic_processes_and_exercise#:~:text=Marijuana%20has%20been%20shown%20to,by%20reducing%20stress%20and%20anxiety.

28 Ann Pietrangelo, "The Effects of Caffeine on Your Body," *Healthline*, September 28, 2018, https://www.healthline.com/health/caffeine-effects-on-body.

29 Dawn MacKeen, "Is Coffee Good for You? Yes! But it Depends on the Kind of Coffee and The Quantity," February 13, 2020, Updated November 12, 2021. https://www.nytimes.com/2020/02/13/style/self-care/coffee-benefits.html.

30 Joe Hernandez, "U.S. Sprinter Sha'Carri Richardson Is Suspended After a Positive Marijuana Test," *NPR.org*, July 2, 2021, https://www.npr.org/2021/07/02/1012490073/u-s-sprinter-shacarri-richardson-suspended-after-positive-marijuana-test.

31 David DiSalvo, "What Alcohol Really Does to your Brain," *Forbes,* October 16, 2012, https://www.forbes.com/sites/daviddisalvo/2012/10/16/what-alcohol-really-does-to-your-brain/?sh=4ced2b2d664e.

32 David Nutt, "There Is No Such Thing as a Safe Level of Alcohol Consumption," *The Guardian*, March 7, 2011, https://www.theguardian.com/science/2011/mar/07/safe-level-alcohol-consumption.

33 Francesca M. Filbey et al., "Long-Term Effects of Marijuana Use on the Brain," *Proceedings of the National Academy of Sciences* (2014), doi:10.1073/pnas.1415297111.

34 Jose A. Cortes-Briones et al., "The Psychosis-Like Effects of Tetrahydrocannabinol are Associated with Increased Cortical Noise in Healthy Humans," *Biological Psychiatry* 78, 11 (2015): 805-813, https://doi.org/10.1016/j.biopsych.2015.03.023.

35 J.O. Owolabi, S.Y. Olatunji, and A.J. Olanrewaju, "Caffeine and Cannabis Effects on Vital Neurotransmitters and Enzymes in the Brain tissue of Juvenile Experimental Rats," *Annals of Neurosciences* 24, 2 (2017), doi: 10.1159/000475895.

36   Toby T. Winton-Brown et al. "Modulation of Auditory and Visual Processing by Delta-9-Tetrahydrocannabinol and Cannabidiol: An FMRI Study," Neuropsychopharmacology official publication of the American College of Neuropsychopharmacology vol. 36,7 (2011): 1340-8. doi:10.1038/npp.2011.17.

37   Crystal Raypole, "What Really Happens During an Out-of-Body Experience?" *Healthline, July 30, 2019,* https://www.healthline.com/health/out-of-body-experience#causes.

38   David Nield, "Scientists Have Connected the Brains of 3 People, Enabling Them to Share Thoughts," *ScienceAlert,* October 2, 2018, https://www.sciencealert.com/brain-to-brain-mind-connection-lets-three-people-share-thoughts.

39   Conor Feehly, "Brains Might Sync as People Interact—and That Could Upend Consciousness Research," *Discover Magazine,* July 26, 2021, https://www.discovermagazine.com/mind/brains-might-sync-as-people-interact-and-that-could-upend-consciousness.

40   Natalie L Dyer, PhD, "Intuition and the Filter Theory of Consciousness," *Blog of Dr. Natalie Dyer,* June 17, 2018, https://drnataliedyer.com/blog/intuition-and-the-filter-theory-of-consciousness/.

41   Thea Singer, "How Humans Bond: The Train Chemistry Revealed," *News@ Northeastern,* February 13, 2017, https://news.northeastern.edu/2017/02/13/how-humans-bond-the-brain-chemistry-revealed/.

42   Reginald Reefer, "What is Your Pineal Gland and What Does Cannabis Do for It?" *Cannabis.net,* December 14, 2021, https://cannabis.net/blog/opinion/what-is-your-pineal-gland-and-what-does-cannabis-do-for-it.

43   M. Borowska M., Czarnywojtek, A., Sawicka-Gutaj, N., Woliński, K., Płazińska, M. T., Mikołajczak, P., & Ruchała, M. (2018). "The Effects of Cannabinoids on the Endocrine System," Endokrynologia Polska, 696), 705–719. https://doi.org/10.5603/EP.a2018.0072.

44   P.D. Newman, "AASR, Strassman, & Endogenous DMT," *Graham Hancock Official Website,* January 10, 2018, https://grahamhancock.com/phorum/read.php?8,1130498.

45   Gert-Jan Lokhorst, "Descartes and the Pineal Gland," *Stanford Encyclopedia of Philosophy,* September 18, 2013, https://plato.stanford.edu/entries/pineal-gland/.

46   "Pituitary Gland | You and Your Hormones from the Society for Endocrinology," 2018, *YourHormones.Info,* https://www.yourhormones.info/glands/pituitary-gland/.

47   Erica Matluck, N.D., "A Guide to Opening Your Third Eye & Accessing Your Highest Intuition," *mbgmindfulness,* July 25, 2019, https://www.mind-bodygreen.com/articles/third-eye-chakra-4-techniques-for-opening-up-the-sixth-chakra.

48   Tom Ireland, "What Does Mindfulness Meditation Do to Your Brain?" *Scientific American Blog Network,* June 12, 2014, https://blogs.

scientificamerican.com/guest-blog/what-does-mindfulness-meditatio n-do-to-your-brain/.

[49] L. Fattore & W. Fratta, "How Important are Sex Differences in Cannabinoid Action?" *British Journal of Pharmacology,* June 2010, https://doi.org/10.111 1/j.1476-5381.2010.00776.

[50] Sarah C.P. Williams, "Study Identifies Brain Areas Altered During Hypnotic Trances," *Stanford Medicine News Center,* July 27, 2016, https:// med.stanford.edu/news/all-news/2016/07/study-identifies-brain-area s-altered-during-hypnotic-trances.html.

[51] Hedy Marks, "Dreams," *WebMD,* November 5, 2021, https://www.webmd. com/sleep-disorders/dreaming-overview.

[52] Kendra Cherry, "Why Do We Dream?" *VeryWellMind,* April 7, 2021, https:// www.verywellmind.com/why-do-we-dream-top-dream-theories-2795931.

[53] "Near Death Experiences (NDEs)," *University of Virginia Division of Perceptual Studies,* accessed December 2021, https://med.virginia.edu/ perceptual-studies/our-research/near-death-experiences-ndes/.

[54] Conor Feehly, "The Brain Waves of a Dying Person Have Been Recorded in Detail For the First Time," *Science Alert,* February 24, 2022, https://www. sciencealert.com/for-the-first-time-scientists-have-recorded-the-brain-wa ves-of-a-dying-person.

[55] Shelly Weaver-Cather, "Should You Be Afraid of the Witching Hour?" *Night Cap by Tuft & Needle,* April 5, 2021, https://www.tuftandneedle.com/ resources/what-is-the-witching-hour/.

[56] "Sleep Basics: REM & NREM, Sleep Stages, Good Sleep Habits, and More," *Cleveland Clinic,* accessed September 2021, https://my.clevelandclinic.org/ health/articles/12148-sleep-basics.

[57] Robert Gunmit, MD, "Neither Gods Nor Demons But Misfiring Brains," *Dana Foundation,* April 1, 2014, https://dana.org/article/neither-gods-no r-demons-but-misfiring-brains/.

[58] Zawn Villines, "Exorcisms and Psychology: What's Really Going On?" *Good Therapy Blog,* March 8, 2013, https://www.goodtherapy.org/blog/psycholog y-exorcism-demonic-possession-0308137.

[59] Dean F. Wong et al., "Mechanisms of Dopaminergic and Serotonergic Neurotransmission in Tourette Syndrome: Clues From an in vivo Neurochemistry Study with PET," *Neuropsychopharmacology* 33, 5 (2007): doi:10.1038/sj.npp.1301528.

[60] "Epilepsy—Symptoms and Causes," *Mayo Clinic,* accessed December 2021, https://www.mayoclinic.org/diseases-conditions/epilepsy/symptoms- causes/syc-20350093.

[61] Ralf Brisch et al., "The Role of Dopamine in Schizophrenia from a Neurobiological and Evolutionary Perspective: Old Fashioned, But Still in Vogue," *Frontiers In Psychiatry* 5 (2014): doi:10.3389/fpsyt.2014.00047.

62   Tobias Hecker and Lars Braitmayer and Marjolein van Duijl, "Global Mental Health and Trauma Exposure: The Current Evidence for the Relationship Between Traumatic Experiences and Spirit Possession," *European Journal of Psychotraumatology* 6 (2015): doi:10.3402/ejpt.v6.29126.

63   Erin Maynard, "How Trauma and PTSD Impact the Brain," *VeryWellMind,* February 13, 2020, https://www.verywellmind.com/what-exactly-does-pts d-do-to-the-brain-2797210.

64   William Peters, MFT, "What 'Shared Death Experiences' Are & Why We Need to Discuss Them," *MBG Mindfulness,* February 8, 2022 https://www. mindbodygreen.com/articles/shared-death-experiences.

65   Michelle Roya Red, "The Power of Prayer: Why Does It Work?" *HuffPost Contributor Platform,* October 24, 2011, https://www.huffpost.com/entry/ power-of-prayer_b_1015475.

66   Carey Benedict, "Long-Awaited Medical Study Questions the Power of Prayer," *The New York Times,* March 31, 2006, https://www.nytimes.com/2006/03/31/ health/longawaited-medical-study-questions-the-power-of-prayer.html.

67   "Mediumship," *New World Encyclopedia website,* accessed March 18, 2022, https://www.newworldencyclopedia.org/entry/Mediumship.

68   Arnaud Delorme et al., "Electrocortical Activity Associated with Subjective Communication with the Diseased," *Frontiers In Psychology* 4 (2013): doi:10.3389/fpsyg.2013.00834.

69   "Life After Death," *BBC Website,* Accessed March 2, 2022 https:// www.bbc.co.uk/bitesize/guides/zfts4wx/revision/3#:~:text=Some%20 Buddhists%20believe%20that%20enlightened,for%20that%20 individual%20itself%20ends.

70   Jessica Staveley, "In 1957, Jacqueline and Joanna Were Killed in a Car Accident. The Next Year, They Were 'Reincarnated'," *Mamma Mia,* June 9, 2020, https://www.mamamia.com.au/pollock-twins/.

71   Marc Hartzman, "The Mind-Boggling Tale of Shanti Devi, the Indian Child Who Claimed She Lived Twice," *All That's Interesting,* May 20, 2021, https:// allthatsinteresting.com/shanti-devi.

72   Jim B. Tucker and Ian Stevenson, *Life Before Life* (New York: St. Martin's Press, 2005).

73   Rishi Sriram, "Why Ages 2–7 Matter so Much for Brain Development," *George Lucas Educational Foundation,* June 24, 2020, https://www.edutopia. org/article/why-ages-2-7-matter-so-much-brain-development.

74   Kate Adams, "Why Children See the Invisible," *Psychology Today,* October 18, 2010, https://www.psychologytoday.com/us/blog/childs-play/201010/ when-children-see-the-invisible.

75   "Delirium—Symptoms and Causes," *Mayo Clinic,* accessed September 2021, https://www.mayoclinic.org/diseases-conditions/delirium/symptoms-causes/syc-20371386.

[76] Shahid Ali et al., "Insight Into Delirium," *Innovations in Clinical Neuroscience* (2011): pmid:2213268, https://www.ncbi.nlm.nih.gov/pmc/articles/PMC3225129/.

[77] Youlim Kim et al., "Efficacy of Low-Dose Prophylactic Quetiapine on Delirium Prevention in Critically Ill Patients: A Prospective, Randomized, Double-Blind, Placebo-Controlled Study," *Journal of Clinical Medicine* 9 (2019): doi:10.3390/jcm9010069.

[78] Marcia Purse, "What Are the Symptoms of Paranoia?" *VeryWellMind*, July 6, 2020, https://www.verywellmind.com/what-is-paranoia-378960.

[79] Sohee Park and Megan Ichinose, "Amygdala on the Lookout," *American Journal of Psychiatry* 172, 8 (2015): 704-705, doi:10.1176/appi.ajp.2015.15050646.

[80] Terri D'Arrigo, "What is Paranoid Schizophrenia?" *WebMD*, October 21, 2021, https://www.webmd.com/schizophrenia/schizophrenia-paranoia.

[81] Philip Wang, "What are Dissociative Disorders?" *American Psychiatric Association*, August 2018, https://www.psychiatry.org/patients-families/dissociative-disorders/what-are-dissociative-disorders.

[82] "Dissociative Identity Disorder (Multiple Personality Disorder)," *WebMD*, January 22, 2022, https://www.webmd.com/mental-health/dissociative-identity-disorder-multiple-personality-disorder.

[83] Aisha Ashraf et al., "Dissociative Identity Disorder: A Pathophysiological Phenomenon," *Journal of Cell Science and Therapy*, 7, 5 (2016): doi: 10.4172/2157-7013.1000251.

[84] "Testosterone | You and Your Hormones from the Society for Endocrinology," *You and Your Hormones*, accessed September 2021, https://www.yourhormones.info/hormones/testosterone/.

[85] "The Menstrual Cycle," *University of California San Francisco Center for Reproductive Health*, accessed October 2021, https://crh.ucsf.edu/fertility/fertility_cycle.

[86] Andrea J. Rapkin, Steven M. Berman, and Edythe D. London, "The Cerebellum and Premenstrual Dysphoric Disorder," *AIMS Environmental Science* 1, 2 (2014): 120-141, doi:10.3934/neuroscience.2014.2.120.

[87] Anna Gosline, "Do Women Who Live Together Menstruate Together?" *Scientific American*, December 7, 2007, https://www.scientificamerican.com/article/do-women-who-live-together-menstruate-together/.

[88] "Does Your Period Really Sync With Close Friends?'" *Cleveland Clinic*, January 31, 2022 https://health.clevelandclinic.org/myth-truth-period-really-sync-close-friends/#:~:text=What%20is%20the%20'menstrual%20myth,for%20women%20who%20live%20together.

[89] "Menstrual Cycle May Change Women's Brains," *WebMD*, May 16, 2005, https://www.webmd.com/women/news/20050516/menstrual-cycle-may-change-womens-brains.

90 "What Does Gamma Aminobutyric Acid (GABA) Do?" *Healthline Medical Network,* March 7, 2019, https://www.healthline.com/health/gamma-aminobutyric-acid.

91 WebMD Editorial Contributors, Medically reviewed by Dan Brennan, M.D., "What Is Tantric Sex?" *WebMD,* June 30, 2021, https://www.webmd.com/sex/what-is-tantric-sex.

92 Michelle Clark, "What's Going On With Hormones And Neurotransmitters During Sex?" *Atlas Blog,* June 25, 2021, https://atlasbiomed.com/blog/whats-going-on-with-hormones-and-neurotransmitters-during-sex/.

93 Julia Layton, "How Intelligent Design Works," *HowStuffWorks,* accessed September 2021, https://people.howstuffworks.com/intelligent-design.htm.

94 Ellen Bernstein, "Jack Kevorkian—American Physician," *Encyclopedia Britannica,* accessed December 2021, https://www.britannica.com/biography/Jack-Kevorkian.

95 Rachael Brennan, "48 End of Life Care Costs and Statistics," *Quickquote.com,* July 19, 2021, https://www.quickquote.com/end-of-life-care-costs-statistics/.

96 Cindy Tran, "'I had morning sickness and my twin didn't even know she was pregnant': Meet the identical twins who feel each other's pain, get ill at the same time and can read their sibling's mind," *Daily Mail Australia,* May 22, 2015, https://www.dailymail.co.uk/news/article-3090703/I-morning-sickness-twin-didn-t-know-pregnant-Meet-identical-twins-feel-s-pain-ill-time-read-sibling-s-mind.html.

97 "Duncan MacDougall (Doctor)," *Alchetron, the Free Social Encyclopedia,* accessed September 2021, https://alchetron.com/Duncan-MacDougall-(doctor).

98 Dheeraj DeeKay, "Conversations: On Existence of Soul and Two 'Scientific' Experiments That Prove One," *Extra Newsfeed,* April 23, 2016, https://extranewsfeed.com/conversations-on-existence-of-soul-and-those-two-scientific-experiments-that-prove-one-4cfbb1b4b1a.

99 David Sihaloho and Lihat Iengkapku, "Duncan MacDougall, a Man Who Determine the Weight of Human Soul," Blogspot, April 22, 2016, http://valuexhunter.blogspot.com/2016/04/duncan-macdougall-man-who-determine.html.

100 Ben Thomas, "The Man Who Tried to Weigh the Soul," *Discover Magazine,* November 3, 2015, https://www.discovermagazine.com/mind/the-man-who-tried-to-weigh-the-soul.

101 Alexander Poltorak, "What Is a Soul? I. The Spiritual vs. the Physical," *Times of Israel,* October 22, 2021, https://blogs.timesofisrael.com/what-is-a-soul-i-the-spiritual-vs-the-physical/.

102 Rachel Paula Abrahamson, "Amanda Kloots Believes Nick Cordero's Spirit Entered Their Son's Body," *Today.com,* October 5, 2021, https://www.today.com/parents/amanda-kloots-says-nick-cordero-s-spirit-entered-son-s-t233220.

103   Marie Morales, "Is the World Unreal? Elon Musk, Neil DeGrasse Tyson Theory that the Universe Is a Simulation Proven Wrong," *The Science Times,* December 3, 2021, https://www.sciencetimes.com/articles/34854/20211203/world-unreal-elon-musk-neil-degrasse-tyson-theory-universe-simulation.htm.

104   Przemek Chojecki, "Moore's Law Is Dead. Now What?" *Built In,* November 10, 2021, https://builtin.com/hardware/moores-law.

105   "Butterfly Effect," *Wikipedia,* https://en.wikipedia.org/wiki/Butterfly_effect.

106   Brian Tracy, "Subconscious Mind Power Explained," *Brian Tracy Blog,* Accessed March 2022, https://www.briantracy.com/blog/personal-success/understanding-your-subconscious-mind/.

107   "Belief and the Brain's 'God Spot'," *The Independent,* March 10, 2009, https://www.independent.co.uk/news/science/belief-and-the-brain-s-god-spot-1641022.html.

108   Tom Chivers, "What Can Occam's Razor Tell Us about God?" *Unherd,* September 17, 2018, https://unherd.com/2018/09/can-occams-razor-prove-god-doesnt-exist/.

109   "What Does the Word 'Heaven' Mean In Hebrew and Greek?" *Misfit Ministries Blog,* January 28, 2020, https://misfitministries.org/word-heaven-in-hebrew-and-greek/.

110   "How Old Is the Earth?" *RealFaith by Mark Driscoll,* accessed January 2022, https://realfaith.com/what-christians-believe/old-earth/.

111   Zeke Hausfather, "Factcheck: What Greenland Ice Cores Say About Past and Present Climate Change", *Carbon Brief: Clear on Climate,* March 5, 2019 https://www.carbonbrief.org/factcheck-what-greenland-ice-cores-say-about-past-and-present-climate-change/#:~:text=Ice%20cores%20are%20one%20of,with%20temperature%2C%20but%20imperfectly%20so

112   Mike Walsh, "Woman Unloads On Guy at Gym After He Tries to 'Help' Her Mid-Lift Without Her Consent," *Comic Sands,* December 16, 2021, https://www.comicsands.com/woman-guy-gym-unwanted-help-2656054463.html.

Made in USA - North Chelmsford, MA
1332290_9781647045968
09.13.2022 1723